The Fi
John G. A

The Films of John G. Avildsen

Rocky, The Karate Kid and
Other Underdogs

Larry Powell *and* Tom Garrett
Foreword by Jean Bodon

McFarland & Company, Inc., Publishers
Jefferson, North Carolina, and London

ALSO OF INTEREST

Black Barons of Birmingham: The South's Greatest Negro League Team and Its Players, by Larry Powell (McFarland 2009)

LIBRARY OF CONGRESS CATALOGUING-IN-PUBLICATION DATA

Powell, Larry, 1948–
    The films of John G. Avildsen : Rocky, The karate kid and other underdogs / Larry Powell and Tom Garrett ; foreword by Jean Bodon.
        p.   cm.
    Includes bibliographical references and index.

ISBN 978-0-7864-6692-4

softcover : acid free paper ∞

    1. Avildsen, John G., 1936– —Criticism and interpretation.
2. Motion picture producers and directors—United States.
I. Garrett, Tom, 1959–   II. Title.
PN1998.3.A85P69 2014
791.4302'33092—dc23
[B]   2013042069

BRITISH LIBRARY CATALOGUING DATA ARE AVAILABLE

Front cover: A frame from John Avildsen's 8mm home movie of the filming of *Rocky*. From left: Sasha Stallone, wife of Sylvester Stallone and still photographer on the Philadelphia shoot; assistant cameraman Ralph Hotchkiss; John Avildsen at the camera; Sylvester Stallone in his iconic pose; and gaffer Ralf Bode.

Manufactured in the United States of America

McFarland & Company, Inc., Publishers
  Box 611, Jefferson, North Carolina 28640
    www.mcfarlandpub.com

The authors thank Professor Jean Bodon
(Sam Houston State University)
for his assistance in the development of this book

Table of Contents

Foreword by Jean Bodon

Abel Gance wrote, "With film, death is no longer an absolute." Every filmmaker is well aware that they are embalming time. Every film — including fiction films — becomes a documentary in a sense that it captures a moment in time. *Saturday Night Fever*, for example, has metamorphosed into a documentary. Its storyline has become secondary to the wacky, flamboyant fashion of the late '70s. Filmmaker Jean Delannoy told me once, "My films are cemeteries of beautiful people who once existed." When you direct fiction films, you not only record life but also create life. In effect, you decide when people will get married, when they will die, and what they will do. As Norman Jewison said, "You get to play God for a few months." When you come back to Earth after directing a film, life becomes unbearable, nothing to control; in fact, no one listens to you.

When I was working on the TV series *The Directors*, I had the privilege of interviewing many famous directors and stars. Most of those interviews were disappointing, because most of the interviewees had not learned how to return to Earth — they were just pompous. Some just stayed at the "godlike" level by reaching down to us.

John Avildsen is different. He is a person who knows how to play God's games. On the set, of course he is God, indeed, that is what directors do: creating life for others to see. But John knows how to come back to Earth.

Strangely enough, when John makes a film, he grows a beard, similar to Michelangelo's representation of God. When the film is finished, John shaves his beard. I asked him about that over some vodka and cigarettes, and he told me that he did not have time to shave when making a film. I did not believe him.

I first met John at the Hyatt on Sunset Boulevard to conduct his interview for the *Directors* series. I sat in with John for four hours asking questions. The questions were short and the answers were lengthy. I had a chance to observe him: his sincerity, his mannerisms as well as many other behavioral traits.

1

(Interviewing is like being a psychologist at a first meeting: You observe, you listen, and you draw a conclusions.)

John was passionate about the stories that he was recounting. He became a storyteller, not the pretentious "auteur" who constantly talks about himself. He is sincere, funny and knows the dramatic structure of a story. His most banal answers always had a climax and a resolution.

John is, above all, a storyteller. We were all exposed to storytelling at a young age; we love storytelling and John knows best how to do so because he knows how to displace himself from "auteurism" or self-gratification. For me, sincere storytelling is the greatest skill of a filmmaker.

Mr. Avildsen is loved or hated. Sylvester Stallone hated him at one time, and Jack Lemmon loved him. It is clear that Stallone was the "auteur" of the *Rocky* movie; he created the Rocky story, wrote the script, and insisted on playing the lead part. Furthermore, the film represented his own struggle to succeed in Hollywood.

But only one person was able to tell that story: John Avildsen. *Rocky* became objective, rather than the self-serving version of *Rocky II*, directed by Stallone himself. Stallone himself acknowledged that the Rocky of *Rocky* turned out to be a different character under Avildsen's direction than he had imagined. "Rocky was not a very appealing guy at first," he told the *Hollywood Reporter* in 2012. "His face was bashed in; he didn't like anybody. It was a much harder film, more in the vein of *Mean Streets*. I saw this guy as an embittered fellow who had blown his opportunity and just took out all of his frustrations on the street."

I think that Stallone did not digest the fact that Avildsen received the Academy Award for the film instead of himself. I met Stallone twenty years after the first *Rocky* and he refused to talk about Avildsen. Stallone said, "You are making a documentary on great directors? Avildsen is not a great director! I will talk to you about *Rocky,* but do not ask me any questions about Avildsen." The interview was not pleasant.

Jack Lemmon loved Avildsen and felt indebted to him for his Academy Award for Best Actor with *Save the Tiger.* Four years after my interview with Mr. Lemmon, I invited John Avildsen to lecture for a week at my university. I called Jack Lemmon and asked him if I could come to L.A. to tape a "Welcome to John" for the lectures. Mr. Lemmon told me that he owed John so much and that, of course, he would do it.

I arrived at Mr. Lemmon's office and started to set up the lights and camera. Mr. Lemmon was late. I spoke to his secretary and she said that he was sick, but that he did not want to miss this opportunity to pay homage to John. Jack Lemmon had cancer and I could see that he had changed a lot in just a few years. He said that he just wanted to thank John for having created the most rewarding performance of his career. Mr. Lemmon died a few months later.

Many of us want to thank John because of his great talents as a storyteller. One day, one of the co-writers of this book, Larry Powell, John Avildsen, Rowdy Gaines (Olympic swimming champion) and I had lunch in a restaurant in Birmingham. Rowdy told John that just before the L.A. Games of 1984, the swim team watched *Rocky* to motivate themselves for their races. Rowdy told John that thanks to his film, he won an Olympic gold medal.

The Karate Kid has the same spirit as *Rocky*. That film helped youngsters to achieve their goals, and the same goes with *Power of One* and *Lean on Me*. John is the "auteur" of hope and struggle. Or as Mort Sahl said, "Avildsen is America's Gaurdian of Optimism."

This book will carry you through the passionate films of John Avildsen. Through the detailed, subtle and sensitive scholarship of Larry Powell and Tom Garrett, you will discover a man who makes movies that are larger than life.

John, I hope you will grow your beard back again, very soon. We need you!

Professor Jean Bodon, Ph.D., is the chair of the Department of Mass Communication at Sam Houston State University. He is also a member of the Directors Guild of America and has worked as a feature film director and producer and as a director of documentaries and television commercials.

Preface

Larry Powell

Some movies leave an indelible mark on an audience, leaving them with a desire to see more films featuring the cast and those made by the director. Such was the case with the 1976 film *Rocky*. The movie launched a legendary career for star Sylvester Stallone. John Avildsen had already been a successful director, but the movie made him a household name and a valuable commodity for Hollywood producers.

For me, the experience of seeing *Rocky* was enhanced when I met the director. Avildsen came to my university as a guest lecturer for a week. As one of his co-hosts, I had the chance to attend his presentations and also talk with him informally. I heard an array of interesting stories about his films and his co-workers. He talked about the things that worked and made a film great. He also talked about those things that didn't work, things that went wrong. He was proud of his successes and candid about the films that were not box office winners. Thus we cover the hits — *Rocky, Save the Tiger, The Karate Kid*, and a slew of other successes. But there are also some that the critics and audiences didn't like. And there is at least one small masterpiece (*Happy New Year*) that was overlooked by audiences because they never had a chance to see it.

Those early discussions were the impetus for writing a book about his films. It was a project that had to be delayed, however, because of the demands of being a college professor dealing with classes, administrators, and other writing projects. I finally got serious about it in 2007 and started working on preliminary drafts of some chapters.

The first true break in the effort was when Tom Garrett agreed to join the project as a co-writer. His knowledge of films is impressive; his affinity to Avildsen's work is even more so. Tom made it possible for a true first draft of the entire book to be completed.

The second major break came when Avildsen agreed to review that draft. His suggestions and changes were voluminous. He spent months going over it line by line, spotting mistakes and omissions. Our first draft contained many conjectures about what might have happened during the production of the movies. Avildsen simply eliminated those guesses, providing us with the correct information. His contribution to this final version was invaluable. Without him, we would have produced a book that summarized his films and provided the reader with speculations about each one. With his assistance, the reader will find a book that tells the real story of each production.

That is what the authors wanted and what the readers deserve. Thank you again, John Avildsen, for all your assistance.

CHAPTER 1

The Early Career

Monday, March, 28, 1977. The Dorothy Chandler Pavilion in Los Angeles.

Television cameras capture the stage and the stars as the film world gathers for the 49th annual presentation of the Academy Awards, honoring the best in movies in 1976. Oscar is waiting to find new homes with a host of talented actors, directors, writers, composers, producers, and technicians.

Among those in the audience — John G. Avildsen, known in Hollywood as a director who can squeeze a quality film out of a small budget. Avildsen's work was finally being recognized beyond the Hollywood community. He had, after all, made the best movie of the year.

The names of the nominees were read, with the cameras making the obligatory cuts to the nominees in the audience. Then Jeanne Moreau announced the winner: John G. Avildsen for *Rocky*.

He had come a long way from his childhood film experience. John Guilbert Avildsen was born December 21, 1935. His parents, Clarence John and Ivy Guilbert Avildsen, provided him a middle-class home that would spark his interest in movies and cameras. Avildsen's father, a tool manufacturer in Chicago, made black and white home movies. He started in 1925, an unusual hobby for the time. His father first filmed John when he was 24 hours old, using a 16mm Bell & Howell Filmo camera. The elder Avildsen made his basement into a studio, and young John grew up playing roles in his father's home movies and holding up signs in the front of the camera with the dates of the productions. But John preferred working behind the camera or in the editing room.

Avildsen also learned some important lessons from his mother, who was born in Liverpool, England. A woman with natural comedic talent, she told John a story about attending a vaudeville show as a teenager in Liverpool. One scene featured the hero, with his hands tied behind his back, while the villain carried the captive heroine away. "Oh, but if my hands weren't tied," the hero lamented. Then a voice from the balcony yelled down, "Kick him. Your feet ain't tied!"

Avildsen considered it an important lesson in looking for reality in his films: "You have to remember that the audience is always judging. If it's not real, you lose them."

Another quote from his mother: "You never can tell from where you sit when the lady in the balcony is going to spit." Avildsen explained, "That was her way of saying that you never know what's going to happen. And you never do. So be prepared."

He entered New York University in 1955, taking classes at night while working for an advertising agency, Dowd Redfield & Johnstone, as a copywriter. His dream then was to run his own advertising agency by the time he was thirty. After two and a half years at NYU, he left, thinking he didn't need a degree to do what he wanted to do.

Avildsen lost his job when one Sunday morning in May he was caught publishing a motor scooter magazine on the company's mimeograph machine. The following week, he was hired as Vespa Motor Scooters' advertising and public relations director. He was twenty years old.

In 1958, he quit that position because he expected to be drafted. As a last fling, he rode his Vespa GS from New York to California via Florida. In

Los Angeles he found work as a copywriter in a small agency and studied acting at night with Corey Allen. After three months he returned to New York and landed his best job so far at the prestigious D'Arcy Advertising Agency. There, in the fall of 1958, he met Jack O'Connell, the man who changed Avildsen's life. O'Connell was the copy chief, but wanted to be a movie director. Avildsen caught the directing bug listening to O'Connell musing about how he was going to direct.

He also met a young writer named Norman Wexler, another copywriter at D'Arcy. The two developed a life-long

Avildsen as a 19-year-old copywriter at a Madison Avenue ad agency, June 1955.

Assistant director John G. Avildsen (left) on location shooting *The Greenwich Village Story*, with director Jack O'Connell (center in cap), and Baird Bryant, director of photography, tied to the car, June 1961. Actress Melinda Cordell is behind the steering wheel and Robert Hogan is in the passenger seat.

friendship. In 1969, Wexler would write the script for *Joe*, the film that put Avildsen on the map. Wexler would also write the scripts for *Serpico* and *Saturday Night Fever* plus many others.

In 1959 O'Connell quit his job and left for Italy where he worked for Fellini and Antonioni. At the same time, Avildsen was drafted and became a chaplain's assistant at Fort Sheridan, just outside of Chicago. In the spring of 1961, John was honorably discharged and went to work for O'Connell, who directed his first low-budget film, *The Greenwich Village Story*. Avildsen was the assistant director.

Avildsen first broke onto the Hollywood scene two years later as the assistant director on *Black Like Me*. He had similar credits on other notable films — assistant production manager for *Mickey One* (1964), second unit director for Otto Preminger's *Hurry Sundown* (1967), and director of photography for *Out of It* (1969).

In between, he was production manager for *Una Moglie Americana,* or *Run for Your Wife* (1965) — an Italo-French film shot in the U.S. Meanwhile, he picked up some more experience by directing a few shorts such as *Smiles* and *Light, Sound, Diffuse* while adding to his bank account with some well-paying jobs for directing industrial films, working for such companies as IBM, Clairol, and Shell Oil. It was an ideal training ground for a young filmmaker. He got to shoot and edit each project himself, using any music of his choice to augment the film. As Avildsen later said, the experience "was better than film school."

He was working at D'Arcy for Studebaker when he made his first contribution to popular culture: naming the "Avanti" automobile in 1964. He was one of several people asked to provide possible names for the company's new car. When the request came down, Avildsen had recently returned from Italy where he had visited the manufacturer of Vespa. He had driven a Vespa through a police checkpoint on the highway and remembered the policeman waving him forward and yelling, "Avanti" ("Come forward").

Soon afterwards, he added another vehicle's name to his credit: the Studebaker." Avildsen also came up with the original name of the Jeep Wagoneer. He suggested "Wagonaire" — a name inspired by the sliding-back roof design of the first model.

Avildsen never got credit for either idea. Instead, he was soon fired from the agency after producing an ad for the Lark that never pictured the car. Avildsen described the Lark as the car that "helped put Studebaker out of business."

"It was one ugly, boxy car," he recalled. "I thought we had a better chance of selling it if we didn't show it." Instead, he focused on such features as its braking and handling capabilities. His thinking, he said, was, "Maybe, if we could get them interested in the car, a good salesman could sell it to them on the lot."

Studebaker wasn't amused, calling him to task because the car was never depicted. "That was the whole idea," he explained. "He felt he got screwed," one friend said.

Maybe that's why he is so effective as a director, because he was soon ready to see how well he fit the director's chair. His early efforts were nothing to brag about — three sexploitation efforts (*Turn On to Love, Sweet Dreams,* and *Guess What We Learned in School Today?*) that did little and brought him little attention. Still, there was a hint of talent there. One critic noted that in *Sweet Dreams,* Avildsen demonstrated "a marked ability to handle earthy material with taste."[1] Few people noticed, though; Avildsen failed to find a major distribution for *Sweet Dreams,* which won best feature at the Atlanta Film Festival in 1970. When it was later re-cut and re-released as *Okay Bill,* it still received little notice. But it got him a job at Cannon Films.

Avildsen in Central Park, in New York City, at a script conference with some cast members of *Sweet Dreams*, July 1968.

Hollywood started noticing in 1970 when he made *Joe*, a low-budget effort about a blue-collar racist who blackmails a killer. Despite limited funds and with no margin of error, Avildsen produced a box office sleeper and a cult hit that was a financial and critical success and the highest grossing independent film of 1970. His career seemed to be ready to hit the big time with a major star (Jack Lemmon in *Save the Tiger*) and a major personality (Burt Reynolds in *W.W. and the Dixie Dancekings*). He was beginning to work toward a Best Director Oscar.

Seven of Avildsen's films garnered Oscar nominations. He was the director behind Jack Lemmon's Oscar-winning performance in *Save the Tiger*. *Rocky* received ten nominations, winning three (including Best Picture and Avildsen for Best Director). Six other of his works have also received Oscar nominations: *Joe* (for writing), *The Formula* (for cinematography), *The Karate Kid* (supporting actor, Pat Morita), *The Karate Kid Part II* (song), and 1987's *Happy New Year* (makeup). Avildsen earned a second nomination in 1982 for his documentary *Traveling Hopefully*, about Roger Baldwin, founder of the ACLU.

Some of his movies have become classics. *Rocky* and *The Karate Kid* were audience favorites and the source of a series of sequels. After the terrorist

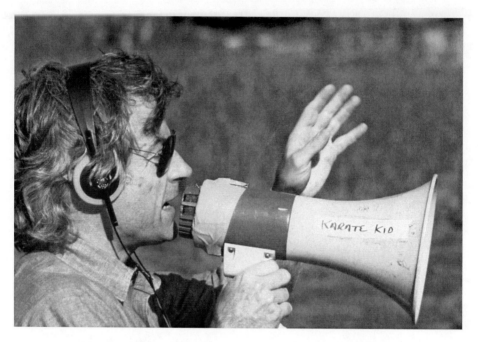

Director John G. Avildsen on the set of *The Karate Kid* (1984).

attacks on September 11, 2001, the government asked Hollywood producers to put together a montage of films that could be used to reflect a positive American experience. Two of his films were included: *Rocky* and *Save the Tiger*. Two other films that he worked on were also included: *Saturday Night Fever* and *Serpico.*

He also dabbled in TV, directing the pilot for *Murder Ink* for CBS in 1983 and directing a public-service special, *From No House to Options House,* which won an Emmy. The production was about a place on Hollywood Boulevard that took in teenage runaways and tried to rehabilitate them.

His movies have included comedy and dramas, patriotic statements with Horatio Alger themes and sexploitation. He sometimes works with offbeat topics, causing some to say, "His view of the fringes of American society varies from acerbic realism to sentimental fantasy."[2]

Avildsen has worked with some of the biggest names in Hollywood: Jack Lemmon, Marlon Brando, George C. Scott, Burt Reynolds. When he finishes a film, though, the audiences remember the star but overlook the director. He's simply not one of those directors who projects star quality himself, but he certainly knows how to bring it out in an actor. That's what a director's supposed to do, isn't it?

From an actor's perspective, he is a meticulous director. His storyboards are detailed, with nearly every shot planned in advance. He did his own cinematography and editing on his early films. On *Rocky* he was his own cameraman-operator for the ten days of shooting in Philadelphia, which accounted for more than one-third of the 28-day schedule. He also prefers editing his own films. "Once the shooting is over, I put on a new hat," he said. "I've always felt that I knew better than anyone how I want the film to look."

He directed some of the best actors in Hollywood, talented artists who have a variety of different personalities. Still, when you watch John Avildsen's movies, the actors lose those personalities and become part of the film, part of the character. Morgan Freeman, for example, is a subdued, easygoing individual who becomes a powerful character in *Lean on Me*. Sylvester Stallone is a talented writer who comes across as semi-literate in *Rocky*. He was so good in the role that many of the Academy voters apparently thought he wasn't acting and didn't vote for him to get an Oscar for his performance. An actor simply cannot turn out such performances without a good director, no matter how good the actor.

He is a man of close relationships. He remained friends with Jack Lemmon up until the day of that great actor's death. Some of his contacts in the directing and technical fields remain lifelong friends.

But he has his enemies. Burt Reynolds had behind-the-scenes arguments with him. He holds the distinction of being fired from some of the best films to come out of Hollywood, including *Saturday Night Fever* and *Serpico*. He turned down some of the best films ever made, including *Kramer vs. Kramer*, *The China Syndrome*, and *The Hunt for Red October*.

Getting fired from *Saturday Night Fever* didn't bother him at the time: He was dismissed on the same day that he received his nomination for an Oscar for *Rocky*. "I was on such a high from the Academy Awards that I couldn't be brought down," he said. He regretted it later, though. If he had made that film, he would have had established a major reputation.

Instead, it was but one of many films that he never completed. He was initially set to direct *Gone Fishing*, starring Joe Pesci and Danny Glover, before a disagreement with a producer and the stars led to his dismissal. "Joe Pesci didn't like short jokes," Avildsen explained. The pivotal point was apparently a scene in which a boat runs out of control and onto the beach, wreaking destruction. Avildsen wanted to cut the scene, arguing that it was a cliché, expensive and dangerous to film. After he was dismissed, the scene was shot and the boat went awry. This resulted in the death of a stuntman while the director of photography lost part of his finger.

Such dismissals often hinge on his personality and artistic differences. Those who dislike him often agree with Burt Reynolds' early assessment: "John Avildsen is very talented, but he's a real prick."

Maybe, but his problem seems to be twofold. On one hand, he has the capacity to truly irritate the actors with whom he works. Is it his personality, though, or merely his directorial technique? Morgan Freeman believes that Avildsen gets on an actor's nerves deliberately, to create an emotional edge for a better performance. Even Burt Reynolds admitted that the better moments in *W.W. and the Dixie Dancekings* came when he was mad at Avildsen.

On the other hand, he sometimes had trouble getting along with the powers that be. That factor seems to be the element that gets him tossed off movies. He still doesn't get along with Irwin Winkler, the producer of *Rocky*. Nor with a lot of the other Hollywood heavyweights. The last Hollywood film that bears his name, *8 Seconds*, was made in 1994.

Still, he has a number of long-time and loyal friends. Freeman has worked with Avildsen on a couple of films, *Lean on Me* and *The Power of One*. Jerry Wintraub produced four movies for Avildsen. Producer Milt Felsen remained a friend. Avildsen and producer Lloyd Kaufman both have liberal political philosophies and maintain a close relationship. Screenwriter Norman Wexler worked with Avildsen on several films and named the lead character in *Saturday Night Fever*—Tony Marinaro—after Avildsen's son Anthony. Wexler, who also wrote *Joe*, named Susan Sarandon's character in that film Melissa after Avildsen's first wife (Anthony's mother).

His personal life—like his career—has been sometimes happy and sometimes controversial. He has three children—Anthony, Jonathan and Bridget—who usually stay out of the public eye. Daughter Bridget is the result of his second marriage; Avildsen and actress Tracy Brooks Swope were married in February 1987.

A young director, John G. Avildsen, on the set of *The Stoolie* (1972)

His favorite hobby is shooting home videos. "I do a lot of birthday parties. I keep the other parents supplied," he has said. "It's a treat for me."[3]

Actually, he shoots video of nearly everything. He takes a digital camera with him to most public events, taping his own interviews. He does it, he says, because he always gets the same questions and he always answers them the same way. He intended to edit the answers into a single clip, showing himself aging as he talks about his films. Instead, his son Anthony did it; the clip is now on YouTube under the title *Rocky Director Spills the Beans.*

CHAPTER 2

Joe

Speed Freaks versus
the Silent Majority

Avildsen first got the attention of Hollywood with a low-budget, shot-on-a-shoestring film. He was both director and cinematographer for the cult classic *Joe*.

Ask any cinema historian — or, for that matter, any filmgoer who took in a steady diet of important works of "New Hollywood" during the late 1960s and early 1970s — and they'll almost certainly cite *Joe* as one of the seminal works of the movement. If you ask a more casual movie lover, though, he or she will probably have little or no knowledge of counter-cultural cinema that extends much beyond *Easy Rider, Midnight Cowboy, MASH* and *Billy Jack*.

It's ironic that *Joe* has not endured to make today's Cliffs Notes shortlist of New Hollywood classics, as its theme of clashing cultures (and its examination of the attendant bigotry) is timeless — especially relative to its contemporary films. Whereas a film like *Easy Rider* is specifically about the collision of hippie culture with establishment culture, *Joe* is much wider in scope, examining not only hippies butting heads with "squares," but also the culture clash of white collar versus blue collar within the establishment. In effect, it becomes a general examination of the friction that results when different value sets are forced to coexist, and its conclusions and cautions can be applied to any two such clashing cultures. As John Bodnar noted, *Joe* was a movie that reflected "a broad political discussion that was endemic to American mass culture."[1]

What's more, *Joe* was a remarkable commercial and critical success, putting a film studio — Cannon Films — on the map and earning an original screenplay Oscar nomination.[2] The film spawned not only the standard sound-

16

track album but also a "Joe Speaks" dialogue LP. Further, *Joe* was popular enough to warrant the development (although never the actual production) of a sequel.

Before it was a successful film, *Joe* was a story idea by Norman Wexler — a writer who, like Avildsen, had a background in advertising.[3] According to the cinema book *The Directors: Take Two*, Avildsen first discussed the idea with Wexler during an encounter at an office when the two men were making advertising industrials.[4]

For one side of the story — which climaxes in the finished film with a white-collar worker and blue-collar worker killing hippies together after some eye-opening experiences in the New York counter-cultural drug scene — Wexler reportedly was inspired by writer Gail Sheehy's "Speed Is of the Essence" piece in *New York Magazine*, concerning drug addiction in the East Village of New York City. For the other, Wexler drew upon the idea of the "Great Silent Majority," a concept then popularized by vice-president Spiro Agnew and President Richard Nixon. Liking the idea, Avildsen pitched it to Cannon (presumably to original company heads Christopher Dewey and Dennis Friedland — twenty-somethings, both), for whom he was directing the sex comedy *Guess What We Learned in School Today?*

As Avildsen recounted in interviews for such books as *Film Directors on Directing*[5] and *The Directors: Take Two*,[6] Cannon initially passed on Wexler's idea, but when the company was later in a predicament — having raised money for another project whose script was "terrible" — Cannon turned to Avildsen for a replacement project. They needed something that could be ready to shoot in four weeks; otherwise they risked losing the money they raised. Avildsen reiterated his interest in doing Wexler's story and Cannon reluctantly capitulated, despite apparent misgivings because "the guy has never written a script before."

It was a valid concern, as Wexler was indeed unproven at the time. *Joe*, his first feature screenwriting credit, earned him an Oscar nomination. His scripting career would continue successfully and include such hit films as *Serpico* (a shared credit with Waldo Salt that earned a second Oscar nomination for Wexler) and *Saturday Night Fever* (a film that would have re-teamed Avildsen with the writer, had Avildsen not been fired during pre-production).

Joe was not Wexler's first writing credit. He had authored an inventive off–Broadway play called "A Week from Tuesday" that Avildsen had seen and enjoyed. The plot involved two women, strangers who run into each other at lunch and strike up a conversation about men. During the course of the play, the audience realizes that the two women are talking about the same man — the husband of one and the lover of the other. The two women part but promise to meet "a week from Tuesday" to continue their conversation.

The play ends with the audience never really sure which woman was the wife and which was the lover. The script impressed Avildsen, who saw Wexler as a writer with talent.

One other point may have contributed to the script for *Joe*. Wexler suffered from bipolar disorder, and his 1972 arrest for threats against the life of President Nixon offers an additional shading to *Joe*'s murderous climax of people willing to kill out of value disagreement.

According to Avildsen, the director jumped into casting during the day and helped Wexler with the screenwriting process at night.[7] As is suggested by Avildsen's comments in *The Directors: Take Two*, the division of writing labor seems to have been Wexler conceiving the plot and dialogue and Avildsen helping to get the content into proper screenplay format: "It was Norman Wexler's story. This was the first movie script he had written, so I worked with him and we got it down on paper."[8] Writing was reportedly completed in a week.

The casting may have moved just as fast but must have been much more frustrating for the director. For the critical blue-collar title role, Avildsen called in Peter Boyle for an audition after seeing his submitted photograph. Boyle brought an unusual background to the role: He became an actor after giving up on a career as a monk. When he married in 1977, the best man at his wedding was former Beatle John Lennon.[9]

The auditioning actors were given dialogue to read that included the line, "You show me a welfare worker who's not a nigger lover, and I'll massage your asshole." Avildsen encouraged Boyle to use his own words. When Boyle delivered the line, he improvised the follow-up, "And I ain't queer." Avildsen said, "You're hired." (Boyle had grown up with people like Joe. "I knew the character so well that when it came to the actual shooting of the movie, I was worried that I would do a caricature," he once said.[10])

Thinking that a highly appropriate ad-lib demonstrated insight into the character, Avildsen wanted Boyle for the role. The powers at Cannon, however, squelched the Boyle casting, reasoning that the actor (then in his mid-thirties) did not look credible as a World War II veteran.

They were right, of course. Despite a full-blown case of male-pattern baldness, Boyle still looked too fresh-faced for the part, especially when acting in the finished film opposite his shared lead, gray-haired actor Dennis Patrick, who was supposed to play Joe's peer despite being Boyle's senior by almost twenty years. When the viewer first hears Boyle's Joe speak of killing men in the war, he or she assumes the character is speaking of Korea, only to learn with surprise later that the two men are supposed to have World War II veteranship in common. One wonders why the script could not have been changed to accommodate Boyle's younger age.

In any case, Avildsen was told by Cannon to cast an older actor as Joe, and the director did — apparently getting an actor with whom he was pleased: "So we went with another older actor who was also very good."[11] This actor has remained nameless in Avildsen's recounting of the *Joe* production, although one source identified him as a veteran of B-gangster films, Lawrence Tierney.[12] Tierney, best known for his title role in the 1945 film *Dillinger*, would have been the right age for the part. However, in such books as *Film Directors on Directing* and *The Directors: Take Two*, Avildsen is not bashful about describing an incident involving the older actor that occurred two days before principal photography began. The actor publicly urinated on a Bloomingdales' escalator and struck a saleslady. That is also consistent with the identification of Tierney as the unnamed first actor, since Tierney had a well-documented problem with incontinence.[13] Apparently, Avildsen was warned by friends that this actor was a drinker and a fighter.[14] The older thespian was no longer considered usable.

Just as with the green-lighting of the film itself, it was Cannon's desperation that allowed Avildsen to get his way. The director made a second push for Boyle, and this time, Cannon allowed it. Boyle, 34 when he took the role of a man who was ten years older, got $3,000 for his work.[15] It was a movie that nobody was supposed to see, so Boyle held nothing back, playing an individual who was philosophically opposite of himself.

The casting of Susan Sarandon in the plot-driving role of a hippie runaway — her first feature film appearance — was relatively uneventful, and with a simple hiring decision, Avildsen launched her movie career which is now in its fifth decade.

Principal photography occurred during a chilly January 1970 in New York, just weeks after the project was okayed by Cannon. Avildsen

Publicity art for *Joe* (1970) featuring Susan Sarandon and Peter Boyle.

doubled as cinematographer. Future Troma Entertainment schlockmeister Lloyd Kaufman was another notable in the crew, serving as production manager. According to *Washington Post* film critic Gary Arnold's August 20, 1970, review, the movie was shot under the working title *The Gap* (doubtless in a reference to certain characters' generational gap). Avildsen later campaigned to change the title to *Joe* because "the story was obviously about this guy."

Following a path blazed by *Easy Rider* the previous year, *Joe* engaged in the new practice of contracting with the National Association of Broadcast Employees and Technicians (NABET — primarily a television union). According to the "Hard Hats and Movie Brats" piece in *Cinema Journal, Joe* eschewed the typical usage of longtime union IATSE for its technical crew, as NABET was trying to make inroads into feature films at the time by inking deals with independent producers.[16] Avildsen was an early organizer for NABET Local 15.

With a budget that has been reported as both $250,000 and $300,000, *Joe* tells the story of young Melissa Compton (Sarandon), who embraces counterculture. However, she also feels conflicted about the hard drug use she sometimes engages in with her live-in boyfriend, Frank Russo (Patrick McDermott). After Frank, a speed dealer and would-be artist, supplies Melissa with drugs that lead to her requiring overdose treatment in a hospital, her father, Bill (Patrick), goes to retrieve Melissa's belongings from Frank's apartment. This results in an argument between the two men, and in a crime of passion, Bill beats Frank to death.

Bill's fatal throttling of Frank is *Joe*'s first minor misstep, due mainly to the casting of the muscular McDermott as Frank. While under other circumstances it might be credible for a button-down middle-aged man to beat a streetwise young man to death (especially if the older man is imbued with rage over his daughter's condition, which Bill is), it doesn't work here because of McDermott's brawny physique. This attention to health (i.e., weightlifting) also seems incongruous with Frank's junky lifestyle. Avildsen, however, noted that Frank was high on drugs at the time of the fight — a condition that made it possible for Bill to overpower Frank.

Nonetheless, Bill is now a murderer, but instead of going straight home, he ducks into a bar to calm his nerves with Scotch. There, he encounters a foundry worker named Joe Curran (Boyle) loudly preaching an anti-hippie, anti-black, anti-liberal rant. Some of Joe's complaints are valid rightist viewpoints (e.g., public welfare money begets a welfare class) but are muddied with ugly bigotry. The rest of Joe's moanings are simply preposterous: "Forty-two percent of all liberals are queer — and that's a fact. Some Wallace people took a poll." Despite the dissimilarity of Bill — a $60k-per-year Madison Avenue ad man — to Joe, Bill lets slip that he just murdered a hippie.

With Melissa detoxing at her parents' ritzy apartment, and with Frank's murder being attributed to a drug-related robbery, and with Bill and Joe bonding over Bill's recent act of establishment backlash, there would not seem to be any source of tension for the next 30 minutes of *Joe*. But in the skillful storytelling hands of Avildsen and Wexler, this section of *Joe* is marvelously tense. The tension derives only slightly from Joe's mention of blackmail to Bill; Joe laughs it off almost immediately after broaching the subject. Still, the possibility stays in the back of the viewer's mind—as we're sure it does in Bill's. The main source of tension is the uneasiness that bubbles under the surface as the blue-collar man and the white-collar man strain to develop a friendship. This is the more subtle culture clash of *Joe*.

Joe is a man of base desires. He swills Millers after a long day's work, likes "a little on the side once in a while," and exhibits pride and anger as two of his prominent personality traits (Bill's wife likens him to a powderkeg). The viewer watches in perpetual fear that Joe will feel foolish in the educated company of Bill, take offense and lash out angrily—or even violently. The movie offers plenty of near-miss moments on this count. At one point over beers, he demands, "You find it hard talking to me?" Later, during a dinner with Bill and his wife, Joe angrily shouts, "The *what*?!" when a word outside his vocabulary is used. During the same dinner, when Joe feels his wife is droning on to an embarrassing point, he cuts her off mid-sentence to the horror of everyone in the room. (This often-boorish characterization of Joe is somewhat ironic in Avildsen's oeuvre, as working-class people are the shining heroes in the director's films that feature his career-defining "plight of the underdog" theme.)

Equally tense is Bill's borderline tolerance of Joe. He doesn't want to look at Joe's gun collection. He doesn't want to bowl with Joe and his friends. He doesn't want the Chinese take-out that Joe orders for their dinner party with the wives (as indicated by a sneaky grab for mixed nuts). The script gives Bill lines about how much he enjoys spending time with Joe, but the viewer's knowledge of universal, emotional and behavioral truths leads one to suspect otherwise.

The film's pretexts for keeping these two men together are that (a) Joe idolizes Bill for his murder of Frank and that (b) Bill is better able to rationalize the murder when he spends time with Joe ("Sometimes with him," Bill says, "I almost feel as if what I did was a humanitarian act. I saved the world from another lousy junky"). These pretexts are a little thin but easily forgivable considering the immensely watchable discomfort Avildsen creates through the performances of his two leads.

The film's third act brings more tangible conflict to the story. Melissa has discovered it was her father who killed Frank and she flees into the East

Village drug underground with this incriminating information. Bill and Joe team up to scour the hippie haunts for Melissa, but get sidetracked with a drug-fueled "free love"–style party. The two men quickly forget about questioning young female peaceniks and become more interested in copulating with them. In a state of undress, Bill and Joe are rolled for their wallets by the hippies.

Angry, and perhaps with a little bloodlust, the two men pursue the counter-cultural pickpockets to a commune. Joe has packed a rifle and a shotgun in the trunk of his car, and the ammo easily finds its way into the unarmed hippie targets as they beg for mercy.

A certain genius to *Joe*'s ending is how the preceding 12-minute sex-party sequence is such an effectively distractive tangent; it causes the viewer to forget about the quest for Melissa. Thus, it's with pure surprise that, when Bill raises his shotgun and discharges a round into the back of a young hippie, it turns out to be his daughter.

The ending, which applies a long frozen frame on Melissa the split second before the ammunition enters her back, is a masterful and haunting way to reveal the identity of this final shooting victim. In this way, *Joe* almost perfectly recalls Monte Hellman's *The Shooting*, a 1967 western that has taken on an art-film reputation. In *The Shooting*, the powerful final shot is a slow-motion reveal of its surprising shooting victim: the twin brother of the protagonist.

Despite *Joe*'s success, Avildsen seems to dislike the way the ending was handled in the editing. He often prefers to do his own editing, but he initially turned down the offer to edit *Joe*. When he later changed his mind, the producers' answer was that they would get back to him on that. As the production continued, Avildsen heard no word on the editing job. He eventually shut down shooting for a couple of hours to push for a decision. After those two hours, he was told he had the editing job. However, when shooting was completed and he returned to edit, he was fired immediately. Thus, the final cut was different from what he envisioned. As he told John Andrew Gallagher in *Film Directors on Directing*:

> I wasn't really that happy with *Joe* because I wasn't allowed to cut it. I always thought it was much more exploitive than it might have been. Also, the ending of it wasn't the ending it was supposed to have. If you recollect, the guy shoots his daughter and runs out of the house and we go out. That's how it ended. It was supposed to end a few seconds later when Joe walks out, sees what's happened, drops his rifle, and we go out on him where maybe he's beginning to realize that this isn't the solution.[17]

Nonetheless, *Joe* was not received as exploitation but rather as an important film, highly relevant to the social issues of its day. Its relevance was bolstered by the May 1970 "Hard Hat Riot" (which saw approximately 200 New

York City construction workers clash violently with antiwar demonstrators near Wall Street) that preceded *Joe*'s summer release by only two months. The riot was the very type of establishment backlash that the movie predicted, and it involved blue-collar workers and hippies — two of the three main factions in *Joe*.

The film was a cultural phenomenon. Later in 1970, *Life* magazine followed Boyle around after the film's success and recorded all the people who greeted him with the anti-hippie sentiments they, in confusing the actor with the role, wrongly assumed he shared. Rick Perlstein, in his 2007 Boyle obituary for inthesetimes.com, reports that countercultural moviegoers would watch *Joe* and shout at the screen, "I'm going to shoot back, Joe!" after the film's conclusion.

Avildsen remembered the feedback he received in his interview for *Film Directors on Directing*:

> People seemed to like it and could relate to it. I didn't get the reaction, "You must hate hard hats" or "You must hate hippies," which I was glad about, because it didn't take either attitude, hopefully. In other words, it didn't try to judge.[18]

The even-handedness of *Joe* is indeed one of the film's strengths. There are not the cardboard establishment villains of *Easy Rider*, who seemed out to persecute long hairs at every turn. Instead, *Joe* features characters like its drug store clerk from an early scene — a straight-laced establishment character to be sure — who is at first angered when Melissa begins knocking products off the shelves, but becomes caring when she realizes the young woman is suffering from adverse reactions to speed. Similarly, Melissa's parents are forgiving (and willing to admit their share of blame) when they learn their daughter has overdosed.

Nor are all of *Joe*'s hippies peace-loving saints. Frank is a drug dealer who is not above scamming his customers. And the sex party peaceniks have little compunction about thievery.

Besides the Oscar nomination, *Joe* enjoyed its share of critical triumphs. In *Time* magazine, critic Mark Goodman favorably compared Boyle's performance to those of Marlon Brando and spoke of Boyle's "harsh power." And the role of Joe reportedly got Boyle an offer for one of the leads in the next year's *The French Connection*. Doubts were expressed by such critics as Robin Karney, who wrote, "Although ostensibly critical of its 'hero,' the film moved dangerously close to condoning him."[19] *The New York Times* took a second look at the film in 2000 and described it as "a cheaply made political button-pusher" that mixed "social satire with confrontational carnage."[20]

If *Joe* had the result of trying to pigeonhole Boyle into establishment roles, it also effectively linked Avildsen for a time with countercul- ture. The director's first studio film, 1973's *Save the Tiger*, would fill in the subplot nooks and cran- nies of its fashion-indus- try story with glimpses of counterculture (as mainly embodied by a hippie hitchhiker). And the Internet Movie Database reports, however uncon- firmed, that Avildsen directed the re-shoots for

Peter Boyle as Joe Curran in *Joe* (1970).

the druggie film *Believe in Me* (1971) without credit. If true, this is amazingly coincidental, as *Believe in Me* was derived directly from the "Speed Is of the Essence" piece in New York Magazine — the same article that served as a roundabout inspiration for Wexler to write *Joe*. But Avildsen is hardly con- sidered a Hopper or Fonda. A few years later, his first sports underdog movie, *Rocky*, would redefine him in a single stroke.

Avildsen did have an idea for a sequel to *Joe*. He envisioned a plot ten years after the end of the film, when Joe would be released from prison and have to deal with a never-before-seen grandson from his son's marriage to a African American woman. He deals with his new environment by joining the Guardian Angels, a volunteer group of unarmed citizens who patrol areas to prevent crime. The idea for the plot came from his son Jonathan, who had joined the Guardian Angels at the age of 14.

The Cannon Group saw potential in a sequel and took out ads in 1980 and 1985 promising first a *Joe II* and then a version called *Citizen Joe*. Those sequels never materialized. Avildsen suggested another idea. Again the plot came from his son Jonathan: The movie would be based on the group's founder, Curtis Sliwa. Sliwa survived an assassination attempt when he was shot five times while inside a New York taxi. John Gotti, Jr., was tried for the crime three times, but each trial ended in a hung jury. It's a great story, but the movie also failed to materialize.

As Avildsen said, "*Joe* was the movie that changed everything." He, Wexler, Boyle and the Cannon Group (which *Time* reported had swelled to 20 employees and six executives after *Joe*) were all on their way. Sarandon would follow in due time.

Production Notes

Directed by: John G. Avildsen. Writers: Norman Wexler. Producers: Christopher C. Dewey, executive producer; Dennis Friedland, executive producer; David Gil, producer; George Manasse, associate producer. Original Music: Bobby Scott. Cinematographer: John G. Avildsen (photographed by). Editor: George T. Norris. Production Managers: George Manasse, production manager; William Sachs, post-production supervisor; Frank Vitale, unit manager. Assistant Director: Harvey Vincent. Art Department: Willard Bond, properties; Hugh Valentine, title art; Sal Vitale, title art. Sound Department: Jack Cooley, sound mixer: Magno Sound; Michael Scott Goldbaum, sound recordist; Charles Hansen, assistant sound recordist; Thomas Kennedy, sound effects editor. Special Effects Department: Louis Antzes, special effects. Visual Effects Department: John Paratore, title designer. Camera and Electrical Department: Ralf Bode, gaffer; Stephen Bower, second assistant camera; Jim Crispi, electrician; Jay Good, still photographer; Ralph Hotchkiss, first assistant camera; Aristedes Pappadas, best boy; Al Sentesy, grip; Aristides Pappidas, electrician (uncredited). Costume and Wardrobe Department: Andy Kay, wardrobe. Editorial Department: Thomas Kennedy, assistant editor. Music Department: Gene Orloff, musical supervisor; Bobby Scott, conductor. Miscellaneous Crew: Tom Feledy, production assistant; Randa Haines, script supervisor; Lloyd Kaufman, production assistant. Filming Location: New York City, New York, USA. Distributors: Cannon Film Distributors (1970) (USA) (theatrical); Valio-Filmi (1971) (Finland) (theatrical); America Video 1996 (Brazil) (VHS); Front Row Video (video); MGM/UA Home Entertainment (2002) (USA) (DVD); Future Film (2010) (Finland) (DVD).

Cast — in credits order: Susan Sarandon, Melissa Compton; Patrick McDermott, Frank Russo; Tim Lewis, Kid in Soda Shop; Estelle Omens, Woman in Bargain Store; Bob O'Connell, Man in Bargain Store; Marlene Warfield, Bellevue Nurse; Dennis Patrick, Bill Compton; Audrey Caire, Joan Compton; Mary Case, Jenny Paine, Teeny Boppers; Peter Boyle, Joe Curran; Reid Cruickshanks, American Bartender; Rudy Churney, Man in Bar; K. Callan, May Lou Curran; Robert Emerick, TV Newscaster; Gloria Hoye, Janine; Bo Enivel, Sam in Bowling Alley; Michael O'Neal, Bartender at Ginger Man; Frank Moon, Gil Richards; Jeanne M. Lange, Phyllis; Perry Gerwitz, Hippie on Street; Morty Schlass, Waiter in Guitar Joint; Frank Vitale, Hippie in Group; Al Sentesy, Poster Shop Proprietor; Patti Caton, Nancy; Gary Weber, George; Claude Robert Simon, Bob; Max Couper, Ronnie; Francine Middleton, Gail.

CHAPTER 3

Cry Uncle

Returning (Already) to His Roots

The early 1970s was a rich cinematic period, partly because actors were hired for their "interesting factor" rather than for any beauty or glamor. But with John Avildsen's lead casting for *Cry Uncle*—of balding, portly character actor Allen Garfield in a role that repeatedly called for him to go fully nude—the practice was taken to a new extreme.

Despite the then-prevailing zeitgeist towards cinematic reality, it was indeed a special circumstance for Garfield—self-described to be then at a weight of 250 lbs.—to not only star in a film, but to do so in various stages of frequent undress. According to *Cry Uncle*'s filmmakers, both Peter Boyle and Rodney Dangerfield turned down the role, and Garfield said he was advised by others not to accept it.[1] Further, the actor said he was "more terrified (to do *Cry Uncle* than any other experience in my life" and that "the biggest acting I did on *Cry Uncle* was showing up every day on the set and pretending that this was a piece of cake to do."

Garfield's schlubby, bumbling character, Jake Masters, is a far cry from the character as written in the source material, the 1968 detective novel *Lie a Little, Die a Little*. The literary version of the character, named Pete McGrath, appeared in ten novels by British crime writer Michael Brett (a *nom de plume* for Miles Barton Tripp), and the original incarnation of the detective has been described as "big, tough and handsome."[2]

But the lead character isn't the only way Avildsen's comedic movie strays from the original story, as Brett's novel was a straight detective yarn. The motion picture rights for *Lie a Little, Die a Little* were purchased by Lee Hessel of porn-exploitation distributor Cambist Films with no apparent intent to transform the material into humor. Somehow—either through 42nd Street cinema owner Bernard "Bingo" Brandt or through *Okay Bill* producer David

Jay Disick (reports conflict)—Hessel was put in touch with Avildsen as a potential director.[3]

After *Joe*, Avildsen had been called out to Hollywood by Warner Brothers for a meeting on a film. In an interview for *Film Directors on Directing*, he said he was turned off by the "assembly line" nature of the studio, so he declined to do the film and returned to New York.[4] When he was approached about adapting *Lie a Little, Die a Little*, Avildsen suggested his friend, writer David Odell, make the adaptation. Odell, who would strike it big in the 1980s with fantasy screenplays for *The Dark Crystal*, *Supergirl*, and *Masters of the Universe*, suggested using the film to parody the detective archetype.[5]

When asked whether *Lie a Little* option-holder Hessel minded his property being taken in a drastically new direction, producer Disick indicated that Hessel was, firstly, willing to give leeway because he was pleased to be working with Avildsen (Hessel had screened *Joe* prior to its release) and, secondly, placated by the fact that there would be plenty of nudity. In fact, Hessel's main concern was that there be both "hot" and "cold" versions of the nudity, apparently unaware that they weren't transforming the novel into straight pornography.[6]

The $185,000 production had Avildsen serving as director, cinematographer, and editor. Many other crew members also pulled double duty by playing roles in the film. Even writer Odell, who would later collaborate with Avildsen on *Fore Play*, played a small part as an angry man in a parking lot and voiced many of the off-screen characters. Lighting director Ralf Bode supplied his automobile as the lead character's car, as he had previously done for *Joe*.

Four rooms at the Windermere hotel on Manhattan's Upper West Side were used as their "studio," and the rooms served as both production offices and interior locations. Rooms would be shot for one scene and then painted so they could be used as other settings. "You'll notice all the interior rooms in this movie have the same kinds of configurations," says Avildsen on *Cry Uncle*'s DVD commentary track.[7] The low-budget maneuvering also applied to outdoor shots. Production manager Lloyd Kaufman remembers shooting one exterior (which involved handguns, no less) on a New York street without any permits or police permission.[8]

Despite the low-budget, almost guerrilla-style shooting conditions, *Cry Uncle* managed some impressive locations through creative and fleet-footed means. An ocean liner was the setting for a couple of scenes, and production manager Kaufman recalls that the location was acquired when Avildsen learned about a cruise ship that had been abandoned in Manhattan harbor as part of a bankruptcy.[9] New York City's La Guardia Airport was shot from the interior, and one scene involved Garfield's character trying to jump into the baggage compartment of a gated airliner. Odell remembers the production nearly missing this because the plane was scheduled to leave the gate.[10]

The *Cry Uncle* version of the story has private detective Jake Masters (Garfield) accepting a job from the wealthy Jason Dominic (David Kirk): Masters must uncover the facts surrounding the murder of a woman named Lucille Reynolds, who had been blackmailing Dominic with a sex film. Naturally, Reynolds' death casts suspicion on Dominic, so if Masters can find the actual killer, his client will be cleared. His main leads are the other women — prostitutes, all — who appear in the film being used for blackmail. Aiding him on the investigation are his teenage nephew Keith (Devin Goldenberg) and Dominic's mistress-for-pay, Cora Merrill (Madeline Le Roux, who was cast after doing a nude play in New York, *The Dirtiest Show in Town*).

Further plot details are unnecessary, since the story exists primarily to hang some sex and yuks. However, it wildly succeeds at this. As *New York Times* reviewer Howard Thompson wrote,

> This picture comes on like a fire engine, sparing nothing, and this viewer shook with laughter for a good — or shocked ten minutes. Some of the dialogue, slamming away at everything from television vigils to police procedure, prostitution and dope addiction, lands on target hilariously. The language is Anglo-Saxon, veering toward latter-day English. And the cast, gave it their all and we're not kidding.[11]

The sexual content goes far beyond the nudity of typical exploitation fare. One scene involves Masters screening the blackmail sex film (actually a negative thereof; perhaps the only way the graphic content could escape censorship), and we appear to see actual fellatio and what looks to be the simulated sodomy of a man by a woman with a strap-on dildo. Of course, this scene exists in the "hot" version; apparently Hessel's request for two versions was fulfilled, and these acts are likely not in the "cold" version.

The most notorious scene in the movie involves necrophilia, as Masters has sex with a recently deceased woman he mistakes for unconscious. The scene had to be shot twice, because it was shot originally incorrectly as a night scene and was shot over again as a day scene. According to Garfield, the later dialogue that referred back to that scene was spoken by Mel Stewart, playing police Lt. Fowler, on the front steps of the precinct house ("The first rule you learn at the Police Academy — don't fuck 'em if they stop breathing") is routinely quoted to him when he's recognized in public.[12]

As for the humor, there is surprisingly little parody-style subversion of the hard-boiled genre outside of the protagonist being an overweight gumshoe who prefers milk to booze and who prefers kinky sex to heroics. A few moments subtly parody the detective genre. In the scene in which Dominic hires Masters, there is the usual amount of exposition, with the client rattling off names and providing leads. In a normal detective story, this exchange of information would go smoothly, and the hero would immediately be off tracking the first lead. But in *Cry Uncle*, Masters clumsily requires spellings on all the names his client throws around as leads—smartly lampooning the too-easy nature of the archetypal "hire" scene.

The film could have gone much further in its genre spoofing; *Cry Uncle* has voice-over narration, but it is not in the hard-boiled style, and it's not even delivered by Garfield. (His only voice-over comes in the necrophilia scene, which was apparently done in post-production as an afterthought to solve pacing issues.) Instead, *Cry Uncle* spends most of its comedic energies on random sex jokes—totally unrelated to the story—that manage to cram in yet more off-color content. Every character has some prurient bit of business. For instance, when Masters runs into trouble with airport security, they confiscate his paperback novel *Swallow the Leader*. Our first glance of Dominic finds him reading *Screw* magazine. And when Jake locates one of his male suspects, he catches him masturbating. This is not to say that the film doesn't attempt social critique in minor ways, but they come off largely as cheap shots.

If Avildsen presented a balanced criticism of both conventional society and counterculture in *Joe*, *Cry Uncle* is a little more in lockstep with its time, mainly thumbing its nose at traditional values. An early scene has a naked woman preparing to use a red-white-and-blue sex toy (a similar gag is used later in the film with flag-themed rolling papers), and another scene has Cora having sex with the teenaged Keith while the national anthem plays on the television ("A powerful political statement, my bit for the anti-war effort," jokes Odell about this scene on the DVD commentary track). Later, Masters interrogates a prostitute while having sex with her next to a painting of Jesus.

In fairness, there are also a few jokes aimed at counterculture occurring in a scene where a room full of stoned hippies, the most vocal being Lloyd Kaufman, wonder whether the events they spy in the motel parking lot are real or merely part of their hallucinations.

One event happened

Mistress-for-pay, Cora Merrill (Madeline Le Roux), in a scene from *Cry Uncle* (1971).

during production that didn't make it into the film. Production assistant Steve Tisch (who also had a bit part as a motel manager) was in charge of delivering a prop police car for a scene. He drove up to the motel in the suburbs, where many in the cast and crew were staying, and playfully hit the siren on the car. The sound triggered a rush of people flushing marijuana down toilets before they realized they were not the target of a real police raid. Tisch withstood the wrath of the others for the rest of the film and well into his budding producing career. Years later he won the 1995 Best Picture Oscar for *Forrest Gump.*

This strange concoction of humor, sex and mystery was edited by Avildsen. When the film was ready to screen, publicist Arthur Rubin was able to attract critics who would not normally attend such a film. As Avildsen and Odell remember, this was because of the publicist's association with a highbrow outfit like Janus Films.[13] Among *Cry Uncle*'s reviewers was *Time*'s Stefan Kanfer, who praised it for busting the clichés of soft-core pornography — especially for casting a male lead who was not a "nude superman" and who likely would be known for posterity as being "the first blue-movie comedian."[14] Kanfer praised Garfield's performance too, writing that the actor "lends each scene a Rabelaisian gusto and surprise."

Such high praise from a prestigious publication may make it easier to swallow that Avildsen — fresh from directing *Joe*, a film that would become a mainstream hit — would return immediately to low-budget sexploitation. However, it should be remembered that *Cry Uncle* was made before *Joe*'s release and subsequent triumph. As Avildsen said in an interview in *The Directors: Take Two*, "After *Joe* was finished I was anxious to make another picture" because it pays the rent.[15] What's more, had it not been a surprise hit, *Joe*, with its orgy scene and plentiful nudity might have gone down in cinema history (albeit mistakenly) with a "sexploitation" label. So perhaps Avildsen didn't see *Joe* as much of a deviation between his early sexploitation films (*Turn on to Love, Guess What We Learned in School Today*) and *Cry Uncle.*

Further, *Cry Uncle* should be viewed in the context of the 1970s popularity of sex in the cinema. The pornographic features *Deep Throat* (1972), *Behind the Green Door* (1972) and *The Devil in Miss Jones* (1973) attracted mainstream viewers of both sexes during a period now referred to as "porno chic." There was not the stigmatization of on-screen sex that existed before or after, especially in Avildsen's home base of New York City. It seems that, given the acceptance (and even vogue) of the Sex Film, that Avildsen's flourishes as a filmmaker were able to be appreciated as true artistry, even when he was working with blue subject matter. In fact, Garfield recalls seeing Avildsen films in New York in the 1960s and considering them "art films."[16]

Returning to sexual subject matter after critical success is a pattern Avildsen would repeat. His segment for the sex-comedy anthology *Fore Play* came shortly after directing Jack Lemmon to an Oscar in *Save the Tiger*. This seems to indicate that sexual subject matter was something that interested Avildsen and, as long as it was acceptable mainstream commercial product (as it was in the 1970s), Avildsen wanted to mix it into his *oeuvre*. Avildsen reportedly even entertained the idea of a sequel, to be named *The Stiff Dick* (a play off *Cry Uncle*'s British release title of *Super Dick* and the necrophilia content, which was to be bumped up in the sequel). In that story Jake Masters would get the job of transporting a corpse from London to San Francisco and then become involved with an international necrophilia ring.

In any case, *Cry Uncle* did not stigmatize its personnel. Garfield would round out the rest of the decade as an in-demand character actor, working for the 1970s' most prestigious directors, Francis Ford Coppola, Robert Altman and William Friedkin. Avildsen's most attention-getting work was soon to come. And although they were less strongly associated with *Cry Uncle*, bit player Paul Sorvino (*Goodfellas*, TV's *Law and Order*) and production assistant Tisch would go on to long careers in Hollywood. Sorvino had another important milestone during the movie. Avildsen drove him home after a day of shooting, and Sorvino bragged about the recent birth of his daughter — a future actress named Mira Sorvino who would win a Supporting Actress Oscar for her role in *Mighty Aphrodite* (1995). She was born September 28, 1967. And character actor Mel Stewart, who played Lt. Fowler, had a long career and later gained fame for playing Henry Jefferson on TV's *All in the Family*.

Besides symbolizing Avildsen's interest in lowbrow material, *Cry Uncle* is also emblematic of the loyalty the director instilled in his cast and crew. For many actors (Devin Goldenberg and five other cast members) and crew members (Kaufman and almost ten others), the film represented a repeat occasion of working with Avildsen. Goldenberg had previously worked with Avildsen on *Guess What We Learned in School Today?*. And many of the personnel would go on to work with the director again (perhaps most notably Sorvino, who would star in Avildsen's *Slow Dancing in the Big City*). Only Boyle and his *Joe* cast mate K Callan (who was offended by the script, according to Avildsen) are known to have turned down roles in *Cry Uncle*.[17]

Production Notes

Directed by: John G. Avildsen. Writers: Novel "Lie A Little, Die A Little," Michael Brett; Screenplay: David Odell; Additional dialogue: Allen Garfield and John G. Avildsen. Producers: David Jay Disick, producer; Ian Merrick, executive producer; Frank Vitale, associate producer. Original Music: Harper MacKay. Cinematographer: John G. Avildsen. Editor: John G. Avildsen. Art Director: Henry M. Shrady III. Make Up Department:

Richard P. Wolkis, hair stylist: Marcia Jean Kurtz. Production Manager: Lloyd Kaufman, production manager. Second Unit Directors or Assistant Directors: Dick Carballo, assistant director. Art Department: Nick Kaufman, assistant art director. Sound Department: Jack Cooley, sound re-recording mixer; Michael Scott Goldbaum, sound mixer; Charles Hansen, boom operator. Camera and Electrical Department: Ralf D. Bode, lighting director; Stephen Bower, second assistant camera; Jay Good, still photographer; Ralf Hotchkiss, first assistant camera; Nikko Karant, still photographer; Aristedes Pappidas, gaffer; Al Sentesy, grip. Editorial Department: Sam Bender, assistant editor; Stan Bochner, assistant editor. Music Department: Harper MacKay, conductor. Miscellaneous Crew: Patricia Greene, script supervisor; Sheppard Greene, production assistant; Jay Lewin, production assistant; Joyce Lippmann, production assistant; Mary Sparacio, production assistant; Marc Stone, title designer; Steven Tisch, production assistant. Filming Locations: LaGuardia Airport, Queens, New York City, New York, USA Production Company: 15th Street Films. Distributors: Cambist Films (1971) (USA) (theatrical); Cinépix Film Properties (CFP) (1972) (Canada) (theatrical); Troma Team Video (1999) (USA) (DVD).

Cast — in credits order ; Allen Garfield, Jake Masters; Madeleine Le Roux, Cora Merrill; Devin Goldenberg, Keith; David Kirk, Jason Dominic; Sean Walsh, Gene Sprigg; Melvin Stuart, Lt. Fowler; Debbi Morgan, Olga Winter; Pamela Gruen, Renee; Maureen Byrnes, Lena Right; Bruce Pecheur, Larry Caulk; Nancy Salmon, Connie; Marcia Jean Kurtz, Russian Girl; Reuben Schafer, Russian; Chuck Pfeiffer, Texas; Paul Sorvino, Coughing Cop; Ray Barron, Bald Cop; Joe Young, Masochist; Dean Tait, Spike; Patricia Wheel, Keith's Mother; Jan Saint, Bar Tender; Aaron Banks, Cop; Jackson Beck, Narrator (voice); Frank Vitale, 1st Hippie; Lloyd Kaufman, 2nd Hippie; Liz Ferroll, Girl.

CHAPTER 4

The Stoolie

At Odds with the Star

Rocky and *The Karate Kid* may be Avildsen's most famous underdogs, but perhaps the biggest underdog of his film career was Roger Pitman — Jackie Mason's lead character in *The Stoolie* (1972). It was Mason's first film role. It was also an early film marred by an argument with the star, one that eventually led to Avildsen being fired from the project.

Jackie Mason's lead role was reminiscent of Allen Garfield's starring performance in *Cry Uncle* the year before. But *The Stoolie* is a step forward — an interesting little film that prepares Avildsen for the Oscar-winning performance that he elicits from Jack Lemmon in *Save the Tiger*, the 1973 film that turned Avildsen into a major director in the eyes of Hollywood.

Jackie Mason[1] stars as Roger Pitman, a loser from Weehawken, New Jersey, who makes an occasional hundred dollars by setting up his friends for the cops. Nobody respects him. The criminals he deals with don't bother to pay him his part of the score. Former friends don't want him hanging around. Even the drug dealer who owns the local pool hall asks him to leave, saying, "I run a respectable joint."

Avildsen was impressed with Mason's acting skills. "Jackie had a very Chaplin-esque quality to him and he did a terrific job with his character," Avildsen once said. "He was very touching and funny and when we needed straight dramatic scenes, he could do that too."[2]

Marcia Jean Kurtz is believable in the role of the female lead as Sheila Morrison. The film was Kurtz's second consecutive role with Avildsen, having also appeared in a small role in his previous film *Cry Uncle*.

Dan Frazer provides a solid performance as detective sergeant Alex Brogan. Frazer would later become better known for his six years as Captain Frank McNeil on *Kojak*.[3] Thayer David, who would later appear in *Fore Play*, played the crooked Lattimore, the target of "the stoolie." David would also appear in *Rocky* as the fight promoter.

The sometimes clever script was the product of writers Larry Alexander, Eugene Price and Marc B. Ray. It was the first movie script for Alexander, who would later become active in writing for television on *The Six Million Dollar Man, Marcus Welby, MD, Matt Helm, Ellery Queen, Baretta, Fantasy Island, CHiPs,* and *MacGyver.*

Price, who also co-authored with Avildsen *Guess What We Learned in School Today?*, later wrote for television, including scripts for *Kung Fu, The Streets of San Francisco, One Life to Live,* and several episodes of *Marcus Welby, MD.* Ray's credits included work on the *Ellery Queen* television series.

William Goldstein got his first shot in films by providing the music for *The Stoolie.* He would later serve a similar role for the TV series *Fame.*

Avildsen served as chief cameraman for the shoot, but he had help from Charlie Clifton and Ralf Bode. Bode had previously worked with Avildsen on *Guess What We Learned in School Today?* and *Joe,* and would work with Avildsen in *Fore Play* and *Slow Dancing in the Big City*; he also worked as director of photography for *Saturday Night Fever* and won an Oscar for his work on *Coal Miner's Daughter.*

The early scenes were shot on location in Weehawken, with most of the remaining work done on location in Miami. The film opens with a hijacked truck, loaded with television sets, racing through the back streets of Weehawken. Pitman directs the two thieves (Josip Elic and Reid Cruickshanks, who was the bartender in *Joe*) to a warehouse to store their booty. They unload the truck, giving Pitman $50 for his work and then taking it back when he complains that it's not much.

Pitman leaves the scene and wanders the streets, first stopping at a friend's house and then moving on to a local pool hall full of various hustlers. He's in his element here, as the stands at the bar while drug deals are carried on around him.

Pitman's transformation begins at the bar when he alerts the cops to a friend (Marco Ruiz, played by Richard "Dick" Carballo, the star of *Guess What We Learned in School Today?*) with a stash of stolen jewelry. Cop Brogan shows up and fires his gun into the ceiling. The frightened Ruiz drops his stash and runs outside — directly and fatally into the path of a Hertz rental truck.

The death of his friend shakes Pitman, but not Brogan. When the truck driver tries to explain that it was not his fault ("I just had the brakes checked"), Brogan dismisses his concern. "Don't worry about it. Small town creep. He's nothing," Brogan tells the driver.

The denigration of his friend obviously bothers Pitman. In the next scene, he is the only mourner as Ruiz is buried in a pauper's grave on Hart Island, entombed in a pine box. The scene was shot on location at Hart Island, New York potter's field. "I think we're the only movie to ever shoot there," Avildsen said.

Pitman is soon back to work, but his goal has changed. On his next job, he's asked to set up a major criminal named Lattimore (Thayer David). "Don't worry," Pitman assures Alex, "Lattimore is one of my best friends."

The deal involves getting Lattimore to accept a payment of $7,500 from Pitman. Once the deal is done, Alex will step in and arrest the crime boss. But Pitman double crosses the cops and keeps the money for himself. He steals the cop's car, drives it to the airport, and catches a flight to Miami. A limo ride from the airport puts him at the door of Miami's plush Doral Hotel, where he has a reservation under the name Roger Smith.

When the grungy-looking Pitman approaches the hotel clerk (Jack Nagel) about the reservation, he is told that Mr. Smith has not yet checked in. Pitman has to identify himself as Smith to get the room.

The scene cuts back to Weehawken, where detective Alex Brogan is talking with his boss, the Weehawken police chief (Lee Steele). The $7,500 that Roger scammed from Alex was the department's entire discretionary budget. Alex is facing discipline — possibly firing — for letting Roger steal the money. With a week remaining before a report must be filed, Alex turns in his badge and his gun and asks for a week's leave to track down Roger and recover the money.

Cut back to the hotel, where Roger starts on a personal program of remaking himself— shave, shower, and a round of shopping for new clothes in the hotel shops. His choice of clothes is atrocious, but by the end of the day he is clean and more presentable.

The new Roger Pitman quickly starts looking for female companionship. His first move, on a gorgeous lifeguard (Gigi Gaus), fails when she responds in German and seemingly doesn't understand his advances. He seems to make more progress when a blonde (Lee Meredith) accepts his offer to rub suntan lotion on her back, and she asks him to undo her strap. He quickly offers to expand his duties, saying, "I'm a real expert at rubbing people's fronts." That idea is squashed when the girl's hunk of a boyfriend (Robert "Big Daddy" Knapp) returns and says, "Maybe you'd like to rub mine."

Cut back to Alex, who has traced Pitman's flight to Miami and drives overnight to catch up with his prey. He stops for gas outside of Miami and becomes victim to a crooked station owner (William "Bill" McCutcheon, who will appear three years later as a benign station owner in *W.W. and the Dixie Dancekings*). The greasy mechanic offers to check his oil and, while under the hood, carefully removes the distributor cap from the engine. He then looks up from the motor and asks Alex how the car had been running. When Alex says everything was fine, the mechanic responds that he has mechanical problems and was lucky to have made it as far as he had. Alex tries to crank the car, but with no success. He ends up staying overnight while the mechanic orders a part to be delivered the next morning.

Pitman is still searching for female companionship. His next effort is to attend a show featuring a beautiful solo singer (Ann Marie). The brunette finishes her set by strolling to his table and seductively singing the last few lines "Besema Mucho" to him. The final bars are done with her lips almost touching his. When the show is over, he heads backstage, grinning broadly, and knocks on her door. She cracks the door, and looks him over. Roger asks, "What does Besema Mucho mean?" She replies, "Beat it, creep, or I'll call my boyfriend."

He runs into a guy in the hallway, airs his complaints, and is advised to try another show with more willing participants. That turns out to be a haven for the elderly, with a middle-age-plus singer (Peppy Fields, playing herself in her film debut) who dishes out bromides for her audience ("Start living your life like you want to live, as long as you don't hurt anybody"). After he leaves, the camera picks him up walking over one of Miami's many bridges. When he approaches the mid-point of the span, he finds a young brunette (Marcia Jean Kurtz) staring over the edge toward the water. She hears him approach, turns and says, "Are you thinking about jumping?"

"I was about to ask you the same thing," Pitman replies.

They start talking about their lonely lives and eventually end up at a diner to continue the conversation over coffee. When she confesses that she's still a virgin, he asks, "Would you like to go to bed with me?"

She turns him down. "Nothing personal," she adds. "I don't even know your name." They exchange names, continue the conversation, and agree to a date for the next day when she will show him some of the tourists sites in Miami.

Cut back to Alex, the next morning. The part for his car has "arrived on the morning Greyhound" and his car is ready to return to the road. Alex pays his $28 bill and mentions that he's a policeman searching for a fugitive thief. The mechanic wishes him luck, adding "If there's anything I can't stand, it's a thief."

Cut back to Miami. Pitman (dressed more conservatively than the previous day) and Sheila are visiting the Parrot Jungle and strolling through flamingo-stocked gardens and parks. As they stroll, they talk — with Pitman opening up with new levels (for him) of self-disclosure. He enjoys being with Sheila, but admits he's reluctant to get optimistic about their relationship. "For some reason, nothing seems to work out for me," he says. "I'm afraid to get excited about anything."

Sheila quickly notices his problem. "You hide behind a front," she says. "Everybody does."

He's not convinced. "But what if what defines you on the outside is really real?" he asks. "And down inside is the phony person?"

We don't get an immediate answer. The scene cuts to Alex, in his car, pulled over by a local sheriff of Climpton County (Burtt Harris, who worked with Avildsen in 1964 on Otto Preminger's *Hurry Sundown*) for doing 80 in a 50-mph zone. Alex tries to appeal for leniency, using the "from-one-cop-to-another-cop" line. Without his badge, though, that doesn't work. After being threatened with jail time, Alex is allowed to leave after paying a $75 "fine-bribe."

Cut back to Miami. Pitman and Sheila are at the local dog track. The lead dog crosses the line, and Pitman tears up his ticket. The poor guy is still losing. But he's doing better in the next scene: He and Sheila are dining on Beef Stroganoff at a nice restaurant. Roger doesn't really know what he's eating, but knows it tastes good. Both are dressed for the occasion, Roger in a white suit and Sheila in the proverbial "little black dress." This is the scene that got Avildsen fired. But more about that later.

They leave for Sheila's hotel room. Sheila is a little tipsy as she fumbles with her key, but they open the door and enter the darkened room. She walks over to the beds and turns on a light, causing Pitman to say, "So this is your room. I never thought I'd get a chance to see it."

That triggers some awkward movements from both parties before they finally kiss and end up in bed together. Sheila is still a bit reluctant, and asks, "You do love me?"

"Of course I do," Roger answers. "I never loved anybody else. Not even me. That's the truth." That satisfies her, and the two get into bed.

Meanwhile, Alex has finally made it to Miami and is checking in with the Miami Police Chief (Phil Philbin). He shows his local counterpart photos of Pitman, without revealing what Pitman did. The cop already knows. After pretending to ask Alex for some "big city" advice and describing Pitman as looking like he is part Puerto Rican and part Jew, the local cop says, "How could you give 7,500 bucks to someone with a face like that?"

While the two cops talk, Pitman and Sheila are up and strolling around a local garden. They stop to gaze at a statue of Venus. She is still a little cautious about their relationship, wondering if he's going to leave her now that they've had sex. Pitman dismisses the idea, saying that he wants to marry her. Sheila isn't sure he means it, and neither is Pitman. But after thinking about it a moment, he says he must mean it. She accepts.

In the next scene, Pitman enters his hotel room, smiling. He keeps smiling as he opens the curtains, but the happy attitude comes to an abrupt stop when he opens a door to find Alex staring back at him.

Alex knocks Pitman to the floor and starts looking for his money. "Where is it?" he asks Pitman. "It's gone," is the only reply.

"My career, my whole life, down the drain," Alex complains, while kicking Pitman. Sheila enters, spots the attack, and throws her body over Pitman in an attempt to protect him. Alex does stop the kicking and resumes his search for the money.

Pitman, still sprawled on the floor, reaches into a pocket and gives Sheila a small jewelry box holding a diamond ring. Alex spots the move and takes the ring. Pitman protests, saying he bought it for Sheila. "I paid 1,800 for it." Alex pockets the ring anyway, planning to get a refund.

Cut to the jewelry shop, with Alex standing behind Pitman and Sheila and requesting a refund on the ring. The ring was purchased with stolen money, Alex explains, and he has come from New Jersey to take the culprit and the stolen money back to the state. The problem: Alex cannot show his badge. The owner (Frank Goldstein) is firm: no refunds. And, since Alex has no police authority, he won't give it back as stolen money either. He does offer to buy the ring back for $600. Pitman negotiates a $1,000 price.

They're still short on money, and Alex demands the full sum. Pitman has one possibility, a cousin Ralphie (Jerome Rudolph) who now lives in Miami. This falls flat, though, with Ralphie dismissing his cousin as a loser who always gets into trouble. This character was not in the script that Avildsen shot.

That leaves Alex, Pitman and Sheila still short of money. They find rooms at a $5-a-night boarding house while Alex and Pitman think of ways to get the funds. Sheila argues that Alex should let them go.

Pitman comes up with one idea and leaves. He's next seen in a gun store, buying a pistol. After purchasing the gun, and letting the store owner (Richard McKenzie) show him how to use it, he points the gun at the man and demands the money from the cash register. "I hate to do this, but I've got a problem," Pitman says.

The store owner laughs and says, "You've got a bigger problem than you think." Pitman picked up an unloaded gun, the man continues, and he dares Pitman to shoot. Meanwhile, he picks up the other gun and aims it at Pitman.

Pitman can't shoot and instead turns and runs toward the door. The owner takes aim and pulls the trigger, but the gun doesn't fire. He then realizes Alex had the loaded gun all the time.

The next day, they try a third option: taking out a loan for $7,000. The problem with that approach is that Pitman is from out of town, has no job and no collateral. The bank's loan office (Hope Pomerance) won't approve a loan without a co-signer. Pitman approaches Alex about co-signing, but the cop vetoes that idea.

By that night, they're no further along than they were two days before. Sheila has felt the call of domestication: She's cooking for the boys, using an outdoor grill. Sheila asks Alex how he would get the money if he were in a similar situation. "Honestly?" he asks. Then adds, "I don't know of an honest way to get it."

The response tells Pitman that his days of freedom are numbered. "I have to go to jail, 10, 15 years."

Sheila refuses to accept that option: "Nope. I waited too long for you to come along." Later, in bed, Pitman has been picked up by her optimism and he talks to Sheila about the kids they will have together.

The next morning, Alex returns to the boarding house with a morning paper. He reads aloud a front-page story about drug trafficking in Miami. His idea: They locate some of the drug dealers and get the reward for their arrest.

All three get in Alex's car as they drive through some of Miami's seedy sections, looking for drugs. They finally pull over near a small grocery store, where Alex gets out to buy a pack of cigarettes. He looks around before returning to the car and decides to sit there awhile.

Soon a vehicle pulls in front of the store. The driver gets out, unlocks the trunk and enters the store. A second person walks up to the car with a bag of groceries, places them in the trunk, and closes the lid. The driver quickly returns to the car and drives away. Alex identifies the driver as a dealer. He cranks his car and follows, while Pitman and Sheila seemed confused.

They follow the driver until he turns off into a deserted industrial area. When he stops, Alex parks two buildings away, draws his gun, and gets out of the car. Pitman and Sheila ask what he's doing, and he tells them to just stay in the car.

The director who replaced Avildsen used a long shot from an elevated pedestal for the next scene. From a distance, the viewer sees the driver get out of the car and remove the bag of groceries from his trunk. When the gangster reaches the corner with his grocery bag, Alex gets the drop on him, pushes him up against the wall, takes the bag, and knocks the man to the ground.

He rushes back to the car and hurriedly drives off as Pitman and Sheila asks what happened. When they get a safe distance from the robbery, Alex stops and tears the bag apart to see what's inside.

He hits the jackpot: Ten thousand dollars in cash plus a stash of white powder that Alex says will bring $15,000 on the streets in Weehawken. He gets out of the car and stashes the drugs in a hollow spot in the bumper of his car.

Pitman and Sheila are appalled. "What, you think I'm the only cop with a hollow bumper in New Jersey?" Alex asks. Pitman, by now fully reformed, wants nothing to do with this new deal. Sheila agrees. Alex, still elated with his newfound riches, agrees to let them go. "I'll drop you both off; you're off the hook," he says. "I'll sell this stuff in Jersey and put in for retirement."

Alex puts them out on the street and offers Pitman a $100 bill. Pitman refuses, and he and Sheila get out. Alex calls Pitman back and stuffs the hundred dollars into his shirt pocket, telling him he'll have to have money to eat.

Alex then returns to the car and drives off, with his bumper leaking a trail of white dust as he drives. Roger and Sheila see the white trail, smile at each other and walk away as the final credits roll.

The ending is satisfying, leaving the viewer with the sense that Roger Pitman has finally come out a winner.

Still, much of the movie is sad. All of the major characters are victims. Victimage is portrayed as something that none can avoid. Thus, even though lead actor Mason is a comedian, there is little humor in the overall move.

Mason once said that comedy "is a great escape for anyone who wants

Jackie Mason as Roger Pittman in *The Stoolie* (1972), which may have been Avildsen's biggest underdog of his film career.

to complain."[4] Along that line, one reviewer described *The Stoolie* as "slow pathos masquerading as comedy."[5] But this movie doesn't fit well within the comedy category. Most people will have trouble finding much humor in it. The focus, instead, is on the pathos of losers.

Overall, *The Stoolie* is a commendable effort for a young director. At times, it seems to be an experimental movie, one in which the director is testing his skills and expanding his repertoire of techniques. He would use some of them later.

The opening scene, for example, uses a single camera to capture the speeding truck as it races toward the warehouse and the stoolie. Avildsen would later use a similar technique in the opening scene of *Rocky*.

Another minor problem is that Sheila's hair changes length a couple of times, suddenly shorter and then back to original length again. The shorter hair appears in scenes inside Alex's car, while the trio is driving around looking for money ideas.

That continuity problem appears to be a result of Avildsen getting fired from the film — the first of several firings in his directorial career. The scene that triggered his dismissal was the restaurant scene: Roger and Sheila dining as the sun sets on the picturesque hotel. A second scene was scheduled for the same day: Roger at the floor show that features brunette Ann Marie. The first shot required only Mason and Kurtz. The second required a band, dancing girls, and dozens of extras.

The problem: Avildsen, intent on getting a great sunset shot, kept shooting and re-shooting the first scene. Meanwhile, the band, the dancers, and the extras sat around waiting for their shot — with their fees mounting by the hour. Mason, who was really the boss of the film, fired Avildsen that night.

"It was really my error," Avildsen said later. "I should have shot the big scene first and then, after all those people went away, shot the simple scene of two people at the table. I didn't do that. So Jackie fired me."[6]

Avildsen went to Mason's hotel room the next morning to apologize and ask for his job back. Mason wouldn't even open the door for him. Avildsen ended up lying on the floor, talking to the actor under the door. He even offered to pay for the last few days of shooting himself, but Mason wouldn't budge.[7]

Although Avildsen accepted much of the blame, he has always believed that two other people involved in the movie were conspiring against him. One of his former girlfriends, Ronnie Mellen, had gotten a job as a still photographer and a small part as a girl working at the Hertz counter. She brought along her new husband, Chase Mellen III, to the shooting. Avildsen believed the two worked to get him fired. Mellen, who is listed as the film's producer, ended up directing the remaining scenes. Their credits on *The Stoolie* remains the only film credits for either of the pair to date.

After the production shut down, Avildsen went off to take a job directing Jack Lemmon in *Save the Tiger*. Months later, Mason found somebody to finish the shooting. By then, Kurtz had gotten a haircut.

If you disregard the minor mistakes, *The Stoolie* can be viewed as the film that crystallizes the underdog theme Avildsen would use in later movies. For fans who want to follow the development of Avildsen's film vision, *The Stoolie* is a must-see.

Avildsen, though, still has regrets. "I was very disappointed that the picture never got finished and put together properly because I think it could have launched Jackie Mason's movie career a lot sooner and I think he would have surprised a lot more people," Avildsen said. "He had an opportunity that slipped by and it's unfortunate."[8]

Production Notes

Directed by: John G. Avildsen. Writers: Larry Alexander, Eugene Price, Marc B. Ray. Producer: Chase Mellen III, producer. Original Music: William Goldstein. Cinematographers: John G. Avildsen, Ralf Bode, Charlie Clifton. Editors: Stan Bochner, Gerry Greenberg. Casting Director: Edythe Maza. Art Director: Charles Bailey. Production Manager: Fred Caruso, production manager. Second Unit Director or Assistant Director: Burtt Harris, assistant director. Art Department: Clifford L. Benson, stand-by scenic; Larry Goodwin, props; Herbert Gruber, stand-by scenic. Sound Department: Bernard Blynder, sound recordist; Stanley Bochner, sound editor; Lane Childs, boom operator; Al Gramaglia, sound; Charles Hansen, boom operator; Sanford Rackow, sound editor; Michael Scott, sound recordist; Scott Warren, sound recordist. Special Effects Department: Louis Antzes, special effects. Camera and Electrical Department; John G. Avildsen, camera operator; Charlie Clifton, camera operator; William Crawford, grip; Stanley Ford, gaffer; William Garbett III, grip; Charles Guanci, key grip; Wayne Hagan, grip; Ralph M. Hotchkiss, first assistant camera; Ronnie Mellen, still photographer; Mel Noped, key grip; Aristedes Pappidas, gaffer; Carl Teitelbaum, electrician; John A. Wilson, electrician; Marc Wyler, grip. Costume and Wardrobe Department: Lenore Bode, wardrobe. Editorial Department: Irving Rathner, negative cutter. Miscellaneous Crew: Maggie Condon, assistant to producer; Randa Haines, script supervisor; Neil R. Lipes, production assistant; Harold Rand, publicist; Roberta Rose, production secretary; Peter Runfolo, location coordinator; Gene Samuelson, title designer; George Silano, director: additional scenes; Stuart Silverman, assistant to producer; Filming Location: Weehawken, New Jersey; Hart Island, New York; Miami Beach, Florida. Distributors: Jama Films (1972) (USA) (theatrical), American Broadcasting Company (ABC) (1978) (USA) (TV) (original airing), Continental Distributing (1972) (USA) (theatrical), Reel Media International (2007) (worldwide) (all media).

Cast—in credits order: Jackie Mason, Roger Pitman; Josip Elic, 1st Hijacker; Reid Cruickshanks, 2nd Hijacker; Dan Frazer, Sgt. Alex Brogan; Leonard York, Maxie; Richard Carballo, Marco Ruiz; Babette New, Sylvia; Mary McKennedy, Pool Hall Girl; Sean Walch, Truck Driver; Thayer David, Lattimore; Ronnie Mellen, Hertz Girl; Marcie Knight, Limousine "Lady"; Jack Nagel, Doral Desk Clerk; Sonny Sands, Doral Bell Hop; Lee Steele, Weehawken Police Chief; Gigi Gaus, German Girl at Pool; Lee Meredith, Suntan Oil

Girl; Robert "Big Daddy" Knapp, Big Daddy at Pool; William McCutcheon, Gas Station Proprietor; Ann Marie, Nightclub Singer; Peppy Fields, Herself; Marcia Jean Kurtz, Sheila Morrison; Burtt Harris, Climpton County Sheriff; Phil Philbin, Miami Police Chief; Frank Goldstein, Jeweler; Jerome Rudolph, Cousin Ralphie; Mildred Smith, Mrs. Butler; Richard McKenzie, Gun Store Clerk; Hope Pomerance, Bank Officer.

CHAPTER 5

Save the Tiger

Knocking on the Door of the Academy Awards

Avildsen's work on *Joe* attracted the attention of the Hollywood establishment. Soon afterwards, he would land a project that would get the attention of the entire movie industry. *Save the Tiger* (1973) became his first major project, his first Hollywood film, won an Academy Award for star Jack Lemmon, and established Avildsen as an artistic force in cinema.

The film was based on a script by Steven Shagan. Shagan and Avildsen would later collaborate on *The Formula*, a movie critical of the oil industry. This one served as a preview of Shagan's cinematic themes, providing a critical look at the garment industry. Prior to *Save the Tiger*, Shagan had worked as an associate producer on the *Tarzan* television series, hardly anything that would indicate he would make a good scriptwriter. He had written the first draft quickly, out of frustrations that had developed from his own work.

He worked two more years after that to refine and re-work the script until he was satisfied. The polishing worked well, leading to an Oscar nomination for scriptwriting. He approached Lemmon with the finished product in 1970, while Lemmon was working on *April Fools*. As Freedland noted, "Shagan didn't know Lemmon, but that didn't stop him from approaching the star with the script, telling Lemmon that he wanted him to read the script and that he would haunt him until he did."[1]

Lemmon was skeptical. "What have you done before?" he asked. Shagan mentioned his work on the *Tarzan* series, a response that didn't increase his credibility with Lemmon, but must have worked since Lemmon read the script.

"After the first scene, I'm hooked," he said later. "It's so realistic, so honest. It didn't have the smell of cold Hollywood."[2]

44

Still, just because Lemmon liked the project was no guarantee that it would ever be produced. In fact, none of the Hollywood studios were interested. As Lemmon later said, "At that time, they still felt that three-quarters of the movie-going audience was thirty or under. Rightly or wrongly, they felt that younger people wouldn't care. They all respected the script, but they just didn't feel there was an audience."[3]

One problem was that the movie's theme was viewed as un–American. "The men sitting behind the big studio desks were worried that the critique of American morals which *Save the Tiger* represented was nothing less than an attack on their beloved nation," Freedland wrote, adding that some of those executives thought it was anti–Semitic while others viewed it as Communist propaganda.[4]

One Paris studio showed some interest, suggesting that François Truffaut direct it and that Yves Montand take the starring role. Lemmon blocked that because he wanted the part and wanted the film made in Hollywood.

Shagan ended up working as producer himself, eventually making an arrangement with Paramount in which Filmways, Cirandinha, and Jalem Productions shared some of the cost."[5] The participation of Jalem, Lemmon's own company, was critical to making the project work. Lemmon helped cut down the cost by working for the Screen Actors Guild minimum wage. Shagan, meanwhile, devoted himself to the movie. As Freedland noted, "This was his big chance both to say something and to have an international star fronting his product."[6]

The story itself was a surprisingly boring modern morality play. Lemmon played Harry Stoner, a dress manufacturer who is facing bankruptcy and middle age. Stoner is a nice-enough guy, but one who finds himself constantly degraded by his own lack of moral standards. Badly in need of business, he sets up a customer with a prostitute so that he can seal a deal. She almost kills the hapless buyer. Short on cash to fulfill the order, Stoner plots to set fire to his own warehouse so he can use the insurance money to keep the factory running.

The title *Save the Tiger* comes from a brief street scene in which an environmental do-gooder is seen soliciting donations to protect endangered species. Those on the streets are beseeched to "save the tiger" with their donations, a plea that resonates with Stoner's own feelings of being on the endangered list.

Jack Gilford received a Supporting Actor Oscar nomination for his role as Stoner's reluctant partner. Other cast members included Laurie Heineman, Normann Burton, Patricia Smith, Thayer David, and Lara Parker. But Lemmon's character was the center of the story and the center of the film. The entire script covers the 24 hours of Stoner's life leading up to the arson.

The writing is crisp and to the point. At one point, Stoner's partner considers the similarities and differences of the two people assisting in them in their sins, Margo the prostitute and Charlie the arsonist. "Professionals, Charlie and Margo," he says. "One starts the fires, the other one puts them out." Later, Stoner finds himself with a companion, a young girl he met earlier during the day. "How old are you?" he asks. "Twenty," the girl replies. "Nobody's twenty," Stoner says ruefully.

With money, script, and a big-name star in hand, the film needed a director. Shagan suggested Avildsen, touting the job the director had done on the low-budget *Joe*. "I saw *Joe*, which knocked me out," Lemmon later said. "I couldn't believe that it had as much quality on the screen for that amount of money."

A meeting was arranged, one that Avildsen later recalled for the HBO series *The Directors*:

> [Lemmon] had just seen *Joe*, and he was blown away, he thought it was terrific. And he said, "Kid, I got to make a movie with you." And I said to him, "I have always been a fan of your work, but if you do this movie with me, if I direct it, if you choose me to direct it, I don't want to see you in it, I want to see this character. I don't want to see Jack Lemmon, I want to see this guy." He knew just what I was talking about. And he said, "Keep your eyes open, kid."

Avildsen's editing experience was apparent in one dramatic scene in which Lemmon delivers a speech before a large audience. As he speaks to the audience of men, he recalls his own war experiences. Avildsen deftly intersperses the speech scenes with depictions of bodies of soldiers. Lemmon struggles to maintain his composure as he seemingly perceives the audience transformed from real people into the bodies of his dead comrades from World War II. The scene becomes a pivotal point at which the audience can see Harry Stoner's world falling apart.

Stoner was indeed a complex man, and Lemmon had to delve into that complexity. Though drowning in debt and facing bankruptcy, he insisted on wearing expensive suits — so expensive that three characters make a comment about his attire.

Lemmon credited Avildsen with helping him capture the character. "John was a great help to me — no question about that," he told the producers of *The Directors*. "I think my instinct about the part from the beginning was pretty good and pretty well on. And John was happy about that." Avildsen focuses much of his attention on making sure that previous Lemmon characters were not visible to the camera. If Avildsen saw Lemmon using a mannerism that he didn't like, Avildsen would call "cut." In most instances, Lemmon knew why the cut had been called. "You want me to do it without the eyebrow?" he would say.

"Yeah, try it without the eyebrow," Avildsen would reply.

Lemmon also praised Avildsen's ability to adjust to the personality of different actors. "He knew that you don't treat every actor the same way," Lemmon said. "There is a way to reach me, reach you, reach him. There is a way to approach actors differently as you get to know them. And he had a very good instinct on how to reach people."

Maybe. But it wasn't always easy. For one thing, Avildsen insisted on shooting the movie in sequence and on location following two weeks of rehearsal. Both decisions were controversial, because they increased costs for a movie that was strapped for cash.

Jack Lemmon as Harry Stoner in *Save the Tiger* (1973).

Studio productions were cheaper, and — if locations were used — it was more cost-efficient to shoot all of the scenes at one location during the same set-up, rather than returning at a later date to shoot in sequence. Thus, as Freedland noted, "Normally that is a recipe for economic disaster, but he was certain that this particular film needed the extra flow of adrenalin that Harry Stoner's problems *in situ* provided."[7]

At times, Lemmon seemed in awe of Avildsen's skills. He recalled one scene for *The Directors*:

> [The first shot] was going to take place in an office downtown in the garment district. What John did was to track the camera all the way through, showing the factory in the background as we played the scene. The risk when you play a scene like that with a moving camera: You can go all day and never get it because it's so complicated. We got it and got it very rapidly and bang!, we went to my office continuing on. I think we picked up one page and a half or so.

Later he told the authors, "I had such confidence in him. I think if he had asked me to jump out the window, I would have done it."

At other times, Lemmon had trouble accepting Avildsen's ideas. They had a disagreement over one critical scene that Avildsen wanted to shoot at the historic Mayan Theater in Los Angeles: As Freedman recalled:

Because the deal for the arson attempt is struck in a cinema, the director insisted on using a real picture theater — one of the pseudo classical palaces built in the 1930s and now eking out a seedy existence showing blue movies. And because he wanted the degradation being suffered by the men from the garment factory to be emphasized, Avildsen wanted a real film to be shown on the screen as the men talk to their arsonist.

That was too much. Jack asked him to stop the film and dub the soundtrack later — audiences could hear the dialogue, mostly a holier-than-thou commentary on the need for sexual freedom, while the conspirators talked. With a real film being shown, Jack found himself constantly looking at the screen — he had never seen a blue movie before. "Here I was, trying to be disturbed, secretive and frightened while watching one girl make love to another girl with a peach, and then this guy walks in."[8]

A bigger problem may have been the seriousness with which Lemmon approached the project. He immersed himself so totally in the role that, Freedland wrote, "Afterwards, he recognized he had been fairly close to a breakdown without realizing it."[9] At first glance, there seemed to be no major problem. His character was similar to his role in *Days of Wine and Roses*. The difference: For *Save the Tiger*, he spent three years imagining how he might portray the role. As Freedland wrote, "Once more, it was a case of Jack stepping into his character's handmade shoes. Only this time it took on a seriousness that had never occurred before. He needed empathy with every character he played."[10]

Lemmon told Freeman, "It was not important that I liked the character I played. What was very important was that I cared about him and understood him. I didn't agree with anything that the character believed in or one word that he said, but I never cared about a character more."[11]

Once filming started, the role took over his life. He started talking to himself, snapping at those around him. Sometimes, after getting home, he wouldn't talk. "I was so distraught, I couldn't shake it," Lemmon later said. "I couldn't relate to anything else. I couldn't give a damn about anything else. I was too far into this role and I was afraid of losing Harry Stoner."[12] As Freedland wrote:

> He took the dress manufacturer home with him in the evenings.... Worse, he traveled with him to and from the studio. He would be driving down Sunset Boulevard when, for no apparent reason, tears would cascade down his cheeks. He didn't know why — he would just suddenly weep and there was nothing he could do to control it.[13]

Eventually Lemmon realized his role was behind his unusual behavior. His wife Felicia and the rest of his family saved him. Felicia started driving him to work because the crying became such a problem. "If Felicia had not been an actress and understood what I was going through, I really think she might have packed up and left," Lemmon later said.[14]

For Lemmon, the film was an important morality play. When it was completed, he toured the country to lecture on its theme, with stops that included Harvard University and other college campuses.

His first sense of its value may have come when he was in Italy, filming *Avanti!* with director Billy Wilder. Avildsen and Shagan flew to Italy with a cut of the film. Avildsen, Shagan, Lemmon and Wilder viewed the film in a small screening room. The film broke a couple of times, but the trio finally saw all of it. When it was over, Wilder was the first to speak.

"There's only one thing wrong with it," the director said.

When he paused briefly, Avildsen held his breath — waiting for the criticism to follow. Then Wilder added. "The only thing wrong with it is that I didn't direct it."

"That really made me feel good," Avildsen recalled.

Generally, the critics agreed. They were appreciative of Avildsen's direction, but unimpressed with Shagan's script — even though it was nominated for best adapted screenplay and won the Writers Guild of America award for best screenplay. Lemmon's performance got most of the accolades. As Freedland wrote, "It wasn't the Jack Lemmon anyone expected to see."[15] Rex Reed, of the *Los Angeles Times* wrote "It is one of the best films ever to come out of the Hollywood studios and it's unquestionably the summit of Jack Lemmon's acting career."[16]

Another *Times* critic, Charles Champlin, called it "the best thing Lemmon has ever done, which is saying a great deal."[17] Christopher Null praised Lemmon's "harrowing portrayal of Harry Stoner, who at first seems your average self-loathing businessman, but soon enough proves to have a battalion of skeletons in his closet."[18] Similarly, Walter Frith noted that Lemmon had been "a shining example of screen acting in its purest form."[19]

Richard Cuskelly, of the *Herald Examiner*, said Lemmon's role was "one of those hair-raising gut performances that have a life far outside the time and span of the film."[20] Similarly, Clive Hirschhorn, of London's *Sunday Express*, wrote, "There's no denying Jack Lemmon's stunning performance or the skill with which the film had been made."[21]

Karney noted that the movie was one of Lemmon's "few films to concern itself with failure."[22] Karney listed two other Lemmon films — *The China Syndrome* and *Missing*— which were similar in that "Lemmon was encouraged to dig deep into himself, and into his acting skills, and the result was a new economy, a newly mature insight into the characters that gave each film its special depth."[23]

Avildsen's work drew similar praise. "As a testament to questionable business ethics, *Save the Tiger* works," wrote Walter Frith, describing it as "a film that doesn't strain its convictions, it presents them honestly.... Don't mistake it as a preachy, self-indulgent guilt trip on the part of its main characters. What the film is really about is one man's longing for the past to a happier time in his life as he sees his marriage crumble, his business decline and his sanity tested."[24] And Kathleen Carroll of the *New York Daily News* wrote, "Director John Avildsen, as he demonstrated in *Joe*, has a talent for recreating life-like situations. His camera works like a magnet, picking up each squalid detail." Arthur Knight of *Saturday Review* proclaimed, "The first important film of 1973 — and possibly of the seventies."

There were some dissenters. Jay Cocks of *Time* magazine gave Lemmon a backhanded compliment, saying his work was "less febrile here than usual." But he was critical of Avildsen's work, writing that the director "continues to prove himself a master of the visual cliché, the low-slung symbol and the stereophonic anticlimax."[25]

Pauline Kael was critical of the plot and Shagan's script. "The picture is a moral hustle that says this high-living showoff is a victim of American materialism," she wrote, adding that Shagan "appears to think he has created a modern tragic hero, and he's determined to puff the movie up with wit and wisdom."[26] Similarly, Karney noted the movie "provided Jack Lemmon with an Oscar-winning role, but not much pleasure for anyone else."[27]

But such criticisms were the minority opinion at the time. And even those who were critical continued to lavish praise on the performance that Avildsen had elicited from Lemmon. As Null wrote, "Lemmon is undoubtedly the centerpiece here, keeping up with an overdone story and ultimately redeeming the film admirably."[28]

Critical acclaim was followed by success at the award shows. Lemmon, Gilford, and Shagan received Academy Award nominations. Lemmon walked away with his second Oscar and his first as Best Actor, beating out Marlon Brando (*Last Tango in Paris*), Al Pacino (*Serpico*), Jack Nicholson (*The Last Detail*) and Robert Redford (*The Sting*).

Avildsen was elated over the awards, even if his name wasn't on any of them. He was particularly happy for Lemmon. "When Jack Lemmon won the Academy Award for Best Actor, I could not have been more pleased because working with him was such a pleasure," he later told the makers of *The Directors*.

Freedland noted that the award was particularly gratifying to Lemmon because it "proved that there were other things in life than money."[29] Maybe. But it had money going for it too. The film was not a box office success, but for Lemmon, who had worked for minimal salary and helped to finance the production, the film proved to be, as Freedland said, "sufficient reward for his faith and persistence."[30]

The passage of time has increased the credit that Lemmon and Avildsen have received. In 1991, Blockbuster Video listed *Save the Tiger* as one of "the

Avildsen lining up a shot on the set of *Save the Tiger* (1973).

greatest movies of all time," noting: "Lemmon turns in an altogether moving portrayal" and that "Avildsen tersely takes us into the story of an American dream that missed the boat."[31] It was, for both men, a pivotal movie in their careers.

Production Notes

Directed by: John G. Avildsen. Writer: Steve Shagan Writer. Producers: Edward S. Feldman, executive producer; Martin Ransohoff, producer; Steve Shagan, producer. Original Music: Marvin Hamlisch. Cinematographer: Jim Crabe. Editor: David Bretherton.

Casting Director: Caro Jones. Art Director: Jack Collis. Set Decorator: Ray Molyneaux. Make Up Department: Harry Ray, makeup artist. Production Manager: Frank Baur. Second Unit Directors or Assistant Directors: Ron Schwary, second assistant director; Christopher Seiter, assistant director. Art Department: Don Nunley, property master. Sound Department: Bud Alper, sound; Robert I. Knudson, sound. Camera and Electrical Department: Ross Maehl, gaffer; John Murray, key grip; Jack Willoughby, camera operator; Calvin Maehl, best boy electric (uncredited). Costume and Wardrobe Department: John A. Anderson, wardrobe; Joseph Magnin, fashion show wardrobe. Editorial Department: David Ramirez, assistant editor. Music Department: Marvin Hamlisch, conductor. Miscellaneous Crew: Pat Quinn, fashion show consultant; Ray Quiroz, script supervisor. Filming Locations: Downtown, Los Angeles, California, USA; Los Angeles, California, USA; Mayan Theater —1038 Hill Street, Downtown, Los Angeles, California, USA. Production Companies: Filmways Pictures, Cirandinha Productions, Jalem Productions. Distributors: Paramount Pictures (1973) (USA) (theatrical); Columbia Broadcasting System (CBS) (1976) (USA) (TV) (original airing); Paramount Home Video (2005) (USA) (DVD).

Cast — in credits order: Jack Lemmon, Harry Stoner; Jack Gilford, Phil Greene; Laurie Heineman, Myra; Norman Burton, Fred Mirrell; Patricia Smith, Janet Stoner; Thayer David, Charlie Robbins; William Hansen, Meyer; Harvey Jason, Rico; Liv Von Linden, Ula; Lara Parker, Margo; Eloise Hardt, Jackie; Janina, Dusty; Ned Glass, Sid Fivush; Pearl Shear, Cashier; Biff Elliott, Tiger Petitioner; Ben Freedman, Taxi Driver; Madeline Lee, Receptionist. Other credited cast listed alphabetically: Barton MacLane (clips from *High Sierra*) (archive footage).

CHAPTER 6

Fore Play

Sex Comedies That Didn't Work

After finishing his work with Jack Lemmon in *Save the Tiger*, Avildsen signed on in 1973 to work on *Serpico*, the story of a honest cop fighting dishonesty within his own New York Police Department. Avildsen did much of the pre-production work on the film, but was fired by producer Marvin Bregman two weeks before filming started.

Avildsen blamed his dismissal on a conflict that he had with Bregman over who would play the role of Serpico's girlfriend. According to Avildsen, Bregman wanted Cornelia Sharpe (Bregman's girlfriend) in the role. Avildsen refused, explaining, "I thought she just couldn't act to save her life."[1] Once Bregman realized Avildsen wasn't planning to cast Sharpe, he dismissed him from the movie. Sidney Lumet joined the team as director, and Sharpe got the role of Leslie Lane. In retrospect, Avildsen said he didn't handle the situation well. "If I had it to do over again, I would have done it differently, with more finesse," he later said.[2]

Regardless, it left him unemployed. Instead of *Serpico*, he took on a project that he'd been thinking about for years — a sex comedy that became known as *Fore Play* or *The President's Women*. The movie involved four different directors but was never fully developed.

Avildsen gets credit for the idea. During the Johnson administration and Vietnam War, he started thinking about the plot that would invalidate the president and, hence, the war. What would happen, he wondered, if someone should kidnap the president's daughter? And the ransom? Instead of money, what if the President's political power was stripped away by requiring him to have sex with the First Lady on live television?

Nothing came of the idea during the 1960s, but — with *Serpico* under the direction of Lumet — the idea resurfaced, this time inspired by the election of Richard Nixon. "Nixon had become president and the question was what would happen if somebody kidnapped Tricia and the ransom was that Nixon and his wife would have to appear on television and make love if they wanted their daughter back," Avildsen recalled. "I figured this would sort of render Nixon impotent, as it were."[3]

Avildsen approached an investor who had financed his documentary. *Naked,* and the investor liked the idea. Avildsen then approached David Odell, the writer who had produced the script for *Cry Uncle.* Odell turned out a script about a president who wins an election with the aid of Mafia financing.

The resulting script was too short to be a movie by itself. The solution to that problem came by making it one of four vignettes in a bigger story, i.e., four stories under the supervision of four different directors. (That approached led one reviewer to say the film was "structured much like a horror anthology."[4])

That's when things started to break down. Avildsen and three other writers — Terry Southern, Dan Greenberg, and Bruce Jay Friedman — were supposed to do a segment each. The four "features" within the movie were the inspiration for its title, *Fore Play.*

Avildsen quickly began work on his segment. His first choice to play the president had been Rodney Dangerfield, but the comedian refused to be filmed

Avildsen in contemplation with Zero Mostel during a break from filming *Fore Play,* New York City, Summer 1973.

in his underwear.[5] Instead, Zero Mostel signed to play the dual roles of the president and the Mafia don (Don Pasquale) who kidnapped First Daughter Trixie (played by Laurie Heineman), with the name of the daughter bearing a remarkable similarity to that of Nixon's daughter, Tricia). Estelle Parsons played the first lady and a bar maid, so Avildsen's segment had a top-notch cast.

The plot followed Avildsen's original idea. Mostel is elected president with financing from the Mafia. The crime organization's only requirement from the new president is that he promise to make pornography illegal, thus increasing the Mafia's ability to profit from the sale of pornographic movies, magazines, and books. When the president is slow to keep his promise, the bad guys kidnap his daughter. Instead of money, their ransom demand is that the president and First Lady have sex on live television. The couple eventually gives in to the demand.

Meanwhile, the other three teams were supposed to be working on their segments. Like Avildsen's segment, the others had quality casts. In the first segment, Pat Paulsen portrays a man named Norman who buys a blowup doll. He wines and dines the doll in a futile attempt to seduce her. The second segment features the talented Jerry Orbach as a writer named Lorsey who has writer's block and wants to undress a woman.

But the plans didn't work. Greenberg and Friedman worked as writers for the film, with Bruce Malmuth and Robert McCarty taking over directing duties. Those segments never came up to par. Southern never completed his segment at

Poster for *Fore Play* (1975) directed by Avildsen, starring Zero Mostel and Estelle Parsons.

all. That left three unrelated stories that were supposed to be a movie. Even the title was no longer appropriate.

By the time it became apparent that Southern's segment would never arrive, Avildsen had completed filming on his story. Avildsen's segment is the final, and the key, portion of the film. But, with one segment missing, the movie is both aimless and too short (the final version is only 75 minutes). The producer's solution was to contact Mostel, shoot some additional footage, and find a way to have the first two segments incorporated into the plot of the third.

That second round of shooting came 18 months after Avildsen had finished the first shoot. They moved the time forward, to a point where the president is no longer in office. By then, the president is confined to a wheel-chair as he is interviewed for a fictional BBC documentary called "Going Down in History." Michael Clarke-Lawrence played the BBC announcer, and his belated interview with Mostel provides an opportunity to introduce the other two segments — plus Mostel's own segment with Parsons.

Eventually, the title *Fore Play* was abandoned in favor of *The President's Women,* a compromise title that replaced the recommendation of Avildsen and the other principals' suggestion of *All the President's Women.* Nothing really helped. The movie bombed, both at the box office and with critics. "It opened and played down South, didn't do very much," Avildsen said. "I don't think it ever played in New York at all."[6]

The critics were brutal. "Boring, flat, and completely disastrous attempt at sex comedy," one wrote. "This is the type of teaser T & A picture that gives all other T & A pictures a bad name."[7] Winters added that it was "sleep-inducing." An online review from an Internet Movie Database user saved its only positive comments for Avildsen's segment:

> I do wonder how they got such talented actors to do such drivel. My guess is they all lost a bet or something.) There's *maybe* one or two laughs in this whole movie — and they're in the last segment only. This is a stupid, unfunny, smutty movie — even the requisite female nudity is boring! For masochists only.[8]

Avildsen saw some good points in doing the project: "It was a good experience working with Zero and Estelle," he said.[9] "And it helped pay the rent."

Production Notes

Directed by: John G. Avildsen, Bruce Malmuth, Robert McCarty. Writers: Bruce Jay Friedman Story, Dan Greenburg, David Odell, Jack Richardson. Producers: Carl Gurevich, producer, Benni Korzen, producer. Original Music: Gary William Friedman, Stan Vincent.

Cinematographers: Ralf D. Bode, Adam Giffard. Production Manager: Dan Malmuth. Camera and Electrical Department: Aristides Pappidas, gaffer. Editorial Department: Robert Neal Marshall, assistant editor (international version). Miscellaneous Crew: Karen Gilbert, production coordinator. Production Company: Syn-Frank Enterprises. Distributors: Cinema National (1975) (USA) (theatrical); Troma Team Video (USA) (DVD).

Cast — in credits order: Zero Mostel, President/Don Pasquale; Estelle Parsons, 1st Lady/Barmaid; Pat Paulsen, Norman; Jerry Orbach, Jerry Lorsey; George S. Irving, Reverend/Muse. Other credited cast listed alphabetically: Fred Baur, Secret Service/Mafia; Sudie Bond, Norman's Mother; Mark Carvel, Steward; Joe Cirillo, Secret Service/Mafia; Michael Clarke-Lawrence, B.B.C. Announcer; Irwin Corey, Professor Irwin Corey; Ron Cummins, Arnold; Lou David, Secret Service #9; Thayer David, General; Paul Dooley, Salesman; Robert Dryden, Pharmacist; Andrew Duncan, Hurdlemeyer; Garry Goodrow, TV Director; Allan Hahn, Secret Service/Mafia; Laurie Heineman, Trixie; Jack Hollander, Barfly #2; Kathleen Joyce, Kinky Claudia; Alfred Karl, Secret Service/Mafia; George King, Masseur; Annie Korzen, Lady in Street; Deborah Loomis, Doll; Cia Lozell, Mary Ellen; Tom McDermott, Chief Justice McDonald; Mary-Jennifer Mitchell, Housewife; Louisa Moritz, Lt. Sylvia Arliss; Joe Palmieri, Alfredo; George Planco, Secret Service/Mafia; Shelley Plimpton, First Girl; Douglas Richardson, Wet Secret Service Man; Kevin Sanders, T.V. Announcer; Joe Sardello, Barfly #1; Carmen llvarez, Anytime Annie.

CHAPTER 7

W.W. and the Dixie Dancekings

John Avildsen vs. Burt Reynolds

At the memorial for the USS *Arizona* at Pearl Harbor, oil from the sunken battleship still seeps out of the ship's tank, works its way to the surface, and floats along the top of the harbor. The process has been repeating itself for sixty years now, with no major change in the pattern. Visitors can see, on a daily basis, a visual representation of the old adage that oil and water don't mix.

Another example would be John Avildsen and Burt Reynolds. Two giant talents, but as incompatible as oil and water. Neither realized their differences until they had to work together on the 1975 film *W.W. and the Dixie Dancekings*. Reynolds played the first half of the two title roles, a con man who rides around in a 1955 black-and-gold Oldsmobile and takes on the role of promoter for a struggling country band, the Dixie Dancekings. In between gigs, he finances the operation by robbing gas stations owned by the S.O.S. gasoline company. The police find it difficult to catch him, because he shares his loot with the underpaid attendants. They, in turn, give phony descriptions of the thief to the authorities. The company eventually brings in Art Carney, a Bible-quoting lawman.

At first glance, and before filming started, the movie looked like it had a "can't-miss" formula: Take the lovable personality of Reynolds, surround him with some of his country music buddies and capture it all on film. Planned result: a box-office winner. It was, everything considered, an oddball script (courtesy of screenwriter Thomas Rickman) with a oddball cast of characters—a perfect set-up, it would seem, for Reynolds' screen persona.

And it was. In retrospect, *Dancekings* was one of the best films by either Reynolds or Avildsen. It brought Avildsen no awards, but it is well done and entertaining. He did an effective job of tapping into the personalities of the

58

cast and capturing those characters on film. More than 30 years later, it is still a joy to watch. As one critic aptly noted, "This is the rare type film where audiences really get to like the characters, feel comfortable with them, and wish them well."[1]

Reynolds seemed to find his screen persona in the film. His role as the likable con man foreshadows one of his most famous characters, one that reached full expression a year later in *Smokey and the Bandit.* The problem: All of the initial work had been done without consultation with a director. The studio wanted a well-respected Hollywood director to put the ingredients together.

By then Avildsen had developed a reputation as a cost-effective director who could elicit strong performances from actors. He had previously worked with executive producer Steve Shagan on *Save the Tiger.* And he had, after all, gotten an Academy Award performance from Jack Lemmon in that film. Reynolds considered Avildsen a possible choice and asked Lemmon his opinion of the director. Lemmon responded with a rave review of Avildsen and his work, and Reynolds soon had him on board for the film.

Later Burt would say, "Jack Lemmon is not a good person to ask if someone is a good guy. Jack Lemmon would think Hitler was a good house painter. He never said a negative thing about anybody in his life. So we went to lunch and I took him for his word that John Avildsen is a good director."

Reynolds expanded on the story in his autobiography. He recalled running into Lemmon a year later and chastising him for his recommendation, saying, "That John Avildsen is very talented, but he's a real prick."[2]

By then, it was too late. Shooting on the film began in the winter of 1974 at a location outside of Nashville. At first, things went well. "I liked him enormously at the first meeting," Reynolds told the producers of the documentary series *The Directors.*

But trouble soon developed. Avildsen and Reynolds, it turned out, simply didn't like each other. Reynolds was open about his distaste for the director. "He was a picky, arrogant little man, with an entourage of pot-smoking film-school eggheads," Reynolds wrote in his biography.[3]

Avildsen was similarly unimpressed with Reynolds. When interviewed for his segment on Encore's *Directors* series, Avildsen remembered his own frustration with the film: "That proved to be one of the most unhappy experiences of my movie career. And he wanted me to do it. He okayed me. But at a certain point I did not have the knack of getting what I wanted and make him happy."

The press quickly picked up on the dissension, with one early review commenting on the "off-camera discord."[4] Reynolds did nothing to squelch the rumors, saying, "It's always a shock when you work for one of those legends and realize they are not real nice people."[5]

Avildsen also had trouble adapting to Reynolds' entourage of good ol' boys. Reynolds liked to surround himself with a "stock company of regulars"[6] who made appearances in his films. A new movie was often an opportunity for Burt and his buddies to gather and have fun.

Dancekings fits that scenario, with appearances by regulars Ned Beatty, James Hampton, and stuntman Hal Needham. Further, the country-music theme gave Reynolds a chance to hobnob with some of his friends from the Nashville music scene. "I've always been enamored of country people," Reynolds wrote. "You just put a guitar in front of them and they play a song and pass it around. Everybody sings."[7]

He had plenty of singers in *Dancekings*. Connie Van Dyke played the lead singer of the Dancekings. The cast also included recording artists Don Williams, Mel Tillis, and Jerry Reed, the latter best known to music fans as a Grammy-nominated singer, guitar player, and songwriter. *Dancekings* was his film debut; he went on to work in a number of other films, including collaborating with Reynolds in the popular *Smokey and the Bandit* movies.[8]

Avildsen, who gave Reed his first movie role, later said he was particularly impressed with him. "Jerry Reed was very good," he said. "He should have played W.W."[9]

W.W. Bright (Burt Reynolds) and Country Bull (Ned Beatty) in *W.W. and the Dixie Dancekings* (1975).

Some regulars from TV's *Hee Haw* also made brief appearances, including Roni Stoneman and Cathy Baker. Even the legendary Nashville bar owner Tootsie cameoed as herself. It was all one big party, one in which Reynolds freely admitted that he "was whooping it up with my new and special musical friends."[10]

The friend who may have made Avildsen the most uncomfortable wasn't a singer but a guy that Reynolds referred to simply as Ringo. Ringo held the distinction of being the toughest inmate at Reidsville State Prison, the prison that served as the location for *The Longest Yard* (1974) the prison football drama that won a Golden Globe for Best Comedy and garnered Golden Globe nominations for Reynolds, Eddie Arnold and James Hampton. Ringo served as Burt's stand-in during the filming of that movie, and he had been added to the list of Burt's Buddies for *Dancekings*.

It was a critical point in Reynolds' career. Despite his celebrity status, Reynolds' film career had been erratic — a few good films sprinkled among some really bad ones. As Karney noted, "[T]he best that can be said of most of them is that they are amiable. The star's days of glory were due more to personality than quality, and Reynolds has always had personality to spare. [He is] one of the screen's most appealing show-offs."[11]

How they would take advantage of that giant personality seemed to be at the core of the disagreement. Avildsen wanted to work; Reynolds wanted to play. Avildsen's success had been based on attention to details. He carefully planned all of his shots. Key scenes were rehearsed, taped, and reviewed until the director was satisfied that he was capturing what he needed. Reynolds was used to a looser approach to filmmaking, one which allowed his natural personality to emerge on the screen. The two approaches never quite meshed, causing one reviewer to note that the film "occasionally show[ed] its rough edges."[12]

Two points in the film seemed to be the center of antagonism. The first occurred early in the filming when Avildsen showed up on the set with his standard array of storyboards. Reynolds recalled the moment in his autobiography:

> Avildsen walked onto the set the first night surrounded by admiring pupils and holding the most complicated storyboard I'd ever seen. Not only was each scene sketched, there were sketches of sketches. The damn thing was the size of a Superman comic book.
> "You know what, John?" I said. "Why don't I just do a voice-over for those little cartoons and we can release it with Disney."
> "I've worked it all out," he said.
> "John, how the hell do you know where I'm going? Where I'm going to stand? Or what anyone else is going to do?" I said. "It's so unfair to hand-cuff me until you see what I have to offer you. If you hate it, so be it, you're the boss."

"But how do you know you'll hate it? You just might like it."

"I have to follow what that cartoon character in your little picture book wants me to do — no instincts, no sudden magic we can do together? What's the use of any spontaneity any of the actors might have?"[13]

It was a rough beginning. As Reynolds said, "Needless to say, the picture didn't start off well — and it only got worse."[14]

A lot worse. The second defining moment came later when Avildsen was working for the first time with country singer Mel Tillis. Tillis, an icon among country music fans, is well known for performing despite a speech impediment. He has made frequent film appearances using his stuttering mannerisms for comic effect. Avildsen, unfortunately, didn't know who he was or anything about him before preparing to shoot a scene in which Tillis played an attendant at one of the stations targeted by W.W. The resulting events, Reynolds recalled, told him "very early that Avildsen hadn't done a penny's worth of homework about Nashville. He never listened to one minute of country music."[15] This is how Reynolds recalled the incident:

> We were doing a scene at a tiny gas station on a night that was colder than Minnesota. Mel Tillis, playing the attendant, came up to my car and asked, "You w-w-w-ant r-r-r-reg-r-regular or d-d-do..."
>
> "Hold it! Hold it!" Avildsen yelled, interrupting the scene. "Cut the stuttering. It doesn't work."
>
> Jaws dropped with a collective thud. Everybody in the cast and crew gave Avildsen a what-the-hell-did-you-say look. I stepped out of the car and asked the esteemed little director if I could have a word with him around back.... Once we got behind the filling station, I grabbed Avildsen, literally grabbed him, and hoisted him off the ground.
>
> "You insensitive sonuvabitch!" I snarled. "The man has a speech impediment. Anyone who has the least bit of knowledge about country music knows Mel Tillis stutters. He has for his whole life. But in spite of that, he has become a major recording star!"[16]

While Reynolds and Avildsen argued — or as Reynolds wrote, "while I debated whether or not to put Avildsen into orbit"[17] — Tillis found a "fifth of something" and had himself several drinks. Reynolds and Avildsen returned to the scene, and Avildsen said, "Oh, never mind, Tillis, say whatever. Just go ahead and roll it."

It turned out that Tillis didn't stutter when he was drunk. So when Avildsen yelled "Action," the singer said his lines perfectly and with no trace of a stutter.

This time, Reynolds was the embarrassed one. "Since I'd almost strangled the director, I looked like the world's biggest asshole," Reynolds wrote. "But the crew already knew Mel was gassed and Avildsen already had his opinion of me. I never ever worked harder than when I'm inspired by anger."[18]

Perhaps that's why Reynolds liked the final film, despite his conflict with Avildsen. He later called it "an enjoyable and underrated little tale."[19]

"*W.W.* did very well," he later added. "Not a huge hit, but it still has a cult following. It introduced Jerry Reed to acting, which he was born to do. Also I got Don Williams to R.C.A., and he is now considered one of the giants of country music."[20]

But his resentment toward Avildsen remained. "John Avildsen was going to go on and make brilliant films," Reynolds said, "but obviously not with me."[21]

Reynolds was correct. The two men have never worked together since. Still, their only joint collaboration remains a charming work. *Variety* was pleased with "the surprising entertainment and warmth" of the film, calling it "a nice, easygoing, friendly, comfortable comedy-with-drama."[22] The *New York Times* called it "an unexpectedly pleasant surprise," adding that "it's a skylarking sort of movie, full of the good humor and naive optimism with which you start out on an all-day picnic on the hottest day of the year."[23] The *Los Angeles Times* wrote that "*W.W.* is tailored perfectly for Reynolds, but also is a very funny and surprisingly touching film. By now, Reynolds is a master of portraying a self-mocking hustler."[24]

The *New York Times* was particularly complimentary of Avildsen, noting that "one of the charms of the movie is the casual way it seems to discover its story while it wanders from one minor crisis to the next. Mr. Avildsen's manner here is soft sell. It's a tall story, unhurriedly told, which allows the actors, particularly Mr. Reynolds and Mr. Carney, to work some very funny variations on rather conventional roles."[25]

Today, more than thirty years later, the film retains that charm. Still, despite the critical acclaim, it remains one of Reynolds' sleepers — a film that few fans think of immediately when recounting the actor's most famous screen roles. Regardless, *W.W. and the Dixie Dancekings* played a pivotal role in developing that screen persona.

Reynolds, it seems, had found his ideal character. And he knew it. The machismo of W.W. Bright was soon transferred into his most famous character, The Bandit. The 1976 release of *Smokey and the Bandit* expanded the character. Two sequels followed, causing Karney to note that he stuck to the character "in a move that at once gave him greater control of his career and gradually eroded it as he worked the vein to death."[26] Only later in his career, with movies such as *Breaking In* and *Boogie Nights*, did he shift away from the tried and true.

There were some negative elements though. For one thing, it made Reynolds a topic of the gossip columns and tabloids. The stimulus was gossip mongering that had nothing to do with anything Reynolds had done. Instead, it all revolved around the death from AIDS of actor Rock Hudson. Soon afterwards, gossip columns were referring to Hudson and Burt as "close personal friends" and "speculating on whether or not he had AIDS."[27] To fuel the fire, some of the columnists lifted lines out of context from *W.W. and the Dixie Dancekings* as evidence of his possible homosexuality. By then, though, Reynolds was a major sex symbol and few doubted his masculinity.

Avildsen, though, was no longer a part of Reynolds' professional ensemble. Reynolds, in retrospect, blamed himself for their troubled relations. "I did not give of myself as much as I should have," he told the producers of the series *The Directors*. "I did not mean it to be a combative relationship, because I liked him. But it became that way mostly because I thought (and quite honestly it was reverse prejudice on my part) this is him not being from the South and not having a sense of what these people were about, that he will have a problem connecting with them.

"Now if I would have just thought back for half a second," he added, "I would have remembered that the best film I have ever made was about the South, was *Deliverance*, and it was directed by an Englishman."

As for Avildsen, he felt he learned something from the experience. "The thing that the film taught me was that I could do something that I had no passion for, that my mechanics were such that I could make it work," he said. "There's some satisfaction to that."[28]

Production Notes

Directed by: John G. Avildsen. Writer: Thomas Rickman. Producers: Stan Canter, producer, Steve Shagan, executive producer. Original Music: Dave Grusin. Cinematographer: James Crabe (director of photography). Editors: Richard Halsey, Robbe Roberts. Art Director: Larry Paull. Set Decorator: Jim Berkey. Make Up Department: Tom Ellingwood, makeup artist; Paul Stanhope, makeup artist; Marlene Williams, hairdresser. Production Manager: William C. Davidson, unit production manager. Second Unit Directors or Assistant Directors: Jerry Grandey, second assistant director, Ric Rondell, assistant director. Art Department: Bob Schultz, property master. Sound Department: Bud Alper, production sound mixer; Don Bassman, sound re-recording mixer; Jerry Whittington, sound effects editor (uncredited). Special Effects Department: Milt Rice, special effects. Stunts: Hal Needham, stunt coordinator; Denny Arnold, stunts (uncredited); John Ashby, stunts (uncredited); James M. Halty, stunts (uncredited); Camera and Electrical Department: Gene Kearney, grip; Calvin Maehl, best boy electric; Ross Maehl, gaffer; Jerry Whittington, electrician (uncredited). Casting Department: Jack Baur, casting: Hollywood; Sandy Liles, casting: Nashville; Shirley Rich, casting: New York. Costume and Wardrobe Department: Dick LaMotte, wardrobe: men. Editorial Department: Glenn Farr, assistant film editor. Music Department: Tommy Tedesco, musician: guitar (uncredited). Miscellaneous Crew: Les Hoyle, script supervisor; Stanley Brossette, unit publicist (uncredited); Filming Locations: Hollywood, Los Angeles, California, USA; Nashville, Tennessee, USA; New York City, New York, USA; Nolensville, Tennessee, USA; Production Company: Twentieth Century–Fox Film Corporation. Distributors: Twentieth Century–Fox Film Corporation

(1975) (USA) (theatrical); American Broadcasting Company (ABC) (1977) (USA) (TV) (original airing)

Cast — in credits order: Burt Reynolds, W.W. Bright; Conny Van Dyke, Dixie; Jerry Reed, Wayne; Ned Beatty, Country Bull; James Hampton, Junior; Don Williams, Leroy; Richard D. Hurst, Butterball; Mel Tillis, Good Ole Boy #2; Furry Lewis, Uncle Furry; Sherman G. Lloyd, Elton Bird; Mort Marshall, Hester Tate; Bill McCutcheon, Good Ole Boy #1; Peg Murray, Della; Sherry Mathis, June Ann; Roni Stoneman Hemrick, Ticket Lady; Charles S. Lamb, Dude; Nancy Andrews, Rosie; Tootsie, Herself; Shirlee Strother, Secretary #1; Virgilia Chew, Elton Bird's Secretary; Stanley Greene, Chauffeur Powell; Frank Moore, June Ann's Boss; Fred Stuthman, Sourface; Cathy Baker, Dixiebelle #1; Heidi Hepler, Dixiebelle #2; Polly Holliday, Mrs. Cozzens; Lorene Mann, Dolorosa Sister #1; Rita M. Figlio, Dolorosa Sister #2; Sudie Callaway, Dolorosa Sister #3; Mickey Salter, Elvis #1; Hal Needham, Trooper Carson; Gil Rogers, Street Preacher; Gil Gilliam, Boy with Radio; Art Carney, Deacon. Other credited cast listed alphabetically: Brad Dourif (uncredited).

CHAPTER 8

Rocky

A Work of Inspiration

The year was 1976, and 17-year-old Rowdy Gaines had decided to become a competitive swimmer. Despite early setbacks, he made quick progress, crowning his swimming career with three gold medals in the 1984 Olympics.

What does an Olympic champion have to do with a Hollywood film director? Plenty, according to Gaines. One of Avildsen's most famous movies — *Rocky*— inspired the young athlete. He said,

> *Rocky* came out about the same time I started swimming. It was about a guy who had been told all his life that he was a loser, someone who wasn't going to amount to anything.
>
> That's how I felt. My whole life I had been told that I was a loser, that I was worthless, and that I wouldn't amount to anything.
>
> I grew up small and gangly, the typical 98-pound weakling. I was always told that I would never make my high school swim team, that I wouldn't make my college team, I wouldn't make the national team, and that I wouldn't make the Olympic team. And I was told that I wasn't going to win a gold medal after I made the Olympic team.
>
> I related to Rocky, because he kind of went through the same thing. In the story, Rocky is the perennial loser. And, up until I started swimming, I was in that Rocky mode.
>
> I can remember exactly where I was when I first saw *Rocky*. I was at the Continental Theater in Winter Haven, Florida, with my girlfriend, Julie Jordan. We went out for barbeque before we went to the movie.
>
> I remember all the details behind the evening. Some people like my mom remember what they were doing and where they were at when they learned that John F. Kennedy was shot. *Rocky* had that effect on me. I remember walking out of that theater and feeling I was on top of the world and that I could be somebody. I wouldn't say the movie turned my life around, but it certainly helped me believe that I was somebody, that I could be somebody, and that's about when I started swimming.

Eight years later, *Rocky* again played a role in Gaines' swimming career. "The Olympic Village in Los Angeles had a number of screening rooms, and a number of movies were shown. One of those was *Rocky*. I had seen it a zillion times by then, but it was the one movie that the head coach [Don Gambil, University of Alabama] wanted us swimmers to watch, because it was just such an inspirational film. Several of us went to see it before the competition." The inspired Gaines subsequently won three gold medals for the U.S. team.

Gaines' reaction typified audience reactions in the 1970s. *Rocky* became a box-office hit and revolutionized movie themes of the day. Its story of a working class, underdog boxer who gets a shot at the heavyweight championship plucked all the right heartstrings for the audiences of the 1970s. Its images and its sound bites are now part of American culture. "As a piece of pop entertainment," one critic later wrote, "*Rocky* is clearly the people's choice.[1]

The catch: The film was often misinterpreted by audiences, critics and marketers — at least in the view of its director. Critics of the day saw the film as espousing conservative values, a film version of the Horatio Alger theme in which a young man from a poor neighborhood becomes somebody important by working hard toward a goal. Robin Wood, for example, described it as a movie "designed to reinstate: racism, sexism, 'democratic' capitalism,"[2] adding that it was the kind of entertainment "that a potentially Fascist culture would be expected to produce and enjoy."[3] But that wasn't the intent of the movie. On the contrary, Avildsen is an avowed liberal. From his perspective, *Rocky* was intended to be an expression of liberal philosophy — the working class hero struggling against the power of the establishment.

Rocky was perhaps Avildsen's most surprising and most rewarding film. This low-budget flick, written by and starring a then-unknown Sylvester Stallone, was a smash in 1976 that grew into a pop-cultural phenomenon that engendered five sequels. As one critic noted, "A description of it would sound like a cliché from beginning to end. But *Rocky* isn't about a story, it's about a hero."

Blockbuster Entertainment still lists it as one of the top 100 films ever made, adding, "This movie rearranged the face of cinema. The underdog's victory theme became a staple of many movies to follow. The simple story of a determined young fighter is exquisitely enhanced by top-notch performances from all who appear."[4]

Rocky added to a long tradition of boxing movies whose stars have included James Cagney (*City for Conquest*), Elvis Presley (*Kid Galahad),* and Paul Newman (*Somebody Up There Likes Me*). Kirk Douglas received his first Academy Award nomination for his role as a boxer in *Champion.* Bogart played a sportswriter, not a boxer in *The Harder They Fall* (1956), a film that included a cameo appearance by former heavyweight champion Jersey Joe Walcott. *Rocky* used a similar technique, with Joe Frazier making a brief appearance.

But *Rocky*'s Horatio Alger theme was different from the others, thanks in part to both its star and its director. The driving force behind the film was Sylvester Stallone, its writer and star.[5] Stallone correctly envisioned *Rocky* as a vehicle that could propel him from obscurity to stardom. After all, life had been pretty tough on the future superstar until that time. Stallone came from a broken home in one of New York's poorest neighborhoods, Manhattan's Hell's Kitchen. After his parents separated, he spent much of his time in foster homes in Maryland and Philadelphia.

He would have been a star high school athlete had he not been expelled from 14 schools in 11 years. Even with such a record, he was still talented enough to get an athletic scholarship to the American College in Switzerland.

He was more interested in acting than in performing in the athletic arena. He left Switzerland for a brief stop in Florida to study drama at the University of Miami. It was in 1971, while he was a student at the university, that he first met Avildsen. Stallone auditioned for a role in *The Stoolie*, the Jackie Mason movie that Avildsen was making in Miami Beach. He didn't get the part. Stallone left Miami without graduating and headed to New York to try his luck as a professional.

He didn't get off to a good start. He earned a living with a number of odd jobs, including driving a truck and working as a short-order cook. He also worked as an usher in the movie theater that *Rocky* opened in five years later. In between jobs, Stallone wrote and landed a few small roles, but found himself in more demand for his physique than for his thespic skills. His stage debut came in the nude Off Broadway production *Score*. In 1968, short on funds and legitimate acting offers, he took a minor role in a porno film, *A Party at Kitty and Stud's Place*. After he became famous, it was re-released as *The Italian Stallion*.

His first major break came in 1971 when he landed a small role in Woody Allen's *Bananas*. That was followed in 1974 with a bigger role in *The Lords of Flatbush*. By 1975, he was still struggling to make it as an actor, but *The Lords of Flatbush* changed his luck. Gene Kirkwood, a friend of Avildsen's who was head of script development for producers Bob Chartoff and Irwin Winkler, had been impressed by Stallone's work in the film. Kirkwood convinced Chartoff to watch the film, and the producer also came away impressed. He had no role for the young actor, but Chartoff wanted to meet him anyway.[6]

Stallone got together with Chartoff and Winkler soon afterwards; the two men found the young actor to be both "charming and forthright."[7] When he mentioned that he was trying to do some screenwriting, they agreed to read his first effort, a script about three brothers in the 1940s called *Paradise Alley*. Chartoff read it, liked it, and invited Stallone back for a second meeting so they could develop it.

Unfortunately, Stallone had not been totally honest with the two producers. He had, in fact, been trying to sell *Paradise Alley* for years and had found no takers. The month before meeting with Chartoff and Winkler, he had sold the option for $500 to get rent money. Apologizing profusely, he offered to write another script, this one about a boxer.[8]

Stallone's version of events usually leaves out the part about the first script and he often credits the producers with suggesting the idea of a boxing story. "*Rocky* is like a grand magnificent accident," Stallone told the producers of the *Great Directors* documentary series (HBO, Encore).

> They say it was like a million-to-one shot, but I say it's more like a billion to one. I don't know what happened. It was a magical time, a really magical time.
>
> I wrote the script very quickly because I realized that I had an opportunity to do a boxing movie, but I did not have a script. I thought, there hasn't been one for a long time, so I went home and wrote, and wrote, and wrote, and I finished it in three days.
>
> It just poured right out of me. I think because it was such a metaphor for my life.[9]

Inspiration for the plot reportedly came from watching a televised match between Muhammad Ali and Chuck Wepner, a.k.a. the "Bayonne Bleeder."[10] Wepner was a 30-to-1 underdog to champion Ali, and predictably lost the fight. Still, as Stallone later recalled, "He won even though he lost the fight. He'd won something for every loser in the world because he showed he could knock down the invincible and go the distance."[11]

The producers liked the script, but thought it risky with a no-name lead. United Artists suggested James Caan as Rocky, but that idea was rejected by Chartoff and Winkler. As studio executive Mike Medavoy noted, "Not only were they morally and contractually committed to Stallone, they were fervent in their belief in him."[12] Ironically, Stallone has subsequently conceded that some of the other actors considered for the role — including Burt Reynolds, Robert Redford, and Ryan O'Neal — likely would have been better for the part.[13]

By then, Medavoy had been brought into the project. Chartoff and Winkler had given him the script to read while on a New York to Los Angeles flight. Medavoy arranged a screening of *The Lords of Flatbush* so that the other studio executives could see Stallone's previous work.

That's when Stallone got lucky. Arthur Krim and Eric Pleskow, the two executives who reviewed the film, were impressed with the work of another actor in the film, Perry King. They mistakenly thought that King was Stallone, the actor they were supposed to be evaluating. They gave the go-ahead for the project, placing a budget limit of $1.25 million on the project. Chartoff and Winkler had to sign an unusual personal guarantee for any expenses that ran over that limit. One executive also insisted on crossing the profits or combining the costs and profits of *Rocky* with another Chartoff-Winkler project, *New York, New York*. After all, *New York, New York* was thought to be a surefire hit; a boxing movie was commercially risky, or so everybody thought. As it turned out, the surefire hit was a bomb, but the little boxing film made enough money for both of them.[14]

Early in the process, the focus was on saving money, not making it. The producer's hiring criteria was simple: people who would work cheaply and efficiently. They turned to Avildsen as the director because he had "a proven knack for getting the most out of every dollar."[15] His work on *Joe* was cited as proof: "He had directed *Joe* on a $300,000 budget and made it look like a $2 million film."[16]

Avildsen was available. He had just returned from Malta where a potential deal for a Richard Burton movie called *Bandersnatch* had fallen through.[17] Ironically, he almost turned down the film that would garner him an Academy Award.

"It came out of left field," Avildsen said. "I was all set to make another movie in the Mediterranean. I had just come back from doing a location search and meeting with Michael Caine and Peter Ustinov, and suddenly that company ran out of dough."

Long-time friend Gene Kirkwood took advantage of the down time and sent him a script, saying, "Take a look at it. It's called *Rocky*, it's about a fighter."

"A prizefighter?" Avildsen asked,

"Yes."

"I'm not interested in a prizefighter," Avildsen added. "That's really dumb, two people getting in a ring and slugging at each other. There are more interesting things to do."

But Kirkwood insisted, and Avildsen finally read the script. "On the third and fourth pages, this guy was talking to his two turtles. I was captivated by this character Rocky Balboa."

They had a star and a director, but they still needed the rest of the cast. Carl Weathers was signed to play Apollo Creed, the reigning heavyweight champion. Weathers, a former professional football player, was a replacement for former heavyweight champion Ken Norton. Norton dropped out of the project after signing with ABC for a television project.[18]

"I think in many ways I was a kind of an afterthought," Weathers later said. "They did not want to see me at first because I was not known, a fairly young actor new to Los Angeles, new to Hollywood, and new to the film business. And I think they were looking for a name."

Stallone was among those waiting when Weathers arrived to read for the part. He immediately noted that Weathers had the right demeanor to play Creed, one that said "I'm very special, and that kind of thing, a big ego," Stallone later recalled.

Stallone was in the back of the room, behind Avildsen and producers Irwin Winkler and Robert Chartoff, watching Weathers. When Weathers was ready to read for the part, Stallone came forward to read Rocky's lines.

Weathers didn't realize the unknown helping him was both the writer and star of the film. Hoping to make a better impression, Weathers turned to Avildsen and said, "You know, if you get a real actor, I could do a lot better."

Avildsen, though, wanted to see something else. The group moved to a larger room, where Stallone and Weathers started boxing. Weathers got three blows to Stallone's head, before stopping and again speaking to Avildsen, saying, "I could do really well if I was with a real boxer."

Stallone interrupted, saying, "Let's hire him right away." Turning to Weathers, he added, "By the way, I'm playing Rocky. You're hired because you've got the body, you've got the looks, and you've got this incredible ego. You're perfect."

Weathers later recalled that he was lucky to get the part. "I insulted the star of the movie, not knowing it. And I didn't mean to; I just mean, 'Give me somebody I can really bounce off of here.'"

Getting Weathers to play Creed was an important element, but other roles were also important. Carrie Snodgress and Susan Sarandon had been considered for the role of Adrian, Rocky's girlfriend. Snodgress wanted too much money, and Sarandon was considered "too beautiful and worldly."[19] Talia Shire, just off her Oscar-nominated performance in *The Godfather Part II*, came in to read. "Talia is beautiful," Stallone has said, "but she really dressed down. Then she gave me a bop on the chin like, 'You get 'em, Rocky.' And she just had it."[20]

Stallone's father Frank got a small part, as did his son Frank Jr. Also among the cast was Christopher Avildsen. Associate producer Lloyd Kaufman made a brief appearance as a drunk that Rocky drapes over his shoulder and takes into the bar. That exterior scene was shot in Philadelphia, with a non-union crew, and Avildsen as cameraman. Ironically, Avildsen was one of the original founders of a filmmakers' union (NADET Local 15). Avildsen shot in Philadelphia for ten days, more than a third of the 28-day schedule. The producers, who never went to Philadelphia, were afraid of being caught with a non-union crew and ordered the unit back to Los Angeles without finishing the exteriors. Kaufman paid for his own airplane ticket to California so that he could appear on Rocky's shoulders when he walks into the bar, which was in Los Angeles.

One of the exteriors not shot in Philadelphia was Rocky's first date with Adrian. It was originally written to take place in a diner. Avildsen suggested that rather than having two actors sitting at a table looking at each other for five or six pages of dialogue, that they go skating and play the scene at a skating rink. They found a rink in downtown Philadelphia and arranged for non-union extras to fill the rink. When they returned to Los Angeles, the producers said the first date would go back to the diner location, since they could not afford all the union extras. Avildsen suggested the rink be closed and therefore there would be no extras. Stallone liked the idea and changed the script to accommodate the empty rink,

Burgess Meredith took the key role of Mickey, the local trainer. The part had been written with Lee J. Cobb in mind, but he rejected it when Avildsen insisted that he read and audition. Lee Strasberg was considered, but his fee ($75,000) was too high for the budget. Avildsen suggested Meredith, having worked with him as a second-unit director on *Hurry Sundown*.[21]

Meredith had to audition in a one-on-one session with Stallone. It didn't go well at first, until Avildsen asked the veteran actor to forget the script and improvise. Meredith ended the scene with a line that wasn't in the script: "Hey Rocky, ever think about retiring? Well, start thinking about it!"

"That's what got him the part," Avildsen said.[22]

One reviewer said it was Meredith's best performance in years; other critics thought so too, awarding him with an Oscar nomination. It would be one of only two Oscars awarded to a sports movie (the other was *Chariots of Fire*, 1981) for more than three decades.[23]

Burt Young also got an Oscar nomination for playing Paulie, Adrian's older brother. One reviewer described Young's role as being "defeated and resentful, loyal and bitter, caring about people enough to hurt them just to draw attention to his grief."

When the producers approached Young for the role, though, they did so apologetically. "They were complaining to me: The kid who wrote the script is too young," Young said. "But they wanted me to do it." Young balked at first, trying to get more money. But the low-budget feature had little room to negotiate, and Young needed the money. Stallone went to Young—the first time they had met—and asked him to take the role.

"Mr. Young, I'm Sylvester Stallone," he said. "You got to do the movie, I wrote the part for you."

Young replied, "Shhh. I'm gonna do the movie. I'm gonna try to twist their arm and get a dollar or two more."

Young was the only actor actively courted for the movie. "I was the only actor that did not have to audition," he recalled. "Even Burgess Meredith and Talia Shire auditioned. I was the highest paid actor over Sylvester. And I was trying to squeeze a couple of bucks from the studio. They were very short with the money."

Once the cast was set, production moved quickly. "It had to be done in 28 days for less than a million bucks, and nobody bothered you because there was so little money involved," Avildsen said.

The 28-day shooting schedule started on location in Philadelphia on November 5, 1975, using a non-union crew. "Everyone was stuck in one little van," producer Winkler later recalled. "Stallone's dressing room, the production office, the wardrobe and props departments were all in this one van. We never had catering—we'd drive the van to an Italian restaurant and order some pizzas. That was lunch for the whole company."[24]

Rocky opens with the camera focused on a painting of Jesus. The camera slowly tilts down and zooms out to reveal the interior of the building—a boxing arena rather than a church—where two pugs awkwardly slug each other. Both fighters look overweight and out of shape. Their slow punches bludgeon the other's body, but not with finesse or skill. It's simply two thugs trying to see which one is the toughest.

Although the scene accurately reflects Stallone's original screenplay, the visuals were improvised on the spot. Avildsen attributed his early work in industrial films for the inspiration. The first time the director saw the old

On the set of *Rocky* (1976) Sylvester Stallone and Avildsen.

building was when they shot the scene. He didn't know the religious painting was on the wall until he arrived, and quickly changed his shot selection to include it.

"That was shot in a gym in South Los Angeles," Avildsen said. "When I walked in and saw that painting, I decided to open with that. It set up a contrast with the action, and offered a chance to identify Rocky with Christ. It puts Rocky in good company from the first shot."

Rocky leaves that bout as a dubious winner, pocketing the small purse. Over the next few scenes, we learn a little about his daily life. This professional "boxer" works a day job as a strong-arm man for a loan shark. He has the muscle for the job, but not the personality. He chases down a guy who owes the "bank" seventy bucks, threatening to break the guy's thumbs, but doesn't have the heart to carry out the threat.

When he's got some spare time — which seems to be fairly often — he works out at a nearby gym where he has a love-hate relationship with the trainer Mickey (Burgess Meredith). The problem: Mickey knows that Rocky had the talent but not the motivation to be a real boxer. The advantages of his strength and athletic skills have been diminished by too much smoking, drinking, and screwing around.

One reason Rocky continues to work out is that he is so socially awkward outside the ring. He's desperately in love with a neighborhood girl (Talia Shire), but she's spent too much time cleaning house and cooking for her brother (Burt Young). Adrian is even more shy than Rocky is. She works at a local pet shop, which Rocky visits to buy food for his pets — two turtles (Cuff and Link) and a goldfish (Moby Dick).

Rocky roams the streets of a dirty and dreary part of Philadelphia, a place with which he became familiar while living in foster homes in the area. Karney (1993) noted that one of the strengths of the film is its convincing "depiction of the crumbling tenements of Philadelphia."[25] Another critic added, "Avildsen correctly isolates Rocky in his urban environment, because this movie shouldn't have a documentary feel, with people hanging out of every window: It's a legend, it's about little people, but it's bigger than life, and you have to set them apart visually so you can isolate them morally."

Adrian has a stormy relationship with her brother. She's looking for something better, but is afraid to look too hard. Her watershed moment comes after an argument with her brother. He's taken a baseball bat to the living room, leaving it in shambles. She sits in the corner of her bedroom, crying, when Rocky enters.

"Do you want a roommate?" she asks quietly, only barely looking at Rocky.

"Absolutely," Rocky answers.

As one critic noted, Rocky's response "is exactly what he should say, and how he should say it, and why *Rocky* is such an immensely involving movie."

Rocky and Adrian finally click in his apartment. The scene ends with a dramatic kiss between the two awkward lovers. One reviewer noted, "When she hesitates before kissing Rocky for the first time, it's a moment so poignant it's like no other."

"They both had colds that day, and it had been a contentious day on the set. Neither of them were in the mood to do it," Avildsen recalled. "It's a tribute to the professionalism of both that they did it so well. The kiss was well choreographed in advance. There would be three kisses, with them collapsing on the floor with the third one."

Outside the walls of the apartment, the drudgery of daily life seems broken only by the rising pathos in the character and the noise of the overhead el trains as they clamor nearby. Avildsen recalled that Stallone approached him after watching the film for the first time and said, "Wasn't it lucky that the train came by then?" he said, referring to a night scene in which Rocky and Talia were walking along deserted streets.

"It wasn't luck at all," Avildsen recalled. "I had a gopher down the track with a walkie-talkie. He'd tell me when the train was approaching, and that's when we'd roll the film." Avildsen also used a common trick to increase the visual appeal of the neighborhood scenes, splashing water on the streets to make them sparkle at night. He was able to enlist the neighborhood kids to wet down the street with buckets of water. There was no budget for a water truck.

While Rocky is roaming somewhat aimlessly around his neighborhood, a real boxer is working on a plan that will change his life. Apollo Creed has an ego that befits the heavyweight champion of the world and the audacity to concoct what could be a major moneymaker for himself: a New Year's Eve bout on the nation's 200th birthday with an unknown fighter.

Creed sees the fight as both a public relations and financial bonanza. He can promote the bout as proof that America is still a land of opportunity, if he can just get the right patsy to take the beating. After discarding several possibilities, he settles on Rocky because of his nickname: the Italian Stallion. It has marquee value and makes for a racial contrast that will generate dollars.

So far, you've got the plot for a typical B-movie. But here's where things start to surprise you. As originally written, when the promoter offers Rocky (who thinks he's being interviewed as a sparring partner) the chance to fight Apollo Creed, Rocky accepts. But Avildsen suggested that Rocky turn down the offer because he's no match for Apollo Creed. Now the promoter has to con Rocky into accepting the fight: "You believe in America, don't you?" the promoter asks Rocky. Now we feel for Rocky. He's being taken advantage of.

Avildsen says, "The original script had Burgess Meredith coming to Rocky and asking to be his manager. Rocky says, 'I don't need a manager,' speaks dismissively to Mickey and exits into his putrid bathroom, slamming the door." Crestfallen, Mickey leaves Rocky's apartment, exits the building and begins to walk up the street. The next cut in the script had Rocky running up the street after Mickey, putting his arm over his shoulder with warmth and affection. What happened? Why the change? Avildsen explains:

> I decided Rocky needed some sort of epiphany, some transcending moment that would lead to a reunion with Burgess's character. I asked Sylvester to improvise and just vent his anger as he stood in the doorway of his bathroom. Then when we see the exterior with Rocky running after Mickey, his anger released, we understand as he shakes hands with his old friend that all is forgiven.
>
> So that's what we did. One take, and he did it perfectly. I said, "That's a print." But my sound guy said, "Not so fast." His batteries had died during the scene, so we had to do it again. On the second take, he did it almost as well, and that's what we used.

After that, Mickey puts Rocky through a rigorous training schedule. Of this part, Karney wrote, "What makes the movie extraordinary is that it doesn't try to surprise us with an original plot, with twists and complications; it wants to involve us on an elemental, a sometimes savage, level. It's about heroism and realizing your potential, about taking your best shot and sticking by your girl. It sounds not only clichéd but corny — and yet it's not, not a bit, because it really does work on those levels."[26]

Because of a limited budget, Avildsen had to occasionally improvise scenes. Those moves typically solidified the script and the movie. Late in the film, for example, there was a scene written in which Rocky would visit Mickey's gym the night before the fight. He would watch newsreel coverage of Apollo's fights on a 16mm movie projector. But there was never the time or money to shoot the newsreel footage for Rocky to watch. So Avildsen suggested that instead of going to the gym, Rocky goes to the huge empty arena. He would be intimidated by the size of the place and realize he doesn't belong. Plus there would never be money to pay extras to fill the place. But this way the audience would see the size of the arena and imagine it full. So it was decided to shoot in the empty arena. There Rocky would see two giant posters depicting Apollo and himself.

Unfortunately, Avildsen had trouble getting the posters produced. They were expensive, and he had to rely on the studio to provide them. By the time the posters arrived, Rocky's poster had him dressed in the wrong colored boxing trunks.

The scene was critical to the development of the plot, but the film had neither the money nor the time to do the posters over again. The solution: Avildsen had Apollo Creed's promoter discover Rocky in the empty arena. Rocky complains to the promoter that the trunks are the wrong color. The promoter assures Rocky that it doesn't matter and leaves Rocky alone and dejected. Now the audience feels again for Rocky, because nobody cares about him.

In another instance, the crew realized that Rocky's boxing robe was too big for him, but there wasn't money in the budget to make another one. The result: The script was rewritten to make a joke of the discrepancy. One critic noted that, time and again, the film demonstrated how to turn "a lack of money into a good thing."[27]

Another example was Rocky and Adrian's first date in an empty skating rink on Thanksgiving Day. Avildsen improvised that scene by having the two young lovers sneak into the rink while it was closed. "Now you've got two people all alone who can't skate and it's a metaphor," Stallone later said. "Alone, they both fall down. But together, maybe they can hold each other up."[28]

Avildsen isolates Rocky for many of the training scenes. Karney noted that this technique was effective because "the emphasis on training and hard work merits the big emotional pay-off Stallone contrives."[29]

Sylvester Stallone and Avildsen on the set of *Rocky* (1976).

The most memorable scene in the movie comes at the culmination of Rocky's training, when he runs up the steps of Philadelphia's art museum, jumps up and shakes his fist in the air. Avildsen had a Steadicam for the scene and used it for maximum effect. As one reviewer wrote, "You know he's sending a message to the whole movie industry that had ignored him for so long."

The climax came in the ring, with Rocky and Apollo squared off against each other. Those scenes posed a particular problem for Avildsen. "I had never seen a boxing match," Avildsen said. "Once I got the job, I watched a lot of boxing movies and thought the boxing looked very phony. And I realized that if we were going to make it look real, we were going to have to practice a great deal."

"We were in the gym day after day," Weathers recalled. "Training, working out, training, working out, boxing, working out, training, working out."

On the first day of boxing practice, Stallone and Weathers got into the ring, started bouncing around, and improvising their moves. Avildsen stopped the process: "Wait a second. This is never going to work," he said.

Turning to Stallone, he said, "Sylvester, why don't you write this out. Go home and write it out; it starts with two lefts and then a right, and then you fall down, and then the other guy falls down, and you do that and he does this. Write it all out, and we'll learn it like a ballet."

Stallone returned the next day with nearly thirty pages of lefts and rights that orchestrated the entire fight. This work led to him getting another listing in the film's credits for choreography.

"We had the ring divided into pretty much like a clock," Weathers recalled. "Within those four sections of the ring, we also had how you would work and what punches and what combinations and what moves you would make."

The fight scene footage was shot with an innovative technique. Garrett Brown, the young cinematographer who had invented the Steadicam, used the camera for the first time to shoot such scenes. In fact, sharp-eyed film buffs can occasionally spot Brown strapped to his camera and stalking the ring in wide shots of the scene.[30]

Avildsen photographed each of the rehearsals with his 8mm home movie camera and showed both actors the footage. The early shots didn't look great, but Avildsen used the footage to motivate both men. "We've got to get a lot better than this," he told them. "Otherwise it's going to look like that and you don't want to look like that."

Both worked harder. "Every day, an hour or two, they practiced and practiced," Avildsen said. "They knew that there was a right, and then a left, and then a this, and a that, and a jab and a punch and they got it down and so they were coming that close to one another. It looked real."

When the fight is over, there's another break from convention: Rocky loses.

There is a dramatic, gut-wrenching scene in which Rocky — although severely injured — summarizes every ounce of his remaining strength, fully intending to win the match. He gets his opportunity, lands the blow, and startles Creed with its strength.

In the end, though, it's not enough. He gave it all he had, but he still loses.

That's one reason the film is so moving. As one critic wrote, "By now, everyone knows who wins, but the scenes before the fight set us up for it so completely, so emotionally, that when it's over we've had it. We're drained."

Another critic agreed: "It involves us emotionally, it makes us commit ourselves: We find, maybe to our surprise after remaining detached during so many movies, that this time we care."

Rocky finds that he cares, too. He lost, but he's still proud. He's proven to himself and the world that "he's not just another bum from the neighborhood."

With the loss comes further realization that his life with Adrian is more important than success in the ring. As the fight ends, he's seeking her — not the adulation of the fans. But even that dramatic ending was improvised, necessitated by a need to make the film reflect the musical score. The original, somber ending merely has a defeated Rocky and Talia Shire leaving the ring and walking into a dark hallway.[31] That melancholy finale simply didn't fit the newly created musical score, even though the shot was used on the movie's poster.[32]

While preparing for the movie, Avildsen showed composer Bill Conti the 8mm rehearsal footage. While watching the 8mm movies, Avildsen played Beethoven's 6th on his tape recorder. "This is the feel I want," Avildsen told Conti. "I want a classical sound, not rock 'n' roll."

Conti was given a $25,000 budget for the music, including his fee, cost of the musicians and studio rental. The theme song, "Gonna Fly Now," established Conti's reputation, and his subsequent work on the sequels and other films made him millions. It also established a creative partnership with John Avildsen that covered 12 different movies, including the *Karate Kid* films, *Lean on Me, Slow Dancing in the City, The Formula,* and *8 Seconds.*[33] Medavoy called the music

> perhaps the most memorable film score of the decade. To this day, the music is a symbol of athletic triumph around the world. Almost every sporting event blasts the inspirational theme song, "Gonna Fly Now." It has sbecome a symbol of the triumph of the human spirit and the courage to take that once-in-a-lifetime chance.[34]

Because budget considerations, Conti's work was limited to a single three-hour scoring session. A problem arose when Conti brought the music for the end of the movie to Avildsen. "It was inspiring," Avildsen remembered, "but I didn't have any footage that would go with the music. If you remember the poster of *Rocky*, that was the image, the boy and the girl walking away from the camera. This music with the footage that I have makes no sense at all."

But Avildsen loved the music. He suggested they keep the music and reshoot the end. Keep Rocky in the ring, yelling for Adrian. Adrian fights her way through the crowd to Rocky's arms. She says "I love you" and Rocky says "I love you" and the movie is over.

The producers agreed. But it meant re-shooting the final scene, and they had no more money. This time it was the producers who improvised, putting together $25,000 of their own money and scrounging help from other movies.[35] At that time, Martin Scorsese was about to do a picture for the same producers. As Avildsen recalled, "Unbeknownst to Marty [who worked for Avildsen as an assistant when he was a student at NYU and Avildsen was making his first short in 1964], I think the producers took his camera gear and they gave us about four hours to take this gear and about twenty-five extras to walk in front of the camera." Those 25 extras walked back and forth on-camera to create the sense of an arena crowd.

Looking back, nearly all of the participants thought the filming had gone well, but nobody expected anything special. After all, it was a low-budget film with few lofty expectations.

"*Rocky* was not an independent film. That's a common misconception," Avildsen said. "It was financed by United Artists, a major studio. They just didn't budget a lot of money for it." Not much at all, by Hollywood standards — a mere $1.1 million. Avildsen couldn't quite do it for that, but he did complete the entire project for just $1,220,011 — only about $100,000 over budget for a film that would gross more than $115 million in the U.S. alone.[36]

Medavoy wrote, "By any standard, *Rocky* was a true labor of love by everyone involved, every step of the way."[37] Avildsen agreed: "The whole production went smoothly, and everybody liked the movie. But there was no anticipation of it being a hit."

One reason for the lack of enthusiasm is that the first cut of the film didn't include the final scene. "The first time we saw *Rocky*, we all agreed it was pretty good," Medavoy wrote. "But it didn't have the final fight scene in it — the one scene that delivers on the promise of the entire movie."[38]

When that scene was added, audiences erupted. "The first time I showed it to about 40 or 50 friends, they all freaked out, so that was encouraging," Avildsen told a reporter.[39] "But I guess when I saw the lines around the block, it began to take on a reality." Later he added, "I thought it was going to be the second half of a double-bill at a drive-in."[40]

Similarly, Burt Young had few expectations. "I never knew what we had.

No one ever knew what we had. The studio did not know. They had to see screening after screening to believe that they had a million dollar movie looking like a thirty million dollar movie. That was all John Avildsen."

Meanwhile, two of the producers and studio executives thought they had something special. Robert Chartoff, Irwin Winkler and Gabe Sumner convinced United Artists that they had "magic in a bottle" with the film.[41] The studio held an industry screening at the Cary Grant Theater on the MGM lot. As Medavoy remembered, "The audience literally got up and cheered during the new final fight scene. 'Hit him Rocky!' they screamed. Even for a friends-and-family screening, this was extraordinary."[42]

The response at the industry screening was so enthusiastic that United Artists scheduled a preview screening at New York's Baronet Theater on Third Avenue, where Stallone had worked as an usher. As Medavoy recalled:

> Again, the audiences went wild. From the moment the screening let out, Stallone was a star. The transformation was almost instant. He stood in the lobby wearing a $20 suit, and people walked up to him and just wanted to touch him. They were calling him "Rock" and talking to him as though he were really the street fighter from Philadelphia who had just gone the distance with the heavyweight champion of the world. This marked the end of the humble guy with the Swiss education I met before we okayed *Rocky*.[43]

Those reactions changed the release schedule for the film. The studio had originally planned to release it to theaters in February 1977. But such a move meant the film would not qualify for the 1976 Academy Awards. United Artists thought it had a winner, so the release date was moved up to December 1976.

Despite the strong audience responses, United Artists decided not to promote the film with a heavy advertising budget. Instead, the film's advertising relied heavily on small-market exposure and word-of-mouth promotion. "If there was ever such a thing as a word-of-mouth strategy, this was it," Medavoy wrote. "We booked the film in smaller theaters that would promise open-ended play dates to allow one person to tell another. Since television advertising was cost-prohibitive relative to the budget, we sent Stallone to as many small towns as possible to give personal interviews to the local newspapers and radio stations."[44]

It also was the beginning of the *Rocky* mythology. Stallone's central message for these tours was simple: "This is a personal film, I'm the little guy, and you know how those big, bad Hollywood studios are — so I need your help."[45]

The problem, as Medavoy recalled, is that "Stallone ended up repeating this promotional mantra so many times that he began to believe that we were the evil corporate robber barons. He forgot that we were the friends of the artists who had agreed to let him star in his own script despite its dubious commercial potential."[46]

Medavoy blamed part of this attitude on producers Chartoff and Winkler. "By the time we started promoting Stallone for the Oscar," Medavoy wrote, "he had been force-fed so many stories from Bob and Irwin about how he stood up to the studios when they wanted to cast a star and buy him off that he now believed them."[47]

The critics picked up on the story. Nye noted that Stallone "staked his whole career on the movie,"[48] adding that Stallone wrote the story but found it hard to convince the studio that he should also star in it. Stallone backed up that view, saying, "They just didn't want me, and it was a film that people laughed at and I heard rumors that after a week they wanted to replace me." The story still circulates today. As Medavoy noted, "The myth has become a reality. In our star-driven culture, Stallone gets to write history the way he chooses."[49]

One critic noted, "*Rocky* is an old-fashioned fairy tale brilliantly revamped to chime in with the depressed mood of the '70s." "Very simply, this is a film that anyone can love," another added. Karney said the film "more than satisfied the audience's need to believe in the American Dream and the happy ending. There was an exuberant feel to Avildsen's direction as the film built to the climactic fight, while the streetwise dialogue and Sylvester Stallone's self-mocking performance as the good-natured pug made the simple, sentimental situations palatable."[50]

Those reviews have held up over time. Griffin has called it "perhaps the greatest of all traditional sports movies."[51] Similarly, Hakari described it as "the ultimate 'hometown schlub makes good' sports movie."[52]

The public responded in droves. *Rocky* became one of the biggest hits in 20 years, drawing in more than $225 million, or more than $500 million in today's dollars. Awards came by the handfuls, including three Oscars, ten Oscar nominations, a Directors Guild nomination for Avildsen, and a Writers Guild nomination for Stallone. Avildsen was elated when he learned he was nominated for a Best Director Oscar. Although initially dismissing the idea of winning, he started considering the possibility when critic Gene Siskel called, asking if he could spend the day of the Oscars with him.[53] His confidence increased when he won the Directors Guild Award, a decision that one critic described as "a jawdropper."[54] But, O'Neil added, "His victory meant that the underdog movie about the triumph of underdogs was the frontrunner to win the Best Picture Oscar."[55]

One critic even contributed to the final version of the film. Pauline Kael[56] of *New Yorker* magazine saw a pre-release version and called Avildsen to compliment him on his work. Avildsen asked her opinion of one particular scene in which Rocky walks a neighborhood preteen girl home, telling her she shouldn't swear or smoke. Kael said she liked the scene because it made Rocky likable. Avildsen asked if she would pass her opinion on to the producers, because they wanted to cut it from the movie. They thought the scene slowed the movie down. Kael agreed with Avildsen, and the scene stayed in.

After that, Avildsen had to wait to discover if his film would actually receive an Oscar nomination. He described the two months of waiting for the announcement as torture. "You soon become obsessed with winning," he said. "It starts dominating your thoughts during all waking hours. Everywhere you go, everything you do, it's back there. At first, people congratulate you for the nomination. But later they start predicting that you'll win. And the desire to win it becomes so dominating. You don't tell that to other people, but it becomes so strong that losing would be devastating. Then when I did win it, the feeling was more of relief than elation. I don't know how I would have handled losing."

On the day of the Oscar award show, Avildsen stayed in the Beverly Hills Hotel while being shadowed by *Chicago Tribune* film critic Gene Siskel.[57] The night before, he had attended a party at Marlo Thomas' home, which is "the size of an English boys' school," he told Siskel,[58] while noting that he met Jack Nicholson there. By three that afternoon, while in the tub at the hotel, Avildsen began to realize that he might win the award. He got out of the tub and starting compiling a thank-you list, a task he continued intermittedly through the rest of the day, including during the award ceremony. Meanwhile, he had to field dozens of phone calls from friends and well-wishers. One magazine interview was rescheduled because the reporter couldn't get any time between phone calls. Avildsen left the hotel later in the day, accompanied by his agent Marvin Moss and Siskel, for a meeting with producer Dino de Laurentiis. The producer wanted to sign Avildsen to his next movie, but they disagreed on the film (Avildsen wanted to do a remake of Errol Flynn's *The Adventures of Robin Hood* while de Laurentiis wanted to do a new script about four women stars).

It didn't matter; Avildsen was already committed to future projects for United Artists and Columbia Pictures. Still, he was impressed with de Laurentiis. "I enjoy dealing with him," Avildsen said. "He makes you think of what the old movie moguls must have been like. He makes deals without consulting anyone else."[59] Avildsen continued with his busy day until it was time to go to the awards show.

There the film walked away with three of the statues, including Best Picture, Best Film Editing, and a Best Director Oscar for Avildsen. Four of the actors were nominated — Stallone, Shire, Young, and Meredith — but all lost out. Conti's theme song, "Gonna Fly Now," lost to Barbra Streisand's rendition of "Evergreen." Stallone was also nominated as the writer of the best original screenplay, but lost. That was no surprise, really, since he had also been nominated but failed to win the same honor earlier from the Writers Guild.[60]

Stallone did get his chance on the stage, though, even if he didn't win. When Robert Chartoff and Irwin Winkler went to the podium to accept their Best Picture Oscars, they took Stallone to the stage with them. Medavoy remembered the moment: "The image of Stallone standing on stage, wearing a tux with a wide, seventies-style shirt collar folded over his lapel, basking in praise from the audience, was the culmination of his transformation into an almost instant mythical figure.[61]

Still, the big prize went to Avildsen. When the winner was announced, Avildsen rose from his seat, hesitant at first, hugged Stallone and walked quickly to the stage. He reached into his pocket, where he had jammed an envelope with some notes on who to think. He found that he had sweated so much that the ink had run on the envelope.[62]

At the 1976 Oscars *Rocky* won for Best Picture, Best Director and Best Editing. Shown from left—Director John G. Avildsen, Producer Robert Chartoff, Jack Nicholson (presenter), Sylvester Stallone and Producer Irwin Winkler.

Avildsen on his Oscar-winning night (© ImageCollect.com/photo by Bob V. Noble, Globe Photos Inc.).

As Avildsen gave his acceptance speech, the TV cameras cut to Stallone in the audience. "Rocky gave a lot of people hope," Avildsen said. "A lot of people gave me things. Stallone gave his guts and his heart and his best shot. Thank you, thank you." Stallone smiled, nodding to acknowledge Avildsen's compliment.

It may have been the last civil exchange between the two men for years. Stallone became a star, but Avildsen got the critical acclaim.

In 1995, while working on the HBO documentary series, "The Great Directors," producer Jean Bodon asked Stallone for an interview regarding another director. When the interview was completed, Bodon mentioned that the series was also going to do an episode on Avildsen and asked Stallone to say something about him for the show. Stallone was cool in his reply: He would talk about *Rocky*, he said, but not about Avildsen.

Why the animosity? Part of it may have been Stallone's chip-on-the-shoulder attitude in his *Rocky* era. He acknowledges that he was arrogant, petty, and selfish. "If I were watching a home movie of my life," he said, "I would shake my head in despair and wonderment."[63]

Avildsen believes part of it stems from his Oscar-winning honors as director, coupled with Stallone's disappointment at winning nothing for the film.

It was Stallone's film. He wrote it; he was the star. But the honors went to Avildsen.

Stallone got overlooked, probably because he was such a newcomer. In retrospect, his performance as the semi-literate boxer was superb, but Academy voters didn't know that at the time. There seemed to be an unstated feeling that Stallone wasn't acting, that the character was too much like himself. His work in writing the script should have dispelled that notion, but some Academy voters apparently didn't consider that.

Still, it was an impressive performance, one that had many critics thinking of him as the next De Niro or Brando.[64] As one critic later wrote, "He must have known it would work because he could see himself in the role, could imagine the conviction he's bringing to it, and I can't think of another actor who could quite have pulled off this performance."

Karney agreed: "His acting is often ridiculed, but within an obviously limited range he is actually quite expressive. Most of his characters have been inarticulate, but it is to the actor's credit that we nevertheless identify with them as much as we do."[65] Indeed, twenty-five years after the movie's release, critics were still describing Rocky Balboa as "one of film's most enduring characters."[66]

So endearing, in fact, that the original *Rocky* frequently showed up on television for more than 35 years. In 2002, Avildsen had to cut his baby — editing out 20 minutes from the original *Rocky*. The original is just a few minutes short of two hours — a perfect length for cable movie channels such as HBO and a good fit for two-and-a-half movie slots on commercial TV. However, with the shift to the 21st century, the distributors wanted to market Rocky in two-hour commercial slots. Another 20 minutes needed to be cut to give the networks and local stations enough commercial time. Avildsen did the cutting himself. "It was either do it myself, or let somebody else do it. And I might not like what they cut," he said.

Rocky, it seems, has stood the test of time. Thirty-five years after its original release, home video releases keep it available to new generations of movie fans.[67] As *Variety* critic Michael Speier noted, the movie "is as appealing as ever even after Hollywood has milked the tough-guy-with-a-heart theme bone dry."[68] Current actors cite it as an influence, including wrestler-turned-actor The Rock. "It's a feel-good, standup type of movie," he said. "I love the story of a guy who fights the odds, and he doesn't have to win — and he doesn't win."[69]

Speier also understood the essence of the movie's appeal: [*Rocky* is] rarely cited as a meaningful or masterful film. It does, however, remain a sweet and simple story extremely well executed, and it showcases America's fascination with feel-good fables and underdogs."[70]

Legendary director Frank Capra agreed. During the 1970s, Capra often complained that Hollywood was losing its ability to move people. The exception, he said in 1977, was *Rocky.* "I think it's the best picture of the last ten years," he told the *New York Times.* "... When I saw it, I said, 'Boy, that's a picture I wish I had made.'"[71]

Production Notes

Directed by: John G. Avildsen. Written by: Sylvester Stallone. Producers: Robert Chartoff, producer; Gene Kirkwood, executive producer; Irwin Winkler, producer. Original Music: Bill Conti. Cinematographer: James Crabe. Editors: Scott Conrad, Richard Halsey. Casting Director: Caro Jones. Production Designer: Bill Cassidy. Art Director: James H. Spencer. Set Decorator: Raymond Molyneaux. Make Up Department: Mike Westmore, makeup creator. Production Managers: Hal Polaire, executive in charge of production; Ted Swanson, production manager. Second Unit Directors or Assistant Directors: Fred Gallo, first assistant director; Steve Perry, second assistant director. Art Department: Mike Miner, props; David Nichols, visual consultant. Sound Department: Ray Alba, post-production sound; B. Eugene Ashbrook, sound mixer; John Farrell, looping editor; Burt Schoenfeld, post-production sound; Harry W. Tetrick, sound; Bud Alper, sound (uncredited); Lyle J. Burbridge, sound (uncredited); Ken Dufva, foley artist (uncredited); William L. McCaughey, sound (uncredited); Donald C. Rogers, sound (uncredited). Stunts: Jim Nickerson, stunt coordinator; Glory Fioramonti, stunts (uncredited); Bob Herron, stunts (uncredited); Gray Johnson, stunts (uncredited); Gene LeBell, stunts (uncredited); Bennie Moore, stunts (uncredited). Camera and Electrical Department: Garrett Brown, special camera effects; Dick Edessa, first assistant camera; Gene Kearney, key grip; Ross Maehl, electrical gaffer; Elliott Marks, still photographer; Jack Willoughby, camera operator; Lou Angeli, dolly grip (uncredited); Ralf D. Bode, director of photography: second unit (uncredited); Mike Chevalier, camera operator (uncredited); Calvin Maehl, best boy electric (uncredited); Aristides Pappidas, gaffer: second unit (uncredited); Serge Poupis, first assistant camera: additional camera (uncredited); Kit Whitmore, focus puller: second unit (uncredited). Casting Department: Mark F. Hill, extras casting (uncredited). Costume and Wardrobe Department: Robert Cambel, costumer; Joanne Hutchinson, costume supervisor. Editorial Department: Janice Hampton, assistant film editor; Geoffrey Rowland, assistant film editor. Music Department: Joseph Tuley, Jr., music editor; Bill Conti, conductor (uncredited); Bill Conti, orchestrator (uncredited); Ami Hadani, music engineer (uncredited). Transportation Department: Mike Grover, transportation captain. Miscellaneous Crew: Joan Arnold, production secretary; Dale Benson, location manager; Janet Crosy, assistant to producer; Jimmy Gambina, technical advisor; Gloria Gonzales, assistant to producer; Lloyd Kaufman, pre-production supervisor; David Kramer, publicist; Joe Letizia, liaison: Philadelphia; Bonnie Prendergast, script supervisor; Carol Rosenstein, assistant to director; Marge Rowland, location auditor; Sylvester Stallone, boxing choreographer; Jeff Kanew, trailer (uncredited) (unconfirmed); Steve Sayre, assistant fight choreographer (uncredited). Thanks: Jane Oliver, dedicatee. Filming Locations: 1818 East Tusculum Street, Kensington, North Philadelphia, Pennsylvania, USA (Rocky's home); 318 S. Main St. Downtown, Los Angeles, California, USA (interior for Mighty Micks Gym); Fairmount Park, Philadelphia, Pennsylvania, USA (running scene); Kensington, North Philadelphia, Pennsylvania, USA; Los Angeles Sports Arena—3939 S. Figueroa Street, Exposition Park, Los Angeles, California, USA; Olympic Auditorium—1801 S. Grand Avenue, Downtown, Los Angeles, California, USA; Pat's King of Steaks—1237 S.

Passyunk Avenue, Philadelphia, Pennsylvania, USA; Philadelphia City Hall —1450 John F. Kennedy Blvd., Philadelphia, Pennsylvania, USA; Philadelphia Museum of Art — 2600 Benjamin Franklin Parkway, Philadelphia, Pennsylvania, USA; Resurrection Gym —1114 S. Lorena Street, East Los Angeles, California, USA (opening shot); Santa Monica, California, USA(skating rink); Shamrock Meats — 3461 E. Vernon Avenue, Vernon, California, USA. Production Companies: Chartoff-Winkler Productions (as a Robert Chartoff— Irwin Winkler production); United Artists. Distributors: United Artists (1976) (USA) (theatrical); Columbia Broadcasting System (CBS) (1979) (USA) (TV) (original airing); Sony Pictures Home Entertainment (2006) (USA) (DVD); 20th Century–Fox Home Entertainment (2009) (USA) (DVD) (Blu-ray) (The Undisputed Collection).

Cast — in credits order: Sylvester Stallone, Rocky Balboa; Talia Shire, Adrian Pennino; Burt Young, Paulie Pennino; Carl Weathers, Apollo Creed; Burgess Meredith, Mickey Goldmill; David Thayer, George Jergens; Joe Spinell, Tony Gazzo; Jimmy Gambina, Mike; Bill Baldwin, Fight Announcer; Al Salvani, Cut Man; George Memmoli, Ice Rink Attendant; Jodi Letizia, Marie; Diana Lewis, George O'Hanlon, TV Commentators; Larry Carroll, TV Interviewer; Stan Shaw, Dipper; Don Sherman, Bartender; Billy Sands, Club Fight Announcer; Pedro Lovell, Spider Rico — Club Fighter; DeForest Covan, Apollo's Corner; Simmy Bow, Club Corner Man; Tony Burton, Apollo's Trainer; Hank Rolike, Apollo Corner Man; Shirley O'Hara, Jergens' Secretary; Kathleen Parker, Paulie's Date; Frank Stallone, Timekeeper; Lloyd Kaufman, Drunk; Jane Marla Robbins, Owner of Pet Shop; Jack Hollander, Fats; Joe Sorbello, Buddy, Gazzo's Bodyguard; Christopher Avildsen, Chiptooth; Frankie Van, Club Fight Referee; Lou Fillipo, Championship Fight Referee; Paris Eagle, Fighter; Frank Stallone, Jr., Streetcorner Singer; Robert L. Tangrea, Peter Glassberg, William E. Ring and Joseph C. Giambelluc, Streetcorner Singers; Joe Frazier, Himself; Butkus Stallone, Rocky's Dog. Other credited cast listed alphabetically: Arnold Johnson, Spectator.

CHAPTER 9

Saturday Night Fever

Missing Out on a Blockbuster

Avildsen was still riding the success of *Rocky* in 1976 when he was crossing a New York street and spotted an old friend, Milt Felsen. "Hey, Milt," he yelled.[1]

Felsen stopped, looked around, and spotted the director approaching.

"What are you doing these days?" Avildsen asked

"The usual," Felsen answered.

"How would you like to produce a movie?" Avildsen asked

"Why not? I've got nothing else to do this afternoon."

With that exchange, the two men walked past Central Park to an office building where Avildsen introduced Felsen to Robert Stigwood. Stigwood was a music producer working with a rock group known as the Bee Gees. He had a script for a movie that was written by Avildsen's friend Norman Wexler, who had written *Joe*. Avildsen had recommended Wexler for the job. The script was based on a 1976 *New York* magazine article by British writer Nik Cohn. It focused on a new dance craze that had captured the imagination of the young people in New York City. It would be released as *Saturday Night Fever*, and Avildsen had already been selected to direct.

But they needed production help. Felsen took the job, was given a copy of the script, and sent downstairs to an office that had already been prepared. "[Stigwood] already had all the money, he just needed everything put together," Felsen recalled. "So I sat down at the desk and started lining up a cast and crew."

It wasn't going to be quite that easy. Three days later, Stigwood approached Felsen with a complaint about Avildsen. "He keeps changing the script," Stigwood said. "He wants to make it into another *Rocky*."

Felsen went to his friend with the complaint.

"I just want to make a few changes," Avildsen said, referring to his desire for the film to have an upbeat ending.

"Well, you're making Stigwood mad," Felsen replied. "Why don't you back off?"

"I will soon," Avildsen said. "I've got a few more things I want to do."

He never got them done. A few days after Felsen's conversation with Avildsen, the director was fired. "John was off the picture and I had to find another director," Felsen recalled. "We had to start shooting within two weeks, because John Travolta was starring in a TV show — *Welcome Back, Kotter* — and his contract had a deadline about when he had to be back for that. I tried to talk Stigwood into giving John another chance, but he wouldn't do it."

Felsen then went to Avildsen to see if he knew he had been fired from the film.

"Yeah," Avildsen said.

"Why didn't you just back off?" Felsen asked. But Avildsen, who had just received his Oscar nomination for *Rocky*, was unrepentant and unconcerned.

"Screw him," Avildsen said. "I don't care."

Avildsen had just been fired from *The Stoolie* and *Serpico*. Those would not be his last. He would later quit *Space Camp* in a creative dispute with Fox studio chief Leonard Goldberg, an executive with a reputation for firing directors.[2] Kit Culkin, father of child star Macaulay Culkin, refused to work with Avildsen (and several other directors) on the *Richie Rich* film.[3] Over the next few years, he would be the initial director of such films as *Kramer vs. Kramer* and *Gone Fishing*. In each case, for one reason or another, he was dismissed and another director placed in charge.

Still, Avildsen would leave his imprint on *Saturday Night Fever*. It wasn't transformed into another *Rocky*, but it did share *Rocky*'s working class theme. And several scenes ended up in the movie that were tributes to the director.

After Avildsen was dismissed, Felsen had to find another director. His initial calls were unsuccessful, with everyone turning him down when told they had only two weeks to prepare. Finally, someone in the production reached John Badham. "He didn't ask any questions, and he agreed to do it," Felsen recalled.

Badham had never been to Brooklyn and knew little of the area. Even worse, the film was still casting and other production details were incomplete. Still, Felsen said, "We had enough of the cast together to start shooting the opening scene."

Things got off to a bad start:. The opening scene had John Travolta walking down the street, under the el, and spotting a fancy shirt in a store window that would look good for the Friday night dance. He stops, looks at it and enters the store.

That portion of the shoot went well. But by the time Travolta emerged from the store, a crowd of teenage girls had gathered on the elevated platform. Travolta's TV fans, it turned out, had gotten word of the shoot and they had turned out to see him. "Travolta was terrified," Felsen said, "and he refused to come back to the store."

The problem was solved by having Travolta's double get into a limo and be driven away from the scene. After the crowd dispersed, Felsen used his own car to drive Travolta to safety.

"We stayed away about two hours before we felt it was safe to return and continue the shoot," Felsen said. "After that, we changed our procedures. We only gave out the location for the next day's shoot at midnight, so word wouldn't leak out."

Meanwhile, Travolta and Badham didn't work well together. "Travolta hated Badham, and Badham hated him," Felsen said. "Every day there was a crisis, with Travolta threatening to quit. We'd have to calm him down and

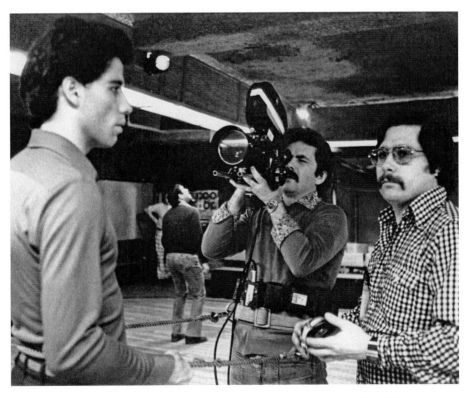

The set of *Saturday Night Fever* (1977) with John Travolta and unidentified crew members.

ask him to stick it out, and then go to Badham and ask him to ease up on Travolta. They were like oil and water. They didn't mix at all."

Meanwhile, another problem was developing with Travolta's co-star. The original script called for Travolta to visit a dance studio where he sees a beautiful young girl dancing. He immediately falls for her and her dancing. The role had not been cast when Badham arrived in New York. Badham, who started doing some of the casting himself, chose the actress for the part.

The problem: She wasn't right for the role. She was in her late twenties — too old for the part — and she couldn't dance. "Now we're already shooting," Felsen recalled, "but the script has to be re-written because you can't shoot the original script with her in that role. We ended up re-writing every day, focusing on the boys instead of the relationship."

The changes were of the very nature that Avildsen had originally been seeking. By being fired from the film, it seems, he created a situation in which the film he wanted was made. "All of the changes worked," Felsen said. "They all made the movie better. It changed from a love story about two dancers to a story about Brooklyn youth in routine jobs who became somebody important every weekend on the dance floor. It made the movie work." Producer Stigwood was happy with the changes, too. "All he wanted was a movie that would showcase the Bee Gees music," Felsen said, "and it did that."

But it also gave the film that same working-class identity that had characterized *Rocky*. Both Rocky and Travolta's Tony Manero began their fictional lives as champions of the working class. Somehow, though, both characters were transformed into successful achievers and icons of conservative values.

Reaganism has been described historically as an era of "heroism revival" and a period of "plastic heroes" fabrication. This climate was quickly exploited by the Hollywood industry which has always been in search of stories with heroic flavors. Simultaneously, the high demand by the public for video cassettes forced the industry to produce in order to meet the new need.

Also, for the benefit of Hollywood, the video industry gave the film industry new economic possibilities after the three-decade decline caused by television. Action-packed movies became the style of choice to fulfill the new demand. Simple "John gets Jane" stories were made, and the process of getting Jane was packed with special effects obstacles.

With the video market on the rise, the distribution of American films exploded abroad. Everyone, from Koreans and Italians to French and Turkish, all were looking for films to rent in video stores. Long dialogues and "intellectual films" did not work for the foreign markets as they had to be translated and understood by other cultures. Action films offered a more interesting aspect to the distributors. Of course, the success of the genre was detrimental to other styles of filmmaking as well as to the foreign film industry.

Rocky and *Saturday Night Fever* may have been the forerunners of that trend. Certainly they were produced during an economically and politically favorable and fertile time. However, *Rocky* and *Saturday Night Fever* were originally developed by filmmakers who had ideological views on the left side of American politics. But both films became icons of the political right. That's one reason they became so popular. What was acceptable to middle America were the ideas articulated in *Rocky* and *Saturday Night Fever*— liberal philosophies that became icons of the political right.

How did this occur? In both cases, the philosophical theme of each movie got separated from the icon each created. *Rocky* was directed by John Avildsen and opened in movie theaters in 1976 at the beginning of the Carter administration. Sylvester Stallone played a kid from a poor neighborhood in Philadelphia who gets a shot to become the boxing's heavyweight world champion. His character became the film embodiment of the conservative America's Horatio Alger theme, i.e., that a poor person can pull themselves up to the top if they will work hard enough. That theme would be the political mantra of Ronald Reagan, and its message would take him all the way to the presidency in 1980. *Saturday Night Fever* followed in 1977.

The initial director, again, was Avildsen, although he was later replaced by Badham. Travolta starred as Tony, a kid from a poor New York neighborhood who has a chance to become a dancing sensation at the local discos. Its theme has obvious similarities to *Rocky*. Tony was named after Avildsen's son Anthony. Wexler had previously named the character that Susan Sarandon played in *Joe* after Anthony's mother Melissa. Tony's bedroom wall is adorned with a poster of *Rocky*. In both cases, a kid from a poor neighborhood looks for a way out of the lower class environment.

This time, the avenue of opportunity was dancing. The resulting popularity of the film and its music sparked the disco era. The free-wheeling, individualistic and improvisational youth dancing of the 1960s was replaced by the carefully choreographed group movements of disco. Musically, at least, *Saturday Night Fever* closed the door on the music of the 1960s and its European influences. It was replaced by a stylistic form that was attuned to the conservative trends of the 1980s.[4] Watching the films, it is clear that Rocky and Tony were not ambassadors of the Reagan era. In fact they were just the opposite: They were the last bastions of the pre-me generation.

But what about the liberal origins in *Rocky*? After making *Rocky*, Avildsen was elected to two terms as president of IA Local 644, the camera union in New York. That position gave him frequent opportunities to meet Milt Felsen, a board member of the Directors Guild of America. At the time, Avildsen had made a few successful films for very little money. His reputation at the time was largely based on two films.

One of those, *Joe*, was a low-budget film that was highly controversial. The other, *Save the Tiger*, featured an Oscar-winning performance by Jack Lemmon, but it was also controversial. The studio was reluctant to produce the movie because of concerns that its anti-establishment theme was too close to Communist propaganda and not something that would attract American audiences. As Lemmon's biographer Michael Freedland noted, "The men sitting behind the big studio desks were worried that the critique of American morals which *Save the Tiger* represented was nothing less than an attack on their beloved nation."[5] The writer behind that attack was Steve Shagan. Shagan would later write another liberal movie, *The Formula* (also directed by Avildsen), in which he attacked the American oil industry, but as Freedland noted, *Save the Tiger* was his first "big chance both to say something and to have an international star fronting his product." The result: Avildsen's first major film was an award-winning effort that took a leftist view of American society.

His next major work would be *Rocky*. Prior to *Rocky*, Sylvester Stallone had never been cast in a major role. He was a struggling actor typecast as a bad guy. The Rocky series became somewhat autobiographical. His character struggles to get out of a social class and, once successful, ignores the values of that class. Rocky was street smart, Stallone was Hollywood smart. When the film was released, producer Irwin Winkler instructed Stallone to tell the press that he was a contender who stood up to the studios. By the time the film became a hit, Stallone had repeated the story so often that he started to believe it. He still believes it.

Both Stallone and Rocky started the metamorphosis of simple man into an invincible icon. *Rocky*, like *Joe* and *Save the Tiger*, were satires of the American system. Indeed, 1976 was the 200-year birthday of the United States. Its celebration was in reality reminiscent of Charles Foster Kane's birthday party: grandiose and egocentric in its nationalism. In *Rocky*, Avildsen pushes the satire mimicking Jimmy Hendrix playing the national anthem at Woodstock, an event that the Americans had not yet digested. The scene was indeed shocking as audiences accepted integration but not to the point of national mockery. But audiences ignored the satire because they started to adore Rocky.

Further, the satirical approach made Rocky's opponent even more dislikable. The love affair with Rocky continued for three more sequels but ground to a halt in *Rocky IV*. What had started with a poster of Rocky, in his red shorts, fighting against a black athlete in an Uncle Sam costume, was gradually transformed. By *Rocky IV*, Rocky is wearing the American flag while he tries to defeat a Russian in red shorts, in front of Gorbachev. Rocky had become Apollo Creed, and audience no longer liked Rocky's film persona.

Political scientist Daniel Franklin[6] argues that political ideologies in movies merely reflect those of the movie audience. If so, Rocky transformed into what the audience wanted. Still, it took four films for Rocky to make the full transition from liberal spokesman for the working class to the icon of the American right. *Saturday Night Fever* did it with one movie. Avildsen was hired to direct the film. On the same day he was fired, Avildsen was nominated for the Academy Award for directing *Rocky*. He later said that he was on such a high from getting the nomination that nothing could bring him down.

Avildsen's biggest concern was the script. Robert Stigwood, the film's producer, was also the producer for the Bee Gees, the musical group whose songs were featured in the movie. Avildsen thought that Stigwood was more interested in the film's music than its story. For Avildsen, the story was the first priority. Even the dancing, which was a focal point of the story, was merely a series of scenes that had to be told with technical precision. They had to be well done, but they contributed little to the story. As Felsen told the authors:

> The producer liked the script the way it was, but John kept changing it. The producer said to me, "If he doesn't want to do this picture — he said he wanted to do it, and he's changing everything — I'm going to have to fire him."
>
> I went to John and said, "John, you're going to get dumped off this film. You agreed to do the film. Do it. It's a good script. We'll change the script when we shoot, as we always do." You always change the script as you shoot. Whatever exigencies arise, you change it. He said, "Okay, I'll do it. I'll make a few of these little changes, but when the producer insists, I'll do it."

Felsen and Lloyd Kaufman decided to stay on the project. Felsen tried to find a replacement for Avildsen, but each director he approached turned down the film. Finally, two weeks before the shoot, Felsen found an unknown director, John Badham, who took the job. It was the beginning of Badham's career, and he was hungry. Badham was raised in a conservative upper class family in Birmingham, Alabama. His stepfather was a Army general and political conservative. Badham was educated in one of Alabama's best prep schools and then went to Yale. There he studied drama with the intention of becoming an actor just like his sister Mary Badham, of *To Kill a Mockingbird* fame. Despite his lack of experience, Badham was well prepared for his first directing assignment. He was a technically astute, hard-working young director who was still discovering New York. He was, in essence, the perfect director for Stigwood. He brought an innocence of the South to the New York scenes.

Unfortunately, few people on the movie liked working with him. Travolta, who was still recovering from the death of his girlfriend, hated working with him. Kaufman, also a Yale graduate, possibly resented the fact that Badham got the job. And Felsen didn't like the fact that Badham was a Republican. As a result, there was constant tension between the cast and the crew. Perhaps this is one reason that the film worked. The conflict between the classes offscreen may have carried over to the finished product: Its "pull-yourself-up-by-your-bootstraps" message caught on quickly with the young people who grew up in lower class neighborhoods.

One such character was Tony, Travolta's character. As mentioned earlier, there was a direct link between this character and Rocky. Avildsen told us that he thinks the poster was intended to be an inside joke. Although he got fired from the film, he still had several friends working on it. He believes they included the poster in the scene for that purpose. Maybe, but it still works. *Rocky* opens with the framing of a painting of Jesus on the cross and dollying to a boxing match — a boxing arena rather than a church — where two over-weight pugs (one of them Rocky) awkwardly slug each other.

That iconic religious connection with Rocky appears again in *Saturday Night Fever*, but in an inverted visual image. This time it's Tony's brother, a priest, who confesses to Tony that he is thinking of leaving the church. That confession is made in front of the *Rocky* poster. Thus, *Rocky* became an icon in its true sense, that is, an image, in *Saturday Night Fever*. The interesting element is that the icon is the film itself, not the character; Tony wants the Rocky success story, not the Rocky image.

Tony needs a way to get out of his own social class. Of course Rocky continues his quest for success *à la* Charles Foster Kane. The films will die in the same manners that Charles Foster Kane, Donald Trump or Howard Hughes did? They all did too much for themselves, often ignoring others on the path. Stallone's Rocky had grown from a man who offered hope for the downtrodden into a sculpted persona of the Me generation. What was at first a satire of a social system became the system: a superman in a superpower with no soul. The post-modernism hero. Travolta and the character of Tony evolved the same way. Muscular with very little compassion.

Stallone, just like Chaplin, could not detach himself from the persona he had created. Indeed, the character Rocky became trapped into a predictable evolution. After the ending of *Rocky*, it was easy to predict that Rocky would win the fight in *Rocky II*. After *Rocky II*, Stallone had to become bigger, better and articulate. The same thing had happened with Chaplin's *Monsieur Verdoux*. When Chaplin abandoned his "Little Tramp" character, the public abandoned Chaplin. Rocky, like Pygmalion, had earned the right to belong to the upper class. Just like Pygmalion, he could no longer return to his roots. Similarly, after *Monsieur Verdoux*, Chaplin could not return to the "Little Tramp." The sequels to *Rocky* were doomed because the story remained the same, with a predictable formula of winning or losing a fight.

Avildsen said that *Rocky* sequels were planned from the beginning, but the actual sequels turned out differently than those originally envisioned. Instead of sticking to the working class theme, the subsequent Rocky movies became success stories. Avildsen summarized the original ideas in this manner:

> When we were making the first movie, we had an idea for a sequel. Actually, it was going to be a trilogy... In the first movie, we had a scene where Rocky goes to meet the mayor of Philadelphia, because here was this Philadelphia boy going to become very famous because he was going to fight the world champion. So the mayor has his picture taken with Rocky. Then everybody leaves his office, and it's just the mayor and Rocky. The mayor's looking over Rocky's arrest record and truancy record from school and say, "You know, you're going to have to do yourself proud. The city is counting on you. And even if you lose, you're going to make quite a bit of money. What are you planning to do with all that money?"
>
> Rocky, with his hat in his hand, says, "I'm going to run for mayor."
>
> Then the second picture would be the campaign. He would run on a reform platform, promise to build playgrounds for the kids, throw out the corrupt politicians, and at the end of the second movie, he wins the election and is now mayor of Philadelphia.
>
> Then the third movie was going to be about his term in office. But, his by-then brother-in-law Paulie — the Burt Young character — gets caught stealing money from the city treasury. Rocky — being the heckuva guy that he is — he takes the fall, he takes the blame and, as a result of taking the blame, gets thrown out of office. The third one would end with him back in that armpit of a boxing arena where we found him in the first place. The announcer would say, "And the former mayor of Philadelphia, Rocky Balboa." He would come out and it would end where it all began.
>
> We were enamored with the idea, but I guess success has its own dictates, and that never went beyond the idea.[7]

Not all sequels suffer from such problems. The James Bond sequels worked because the situations were always different, even if Bond always won. Although Bond always rises to his challenges, those challenges are more complex than a simple uppercut. But sequels would not have worked with some other classic films, because they, too, would become too predictable. Consider, for example, the possible sequels to *On the Waterfront*.[8] In *On the Waterfront II*, Malloy would become a foreman. In *On the Waterfront III*, he would be a manager. By the time we might reach *On the Waterfront IV*, Malloy would be campaigning for mayor. By then, he's part of the establishment that he started out fighting. In *Rocky* and *Saturday Night Fever*, the icons developed because these two characters had the talent and dedication to pay their dues to enter into the capitalist class.

They were not heroes in the true sense of the word. The American heroes at the time were Martin Luther King and Robert Kennedy. Both of them had died in 1968 at the climax of the hippie movement. By the mid–1970s, instead of heroes, being famous became the goal. A hero saves others, a famous person saves himself. A new generation was born and Rocky and Tony were the last of that generation. They were heroes of their peers as characters as was Terry Malloy in *On the Waterfront*. Why this transformation? Part of it was timing. In retrospect, the hippie movement seems to have been the last call for liberalism in the U.S.

Perhaps it was the last social revolution in a capitalist system. The civil rights movement of the 1960s was the beginning of a turn to the left for U.S. politics. At the same time, the young people of the nation were turning to a more liberal view of politics and society, one which was epitomized by the hippie movement. But, in retrospect, that turn was only a small detour in American history. In spite of its death in 1968, elements of political liberalism continued living, though somewhat superficially, through the end of the Vietnam War. Perhaps some members of the left thought they had won the philosophical battle with the end of the war and the collapse of the Nixon administration.

But that was an illusion. By the mid–1970s, the U.S. was ready for a return to the right. Penn State professor Gary Cross summarized the twentieth century in the U.S. by describing it as an all-consuming century in which "commercialism won." That indeed seems to be the case. By the late 1970s and 1980s, American political philosophy had taken a strong turn to the right. Ronald Reagan won the 1980 presidential election with a populist theme of conservative politics and pro-business philosophy. Programs aimed at benefiting the poor were labeled "government handouts," with money going to people who had done nothing to merit the remittance. Even the civil rights movement, which started out as a campaign to uplift the downtrodden, shifted its primary focus to expanding economic opportunities so that blacks could become part of the establishment that was once their enemy. Artistically, the shift to the right was also apparent. The rock 'n' roll revolution ended with Woodstock. After that, it was only imitating itself. The Bee Gees were a mixture of the Beatles and Pat Boone. The disco look was either a fashion or even a disguise (fashion is the link between production and consumption in capitalist society; look at the 2013 version of *The Great Gatsby*), while the hippies' attire was a statement.

The society had changed into a mirror of itself and was recycling itself over and over. Changes were no longer an issue. It was the beginning of postmodernism. Rocky and Tony became the object of fashion and products for consumer consumption. Indeed, the subsequent sequels were profitable for the Hollywood establishment.

Production Notes

Directed by: John Badham. Writers: Magazine article "Tribal Rites of the New Saturday Night," Nik Cohn; Screenplay, Norman Wexler. Producers: Milt Felsen, associate producer; Kevin McCormick, executive producer; Robert Stigwood, producer. Original

Music: Barry Gibb, Maurice Gibb, Robin Gibb. Cinematographer: Ralf D. Bode (director of photography). Editor: David Rawlins. Casting Director: Shirley Rich. Production Designer: Charles Bailey. Set Decorator: George Detitta. Costume Designer: Patrizia Von Brandenstein. Make Up Department: Henriquez, makeup artist; Joe Tubens, hair designer. Production Manager: John Nicolella. Second Unit Directors or Assistant Directors: Joseph Ray, second assistant director; Allan Wertheim, assistant director. Art Department: James Mazzola, property master; William Canfield, set dresser (uncredited). Sound Department: Michael Colgan, sound editor; Robert W. Glass, Jr., sound re-recording mixer; Les Lazarowitz, sound mixer; John T. Reitz, sound re-recording mixer; John K. Wilkinson, sound re-recording mixer. Stunts: Paul Nuckles, stunt coordinator; Lightning Bear, stunts (uncredited). Camera and Electrical Department: Holly Bower, still photographer; James Finnerty, key grip; Tom Priestley, Jr., camera operator; Bill Ward, gaffer; Gary Muller, first assistant camera (uncredited); Robert Paone, second assistant camera (uncredited). Costume and Wardrobe Department: Jennifer Nichols, costumer. Editorial Department: Angelo Corrao, assistant editor (uncredited); Jean-Marc Vasseur, assistant film editor (uncredited). Music Department: John Caper, Jr., music editor; David Shire, composer: additional music; David Shire, music adaptor; Lester Wilson, stager: musical numbers; Dan Wallin, score mixer (uncredited). Miscellaneous Crew: Arlene Albertson, production office coordinator; Lorraine Fields, assistant choreographer; James Gambina, technical consultant; Gary Kalkin, unit publicist; Lloyd Kaufman, location executive; Carl Lotito, assistant: Mr. Stigwood; Joy McMillan, assistant: Mr. Stigwood; Colleen Murphy, assistant: Mr. Badham; Jo-Jo Smith, dance consultant; Ronald Stigwood, assistant: Mr. Stigwood; Renata Stoia, script supervisor; Lester Wilson, choreographer; Deney Terrio, dance instructor (uncredited). Filming Locations: 221 79th Street, Bay Ridge, Brooklyn, New York City, New York, USA (Manero home); 86th Street, Brooklyn, New York City, New York, USA (opening sequence: Tony's Walk); Bay Ridge, Brooklyn, New York City, New York, USA; Bensonhurst, Brooklyn, New York City, New York, USA; Brooklyn Bridge, New York City, New York, USA; Brooklyn Heights Promenade, Brooklyn Heights, Brooklyn, New York City, New York; John J. Carty Park, Bay Ridge, Brooklyn, New York City, New York, USA (basketball court); Kelly's Tavern — 9259 Fourth Avenue, Bay Ridge, Brooklyn, New York City, New York (restaurant); Lenny's Pizza — 1969 86th Street, Bensonhurst, Brooklyn, New York City, New York, USA (opening sequence: Tony's Walk); Manhattan, New York City, New York, USA; Phillips Dance Studio — 1301 W. Seventh Street, Bensonhurst, Brooklyn, New York City, New York (dance studio); Verrazano-Narrows Bridge, New York City, New York. Production Company: Robert Stigwood Organization (RSO). Distributors: Paramount Pictures (1977) (USA) (theatrical); American Broadcasting Company (ABC) (1980) (USA) (TV) (broadcast premiere); Paramount Home Video (2002) (USA) (DVD).

Cast — in credits order: John Travolta, Tony Manero; Karen Lynn Gorney, Stephanie; Barry Miller, Bobby C.; Joseph Cali, Joey; Paul Pape, Double J.; Donna Pescow, Annette; Bruce Ornstein, Gus; Julie Bovasso, Flo; Martin Shakar, Frank Jr.; Sam J. Coppola, Dan Fusco; Nina Hansen, Grandmother; Lisa Peluso, Linda; Denny Dillon, Doreen; Bert Michaels, Pete; Robert Costanza, Paint Store Customer; Robert Weil, Becker; Shelly Batt, Girl in Disco; Fran Drescher, Connie; Donald Gantry, Jay Langhart; Murray Moston, Haberdashery Salesman; William Andrews, Detective; Ann Travolta, Pizza Girl; Helen Travolta, Lady in Paint Store; Ellen March, Bartender; Monti Rock III, The Deejay; Val Bisoglio, Frank Sr.; Other credited cast listed alphabetically: Roy Cheverie, The Wrong Partner (uncredited); Adrienne King, Chere Mauldin, and M.J. Quinn, Dancers (uncredited); Alberto Vazquez, Gang Member (uncredited).

CHAPTER 10

Slow Dancing in the Big City

A Former Sexploitation Director
Tackles Romance

When a director has the biggest hit of his career, it is sometimes most telling to examine the project he chooses immediately afterward, when he presumably has more Hollywood clout and more offers than other times. In this light, Avildsen's *Slow Dancing in the Big City*—a ballet film and old-fashioned romance with no A-list talent — may at first seem a strange follow-up to his Oscar-winning *Rocky*. But when the director's aborted work on *Saturday Night Fever* is viewed as a bridge, it is easier to see how *Slow Dancing* was chosen — almost as if *Fever* put the subject of dance under the director's skin, and the ballet film was his chance to deliver on its promise.

Avildsen described his interest in dance to interviewer John Andrew Gallagher: "I always had a fantasy I was going to do *The Gene Kelly Story* someday, so I'd always had an affinity to dance in the broadest aspects."[1] Decades later, Avildsen would produce (with his son Anthony directing) the documentary *Dancing into the Future* starring Jacques d'Ambrose, which chronicles a collaboration between the National Dance Institute (America) and the Shanghai Song and Dance Ensemble.

One wonders whether Avildsen, upon his firing from *Saturday Night Fever*, was already on the hunt for dance-related material before considering scripts, or whether he did happen to connect, coincidentally, with two successive dance projects. The director says, "I started looking for scripts again. *Slow Dancing* came my way and I was very taken by it."[2]

Actress-turned-writer Barra Grant penned the screenplay, her first to be produced. Apparently, many script changes were made, because when Grant later got a writing-directing deal at 20th Century–Fox, the studio's VP of Creative Affairs Susan Merzbach was quoted as saying, "Most of us saw her

100

original [*Slow Dancing*] screenplay, which was terrific. But successive drafts lessened the impact of the eventual film. It wasn't anything we held against her."[3]

The film's story has chubby human-interest newspaper columnist Lou Friedlander (Paul Sorvino) feeling half-hearted about his casual love interest, Franny (Anita Dangler), despite the fact that she dutifully cooks and cleans for him, and despite the fact that he calls her his muse. Meanwhile, ballet dancer Sarah Gantz (Anne Ditchburn) is butting heads with her wealthy male companion, David Fillmore (Nicolas Coster), over her odd hours of practice in his luxurious home. Sarah ends up taking an apartment in Lou's run-down building, and the two become friendly — and ultimately romantic.

This "odd couple" romance has some clumsy writing in the "getting acquainted" stages. After learning of Sarah's upcoming ballet, for instance, Lou barges into a closed rehearsal and is somehow not thrown out just because he drops his press credentials. Also, the film indicates Lou and Sarah's mutual interest by having them voluntarily trying out each other's diets (deli and pasta fare for Lou, and New Age-y health food for Sarah), but instead of using that a single time, the film repeatedly comes back to the food issue, as if it's only a storytelling trick. Later, when Lou needs medical info about Sarah, he gets it with unrealistic ease for not having her permission or being a relative.

The medical info comes into play when Sarah discovers she has fibromyositis and that she is damaging her body — possibly irrevocably — by continuing to dance. She is in constant pain during rehearsals for the upcoming ballet (entitled "The Primeval Forest," to be performed at Lincoln Center) and is barely passing muster. Sarah's lackluster work distresses her director, because a grant for the ballet company is riding on the quality of "Forest." Unbeknownst to almost everyone, her doctor is insisting on an operation to arrest Sarah's existing muscle damage — a procedure that will prevent the dancer from ever taking the stage again professionally.

This adds up to a lot of conflict in Sarah's life. So that the film isn't lop-sided on conflict, a tacked-on subplot has Lou informally mentoring a young Puerto Rican neighborhood kid — an aspiring drummer named Marty (G. Adam Gifford) — whose older brother is a drug pusher. The subplot ends in Marty's tragic death, which seems more meant to give weight to the proceedings, however artificially, than it rings true to life (we are asked to believe that a fatal drug overdose was "pushed" onto the young Marty by his own brother). But Marty's story thread does offer *Slow Dancing* one well-handled moment of irony: When we first meet the youngster, he is trying to act tough in front of his peer, and he taunts Lou with, "Why don't you go down to 5th Avenue and buy yourself a dress, faggot!" before the two kids run off to play innocently on a seesaw.

Also serving as a minor complication to Lou's potential romance with Sarah is the current woman in his life, Franny. Surprisingly gut-wrenching, the scene in which Lou ends his casual relationship with the waitress is done with minimal dialogue addressing their actual break-up. The script handles the scene as if the forty-something Franny already knows, from previous experience, exactly how this discussion will end, and it is made all the more sad by the possibility that Lou was the aging waitress' last chance for a husband.

Slow Dancing climaxes with the opening night performance of "Primeval Forest," and the scene's tension derives both from the possibility that the heavily attended ballet might be ruined because of Sarah's condition and that the dancer may be doing irreparable harm to her body. Somewhat predictably, her body gives out immediately upon the completion of the ballet, but Avildsen manages to get powerful imagery out of the resulting moment when, in an extreme wide shot, Lou carries Sarah out for her curtain call.

As a ballet film, *Slow Dancing in the Big City* comes chronologically between 1977's *The Turning Point* and 1980's *Fame*. It sandwiches between those two in hipness factor also. *Turning Point* strictly features classical ballet, and the dancers wear traditional leotards. *Fame*, on the other hand, features a raw mix of ballet and modern dance, and the apparel is a fusion of dance clothes and street fashion. *Slow Dancing*'s first dance scene promises a hipper version of ballet, with Sarah dancing furiously to pop music (Carol King's "I Feel the Earth Move"). But then the dancing settles down into classical ballet (albeit with *Fame*-style street-dance fashion) for the remainder of the film, with the one exception of a lunch-break scene, during which the dancers cut loose to some piano rock (provided by composer Bill Conti in a cameo role).

In a way, however, *Slow Dancing* did follow in the footsteps of *The Turning Point*, which launched the acting career of dancer Mikhail Baryshnikov. Similarly, Ditchburn had been a solo dancer and a choreographer for the National Ballet of Canada prior to acting (she maintained a screen career through the 1980s).

Ditchburn was cast after Avildsen spied an energetic photograph of her in the *New York Times*, during the period when she choreographed a ballet at the Metropolitan Opera House. The audition apparently started poorly: "My dramatic acting on the stage had been strictly limited to dance," she recalled. "When I first read the scene, my inexperience showed. But John filmed me over and over again, and I gradually improved."[4]

Avildsen must have been reached somehow by Ditchburn's individual presence, as she was ultimately cast despite not only the rocky audition, but also instead of the many dancers Avildsen saw during a Hollywood casting session. She screen tested with the already cast Sorvino before she was offered the role, and then she underwent two months of acting lessons —five hours daily — before principal photography began.[5]

The dancer-turned-actress received some harsh reviews: "Unfortunately, she does not seem to possess an actress' expressive equipment," wrote Gary Arnold of the *LA Times Washington Post* Service.[6] Steven Smith called her "a clumsy, unintentionally comic actress" in the *Eugene Register-Guard*.[7] Perhaps the general consensus was expressed best by Dan Dinacola when he wrote for *The Schenectady Gazette*, "The best sequences are those in which Ditchburn dances. The worst are those in which she tries to act."[8] Whatever criticisms were levied against Ditchburn's acting, she did make a striking screen debut in some respects, and the Sarah Gantz role earned her a Golden Globe nomination for Best Motion Picture Acting Debut — Female.

Playing opposite her was Sorvino in a role that earned generally positive reviews but which couldn't escape, in almost any review or mention, comparisons to real-life New York City columnist Jimmy Breslin. Lou Friedlander was apparently patterned after the Pulitzer Prize–winning Breslin — a "regular guy" journalist who wrote columns about the common New Yorker — by screenwriter Grant. Apparently the thinly disguised *Slow Dancing* movie character ignited a "continuing verbal duel" between Breslin and Grant's mother, Bess Myerson, herself a minor celebrity for being the first Jewish Miss America.[9]

Paul Sorvino and Anne Ditchburn in *Slow Dancing in the Big City* (1978).

A Breslin-type journalist was a great character for this particular director to oversee. Avildsen's career has shown him to be one of the great New York film directors (although the Philadelphia setting for *Rocky* keeps his association with the Big Apple weaker than a Woody Allen or a Martin Scorsese), and the Breslin-esque Lou Friedlander taps into so many charming New York vignettes through his column.

Many scenes set in the titular "Big City" were reportedly filmed in New Jersey. The Associated Press quoted New Jersey film publicist Henry Rogers as saying that shooting five days in New York's Lincoln Center was going to be cost prohibitive for *Slow Dancing*, so the producers planned to substitute Newark Symphony Hall. Similarly, according to Rogers, a Jersey City Trans-Hudson subway yard would stand-in for a Queens location.[10]

Lou Friedlander's part was beefed up after the film's release. An additional ten minutes of footage involving the character were added near *Slow Dancing*'s beginning when the film was reportedly re-edited as a response to poor reviews.[11] This is perhaps a testament to Sorvino's contribution to the film. The actor had previously worked with Avildsen in a small role in 1971's *Cry Uncle*. That film's star Allen Garfield later revealed that he had campaigned for the Lou Friedlander part in *Slow Dancing*.[12]

The critics were merciless about the on-screen romance between the two. And with good reason. Besides the writing's awkward and improbable scenarios that conspire to put Lou and Sarah together, there is the matter of the setting. *Slow Dancing* spans, roughly, a week's time. Had we seen the exact same meetings between Lou and Sarah but been told, somehow, that these encounters occurred over a three-month time span, the romance would have been more credible.

Ditchburn lashed back at the negative reviews: "I'm not surprised by the adverse reviews (not many critics are romantically minded). There is a razor-fine edge between romanticism and corn, and I think *Slow Dancing* worked against the corn. John's films hit people emotionally; he's a genius at that."[13]

And perhaps *Slow Dancing* was not given a fair shake by the press. The film's several great one-liners (e.g., "Now if you don't mind, I'll see if my door works," Sarah says when shooing Lou out of her newly rented apartment) received no mention in reviews. Further, factual errors were often made; *The Miami News*, for example, described Avildsen as being "most famous for *Roots*."[14] Further, it often didn't get reviewed alone. Newspaper critiques of *Slow Dancing* were sometimes lumped in — as part of the same article — with those of contemporaneous films the reviewers thought were similar: *Paradise Alley* (which had the Stallone connection) and *Ice Castles* (which also concerned a tragedy befalling an arts performer).

The film was a commercial disaster as well as a critical one. *Slow Dancing*'s short theatrical run in (late 1978, early 1979) even made the headlines in a Pittsburgh newspaper for "being the first of the heavily touted Christmas movies to collapse at the box office."[15] It has never been properly available on videotape or DVD. However, fans can find a ten-minute trailer, provided by Avildsen on YouTube. That trailer has drawn some favorable comments from viewers, including one who wrote, "I loved this movie too. I wish that you had the bit in the opening with the Carole King song! That scene is iconic to me as a dancer — the rehearsing hard at home."

Another fan described the film as "my favorite movie ever when I was living in NYC and obsessed with ballet." It was, she added, a "gorgeous movie, gorgeous dancing and a great story." Another wrote, "There has to be a video and DVD of this beautiful story." When told that no DVD was available, another disappointed fan wrote, "I've been looking for this movie for what seems like forever. No wonder I could never find it."

Avildsen may have closed out his seminal decade — the ten-year span that saw the release of *Joe, Save the Tiger* and *Rocky* — on a misstep. But in the 1970s, he had laid a foundation for a whole career's worth of well-deserved second chances.

Production Notes

Directed by: John G. Avildsen. Writer: Barra Grant Writer. Producers: John G. Avildsen, producer; Michael Levee, producer; George Manasse, associate producer. Original Music: Bill Conti. Cinematographer: Ralf D. Bode. Editor: John G. Avildsen. Casting Director: Shirley Rich. Art Director: Henry M. Shrady. Set Decorator: Charles Truhan. Costume Designer: Ruth Morley. Make Up Department: Verne Caruso, hair stylist; Margaret Sunshine, makeup artist; Second Unit Directors or Assistant Directors:; Henry Bronchtein, DGA apprentice; Bill Eustace, second assistant director; Joan Spiegel Feinstein, second assistant director; Dwight Williams, assistant director. Art Department: Michael Badalucco, assistant set dresser; Bill Cassidy, visual design consultant; Stanley Graham, scenic artist; Donald Holtzman, stand-by prop; Susan Kaufman, assistant art director; John Pomponio, assistant set dresser; Tom Tonery, set dresser; Kenneth Weinberg, property master. Sound Department: David B. Cohn, sound editor; Jack Cooley, re-recording mixer: Magnosound; Harriet Fidlow, looping editor; Leslie T. Gaulin, assistant sound editor: Magnofex; Bud Grenzbach, sound mixer: Dolby stereo; Ron Kalish, sound editor; Dennis Maidland 2nd, boom operator; Dennis Maitland, sound mixer; Tod Maitland, sound recordist; David Rosenblum, sound recordist. Camera and Electrical Department: John G. Avildsen, camera operator; Don Biller, second assistant camera; Pedro Bonilla, assistant camera: rehearsal sequence; Holly Bower, still photographer; Ira Brenner, second assistant camera; Maurice Brown, first assistant camera; Catharine Bushnell, still photographer; Joe Coffey, camera operator: rehearsal sequence; Ed Engels, Sr., grip; Jules Fisher, lighting: ballet; Gil Geller, camera operator: Lincoln Center Ballet Sequence; Tom Gilligan, best boy; Bob Haagensen, camera operator: Lincoln Center Ballet Sequence; Craig Haagensen, first assistant camera; Gerald Hirschfeld, director of photography: ballet sequence, Lincoln Center; Marc Hirschfeld, additional focus puller; Charles Meere, best boy; William

Meyerhoff, gaffer; Bob Paone, second assistant camera; Ed Quinn, key grip; Fred Schuler, camera operator: Lincoln Center Ballet Sequence; Jonathan Smith, assistant additional camera operator; Pat Tarzini, first assistant camera; Bill Ward, gaffer; Coulter Watt, additional camera operator;; Robert Shepherd, grip (uncredited). Costume and Wardrobe Department: Al Craine, costumer — men; Jennifer Nichols, costumer — women. Editorial Department: Mindy Byer, apprentice editor; Lou Cangiano, color grader; David Falt, assistant editor; Jane Kurson, apprentice editor; Nicholas Smith, assistant editor. Music Department: Lou Adler, song producer: "I Feel the Earth Move"; Bill Conti, conductor: ballet sequence; Ken Hall, music editor; Tommy Tedesco, musician: guitar (uncredited); Dan Wallin, score mixer (uncredited). Transportation Department: Michael Fennell, transportation captain. Miscellaneous Crew: Chris Avildsen, production assistant; B.J. Bjorkman, script supervisor; Victor Celeste, physical therapist; Roseann Chatterton, production assistant; Celia Costas, production assistant; Bonnie Czekala, production assistant; Anne Ditchburn, choreographer: Roof Ballet; Jo Doster, production assistant; Lyn Fink, assistant production coordinator; Anthony Gittleson, production assistant; Gary Kalkin, unit publicist; William Kegg III, production assistant; Doug Kenny, production assistant; Kobrin, assistant to director; Victoria Frances Levee, assistant to producer; Craig Miller, ballet lighting assistant; Michelle Morán, physical therapist; Florence Nerlinger, production coordinator; Robert North, choreographer; Rich Siegal, production assistant; Jeff Silver, production assistant; Margery Simkin, production assistant; Peter Thompson, dialogue coach. Mark Winter, production assistant. Filming Location: New York City, New York (USA). Production Company: CIP. Distributor: United Artists (1978) (USA) (theatrical).

　　Cast — in credits order: Paul Sorvino, Lou Friedlander; Anne Ditchburn, Sarah Gantz; Nicolas Coster, David Fillmore; Anita Dangler, Franny; Thaao Penghlis, Christopher; Linda Selman, Barbara Bass; Hector Jaime Mercado, Roger Lucas; Dick Carballo, George Washington Monero; Jack Ramage, Doctor Foster; G. Adam Gifford, Marty Olivera; Brenda Joy Kaplan, Punk; Daniel Faraldo, T.C. Olivera; Michael Gorrin, Lester Edelman; Tara Mitton, Diana; Matt Russo, Jeck Guffy; Bill Conti, Rehearsal Pianist; Richard Jamieson, Joe Christy; Susan Doukas, Nurse; Ben Slack, Mort Hoffman; Lloyd Kaufman, Usher; Lee Steele, Baclstage Doorman; Edward Crowley, Graffiti Cop; Danielle Brisebois, Ribi Ciano; Mimi Cecchini, Rose Ciano; Dick Boccelli, Fabrizio; Henry Kaimu Bal, Enrique; Anthony Avildsen and Jonathan Avildsen, Halloween Kids; Clifford Lipson, Larry; Demo DiMartile, Smithfield; Frank Hamilton, Bartender; Peter Marklin, Stage Manager; Mario Todisco, Stagehand; Dee Dee Friedman, Secretary; Don Jay, and Steve James, Voices of Bentleyologist; Barra Grant, Mildred; Helene Alexopoulos, Jacqueline Buglisi, Laura Delano, Gregory Drotar, Florence Fitzgerald, Donlin Foreman, Don Johanson, Elisa Monte, Jerome Sarnat, Ricky Schussel, Barbara Seibert and Harry Streep, Dancers: The Dance Company.

CHAPTER 11

The Formula

Avildsen and Marlon Brando

It seemed like a can't-miss idea: Take two Oscar-winning actors, team them with an Oscar-winning director, and give them a script about the hottest topic in the nation.

Too bad it didn't work.

That's why the 1980 film *The Formula* remains one of Avildsen's more forgettable movies. While there's probably plenty of blame to go around, most of the finger-pointing has been aimed at a Hollywood legend: Marlon Brando.

The genesis of the film began with a novel by Steve Shagan that had taken a jab at the major oil companies. In the novel, the idea of synthetic oil made from coal had been developed by the Nazis during World War II, the major oil companies had the magic formula that would reduce the need for continued consumption of hydrocarbon oil, but they kept that formula secret to protect their profits. A Los Angeles detective stumbles onto the conspiracy while investigating the murder of a friend, and his investigation leads to the death of others.

Shagan not only wrote the novel, but he adapted it into a screenplay and produced the film version. It was, literally, Shagan's film. He was lining up a cast, and he needed a director.

Avildsen, who worked with Shagan on *Save the Tiger*, happened to be available even though he was not enthusiastic about the project. The script, he felt, had too many problems.

Avildsen had been scheduled to direct *The Fiendish Plot of Dr. Fu Manchu*, Peter Sellers' last film. Two weeks before shooting started, Sellers decided *he* wanted to direct that film. "They paid me a lot of money to go away," Avildsen said. "I figured maybe the same thing would happen with *The Formula*. Surely somebody, somewhere along the line would realize this thing didn't work. Well, I was wrong."

Avildsen and producer Steve Shagan relaxing in between takes on the set of *The Formula* (1980).

Shagan, determined to get the film made, went on the road to promote it. Using his book as a ticket, he went on the talk show circuit to let the world know that America "wouldn't have an energy problem were it not for the oil cartels."[1]

Still, little progress had been made by 1977. George C. Scott had been approached about playing the hero who investigates the mysterious formula. But the cast was still lacking someone to play villain Adam Steifel, the businessman behind the oil cartel and the conspiracy to keep the formula a secret.

Realizing that the film was going nowhere, and that the studio producers were growing antsy, Avildsen suggested Brando for the second part. "It wasn't happening with George Scott. The studio was getting cold feet and I said, 'Wait a minute. What if I can get Marlon Brando to go up against Scott, to play the part of the oil guy?'"

What they probably didn't realize was that the elusive Brando was itchy for the part. Well, any part, really, but this one had more attraction than most. It had both the money he needed and a theme he liked.

Money was the top priority. As Schickel noted, "A pattern is evident here: Brando would be idle professionally until he needed some money, then take whatever job seemed to offer the best pay for the least amount of work and, afterwards, withdraw again."[2]

The surprise was that he needed more money so quickly. Brando had taken a big paycheck a few months earlier for his brief appearance in *Superman*: $3.7 million plus a percentage of the gross (and $1.7 million of that guaranteed).[3] But, the cash from that venture seems to have evaporated quickly. As Manso wrote, "It was astounding that within a half-year of shooting *Superman*, Brando was complaining that he needed another paycheck. As several people wondered aloud, where was all the money going?"[4]

Brando openly admitted that he was in financial trouble at the time. "I didn't have any money and I did it for the bucks," he said. "Ten days for three million bucks."[5] It probably helped that he liked the movie's anti-establishment theme. As Manso noted, "Steve Shagan, had criticized the major oil companies in *The Formula*, a theme not without appeal to Brando. After all, the actor had been saying some of the same things that Shagan had pronounced on talk shows — that America wouldn't have an energy problem were it not for the oil cartels — and the attacks on the writer from the oil companies had made the script even more attractive."[6]

Before signing, Brando asked to meet with Avildsen and Shagan. Shagan recalled that they went to Brando's residence on Mulholland Drive where "they were greeted by two Dobermans and two bodyguards."[7] Brando joined them and presented them with bouquets of "Tahitian flowers" that he had grown in California. After that, the three men talked for several hours. The discussion, by one account, lasted until midnight as they hashed out "politics, ecology, and the plight of the American Indian."[8]

> All along, Shagan said, he was conscious that Brando was testing them. Toward the end of the evening the actor began to pace and presented his spiel that any film he did had to have a message. He added that perhaps "portraying the energy cartel in the form of a mystery might be interesting." But most of his comments were so negative that Shagan became sure that Brando would turn down the role. But then there was Brando's impish grin as he suddenly interrupted his doubting remarks. "But you've sold me," he said simply.[9]

Avildsen had a similar recollection of the meeting, and he recalled one portion of the conversation in particular — Brando's interpretation of the character.

"Listen," Brando said. "I have an idea, a particular way that I want to play this guy."

"What's that?" Avildsen asked.

"I see this guy as kind of like a Howard Hughes type of guy, living out in the desert. He's got a beard, a straw hat, and he's very eccentric."

Avildsen disagreed. "Gee, I think this guy should look like he's the head of General Electric. He's the establishment."

Brando suddenly changed direction. "I was just testing you," he said.

Such "tests" were nothing new for Brando. He seemed to like pushing such ideas at directors. For his role in *Superman*, he told director Richard Donner that he thought he should look like a donut. When Donner objected, he had also said, "I was just testing you."

Regardless, Brando took the role, inspired no doubt by the $3 million salary and 11 percent of the gross for two weeks of work. It amounted to, as Manso noted, "a total of five million for what would eventually amount to three scenes in the final release."[10]

The announcement came in September 1977 that he had joined the project and would be working with George C. Scott. Shagan described the pairing as "Patton meets the godfather."[11]

The problem: Brando was in no shape to make a movie. Raising Tahitian flowers may have been good for his soul, but his waistline had also increased dramatically. As the filming schedule for *The Formula* approached, his weight had ballooned up to a reported 243 pounds.[12] Once before, prior to filming *Apocalypse Now*, Brando had checked himself into a hospital so that he could lose weight.

When Avildsen and Shagan approached Brando, he had been idle a little longer than he really cared to be. He had checked himself into St. John's Hospital before working on *Apocalypse Now*, because he was too big for his role. He decided to do that again, checking into St. John's Hospital because, according to Manso, "he knew he'd be self-conscious about his bulk when he stepped before the cameras with George C. Scott in *The Formula*, which after long delays was finally shooting the following month."[13]

From the beginning, there was the potential for trouble. Brando's contract called for only ten days of work, so Avildsen had to shoot his scenes quickly and carefully. But, "Brando, as always, dragged each day's shooting longer and longer by halting scenes to discuss the dialogue."[14]

Further, he provided his own costume. It wasn't anything like the one that he playfully suggested to Avildsen at their original meeting, but it wasn't the clothing of a conservative CEO either. As Manso noted, "He had invented his costume to appear as an aging, fat oil baron, complete with ill-fitting polyester suits, granny glasses, and a few strings of gray hair arranged over a bald pate."[15] The effect, apparently, was to make him look like Occidental Oil's Armand Hammer. Richard Schickel wasn't impressed with the entire image, writing, "His interpretation of this figure is as a foxy old goat, and that robs him — and the film — of menace."[16] Brando also added a hearing aid to the get-up. It was more than a prop. It was an electronic device he had to have because he didn't bother to learn his lines. The "hearing aid" was attached to a tape recorder that played the lines he needed for each scene.

This wasn't the first time he'd taken such a lackadaisical approach to a job. For previous roles, he used off-camera cue cards that he would read when the script called for him to speak. He justified his unstructured approach as a way of bringing authenticity and spontaneity to a role:

> [I] discovered that not memorizing increased the illusion of reality and spontaneity.... When an actor knows what he's going to say, it's easy for the audience to sense that he's giving a writer's speech. But if he hasn't memorized the words, he not only doesn't know what he's going to say, he's not rehearsed *how* he's going to say it or how to move his body or nod his head when he does. Whereas when he *sees* the lines, his mind takes over and responds as if it were expressing a thought for the first time, so that the gestures are spontaneous.[17]

In reality, it created problems for the director. Brando used cue cards, posted at various locations around the set, during the filming of *Apocalypse Now*. As a result, his performance was filled with awkward pauses while his eyes gazed at unseen items off-camera. Those problems had to be corrected in the editing room, with the excess pauses edited out and fake shadows covering his face to disguise the inappropriate eye movements.

For *The Formula*, he tried a new technique — the tape recorder. He read his lines for the next day's shooting into a small recorder every night; the next day, with the recorder taped to his back and a small earphone in place, he used a remote control to play the lines as he needed to say them, listening to his own voice and repeating the lines simultaneously.[18] Brando described the process he used in *The Formula* in his autobiography:

> When I was acting, I turned the tape recorder on and off with a remote hand switch, listened to my voice and repeated the lines simultaneously in the same way that speeches are translated into different languages at the U.N. It took a little practice, but it wasn't hard, and because the earphones were small and hidden, audiences didn't know the difference. Subsequently I came up with a still better system: Instead of a tape recorder, I hid a microphone under my clothes over my chest, put a two-way radio in the small of my back, and tapped sending and receiving antennas on my legs. From about a hundred yards offstage, [assistant] Caroline Barrett, now reads my lines to me into a microphone.... When I repeat the lines simultaneously, the effect is one of spontaneity.[19]

The recorder may have made things easier for Brando, but not for Avildsen. During one day's work, shooting was proceeding on a four-page walking scene with Brando and Scott when Brando suddenly stopped and said, "That's it for today. I'm out of tape." When Avildsen asked for an explanation, Brando explained that he had used up all of the lines that he'd recorded the night before. The crew still had a couple of hours of daylight left, with plenty more shooting to do. But Brando succeeded in shutting them down for the day.

Further, the pairing of Brando and Scott, which looked so good in theory, had its problems. The artistic chemistry expected from pairing the two superstars turned out to be a dud. They never really meshed with each other. As Manso noted, Scott was "an actor whose representation for authenticity and power was close to that of Brando, but who had a real commitment to acting; still, both were notorious mavericks, having rejected Oscars in scene-stealing ways."[20]

Manso recalled one instance in which Scott became irritated with Brando's casual effort. The two had gone through several takes of the scene, with Brando "inventing and reinventing his lines." As the two men took their marks for another take, Scott looked at him and asked, "What are you going

Acting legends George C. Scott and Marlon Brando in a scene from *The Formula* (1980).

to say this time, Marlon?" "What difference does it make?" Brando replied. "You know a cue when you hear one?"[21]

Despite the problems, Avildsen was able to get all three of Brando's scenes shot in the ten days called for in the contract. Then the surprise: Brando asked to stay an extra day or two. He would "donate" the extra days, he said, if the writers would develop an additional scene that would allow him to make a statement about the environment. He also had an idea for the scene: His character would rescue "a frog that was dying from the chlorine in his swimming pool."[22]

"I hope the frog has Blue Cross," he tells the pool man.

Shagan agreed to write the new scene, and Brando stayed over for its shooting. However, as Manso noted, "Since Brando was portraying an oil baron supposedly indifferent to such ecological concerns, the quickly cobbled-up episode made no sense whatsoever."[23] But the line got the biggest laugh in the movie.

That wasn't the end of the trouble. Avildsen and Shagan got into an argument in the post-production editing process, something that Avildsen likes to have full control over. Shagan had written it and produced it. He had his own idea of what it should be like. As one critic noted:

> *The Formula* apparently is a mess because of a post-production fight between Shagan, as writer-producer, and John Avildsen, as director; they exchanged acrimonious letters in the *Los Angeles Times*, and Avildsen failed in an attempt to have his name removed from the picture. The way they tell it, Avildsen wanted the movie to make more sense as a thriller, while Shagan was more concerned with his "message."

Avildsen also wanted the movie to be a half-hour shorter. The feuding delayed the release of the film. It finally made its debut (almost a year after filming was completed) on December 15, 1980. The three Brando scenes were not particularly impressive, causing some observers "to point out that none of his three scenes were worth $1 million apiece."[24]

Brando's pre-filming efforts at dieting had not worked, a problem that *Variety* duly pointed out: "Appearing grotesquely fat and ridiculous, Brando apparently thinks he's making some visual comment on the nature of his character. But it's so overdone, those seeing it are more likely to be so taken by how big Brando has gotten, they'll never think about the corporate fat cats at all."[25]

The result was a movie that even Brando described as a "stinker." It was also a bit confusing, with its message overriding any significant drama. The basic symbols were easy to spot: Brando represented the evil oil companies, while Scott represented the honest but powerless good guys. After that, things get a bit confusing. Scott proceeds to investigate his friend's murder, but only causes more trouble. He talks to a succession of witnesses, each of whom is mysteriously killed soon afterwards. The bad guys, it seems, are all just a wee bit slow about identifying these weak points in their conspiracy.

Meanwhile, other plot elements get tossed in for "message" purpose but serve no useful purpose to the plot. Some, in fact, merely make the plot more confusing. Scott manages to find a European girl (Marthe Keller) who helps him out. Turns out that she's a member of the PLO who was trying to do good deeds because her father was a Nazi who murdered a Jew. Is that really believable? A pro–Jewish Nazi who's a member of the PLO? Maybe it made sense in the original script, but something was lost somewhere along the way.

The critics were brutal. One wrote, "Dull mystery depends solely upon the colossal pairing of Brando and Scott, but even they can't overcome the obvious script." Karney called it "a dull thriller that not even Marlon Brando could save."[26] "Scott and Brando are always worth watching," wrote another, "but writer-producer Steve Shagan telegraphs all his punches." Manso summed up the entire mess by saying, "The general consensus was that the movie was murky, silly, confusing, and boring."[27]

The actors got mixed reviews. Most credited Scott with a credible effort as someone "who fills the crevices of his role with an actor's details that make the cop a human being." Some liked Brando's major speech and his delivery of a one-liner or two ("You're missing the point. We are the Arabs") while others complained that he was "playing some particularly loony tunes."

The one bright spot in the film was the camerawork. Avildsen, a former cinematographer himself, didn't let the script interfere with the visual elements. James Crabe's work earned him an Oscar nomination for Best Cinematography. Crabe was Avildsen's cameraman on eight movies.

One critic summarized the problem: "One of the ironies of *The Formula* is that if it had only been made from an old Hollywood formula — any formula — we might have been able to understand it better.... There can be no joy in unraveling a plot that is a mystery even to itself."

Production Notes

Directed by: John G. Avildsen. Writers: Steve Shagan, Novel; Steve Shagan, Screenplay. Producers: Steve Shagan, producer; Ken Swor, associate producer. Original Music: Bill Conti. Cinematographer: James Crabe. Editor: John Carter. Casting Directors: Renate Arbes, Caro Jones. Production Designer: Herman A. Blumenthal. Set Decorator: Lee Poll. Costume Designer: Bill Thomas. Make Up Department: Del Acevedo, makeup artist; Jo McCarthy, hair stylist; Hasso von Hugo, makeup artist. Production Managers: Dieter Meyer, production manager; Karl W. Schaper, production manager; Ken Swor, unit production manager. Second Unit Directors or Assistant Directors: Candace Allen, second assistant director; Don French, first assistant director; Dan Malmuth, assistant director;

Eva-Maria Schnecker, second assistant director; Dwight Williams, first assistant director. Art Department: Russell Goble, property master; Hans J rgen Kiebach, art director: Europe. Sound Department: Charles Grenzbach, sound re-recording mixer; Jay M. Harding, sound re-recording mixer; Michael J. Kohut, sound re-recording mixer; Al Overton, sound; John Riordan, sound editor. Special Effects Department: Richard Richtsfeld, special effects department. Stunts: Charlie Picerni. Camera and Electrical Department: Mike Benson, camera operator; Garrett Brown, Steadicam operator; David E. Diano, assistant camera; Adam Glick, set lighting technician; Ted Harrison, key grip; Ross A. Maehl, gaffer; Elliott Marks, still photographer; Bob Whitaker, still photographer; George Whitear, still photographer. Casting Department: Shirley Rich, casting consultant. Costume and Wardrobe Department: Tony Scarano, wardrobe. Editorial Department: David Bretherton, supervising editor; Don Dittmar, color timer; Jane Kurson, associate editor; Bob Ramae, assistant editor: Los Angeles. Music Department: Harry V. Lojewski, music supervisor; Joe Tuley, music editor; Dan Wallin, score mixer. Transportation Department: Randy Peters, transportation co-captain. Miscellaneous Crew: Willy Egger, production executive: Germany; Norbert Finck, location manager; Sandy Lawrence, production secretary; Bill Millié, choreographer; Don Morgan, unit publicist; Ana Maria Quintana, script supervisor; Stefan Zürcher, location manager. Filming Locations: Berlin, Germany; CCC-Atelier, Spandau, Berlin, Germany; Los Angeles, California, USA; Switzerlan. Production Companies: CIP Filmproduktion GmbH; Metro-Goldwyn-Mayer (MGM). Distributors: Metro-Goldwyn-Mayer (MGM) (1980) (USA) (theatrical); MGM/UA Home Entertainment (1997) (USA) (video) (laserdisc); Warner Home Video (2006) (USA) (DVD).

Cast — in credits order: George C. Scott, Lt. Barney Caine LAPD; Marlon Brando, Adam Steiffel, Chairman Titan Oil; Marthe Keller, Lisa Spangler; John Gielgud, Dr. Abraham Esau, Director Reich Energy; G.D. Spradlin, Arthur Clements; Beatrice Straight, Kay Neeley; Richard Lynch, General Helmut Kladen/Frank Tedesco; John Van Dreelen, Hans Lehman, Prefect of Police Berlin; Robin Clarke, Major Tom Neeley; Ike Eisenmann, Tony; Marshall Thompson, Geologist #1; Dieter Schidor, Assassin; Werner Kreindl, Schellenberg; Jan Niklas, Gestapo Captain; Wolfgang Preiss, Franz Tauber, Swiss businessman; Calvin Jung, Sergeant Louis Yosuta LAPD Tactical Squad; Alan North, John Nolan, Chief of Tactical Squad LAPD; David Byrd, Paul Obermann, Chief Engineer Berlin Power & Light Co.; Ferdy Mayne, Professor Siebold; Gerry Murphy, Herbert Glenn, Clement's Chauffeur; Francisco Prado, Mendosa; Louis Basile, Sgt. Vince Rizzo — LAPD Metro Homicide; Ric Mancini, Printman; Weston Gavin, U.S. Army Captain; Craig T. Nelson, Geologist #2; Herb Voland, Geologist #3; Diane Tyler, Telex Operator; Jim Brewer, Security Guard; Lavelle Roby, Secretary; Albert Carrier, Butler; Ernie Fuentes, Pool Man; Stephanie Edwards, Nathan Roberts and Tom Hall, Reporters; Reinhard Vom Bauer, Dr. Esau (young); János Gönczöl, Dr. Karl Saur, Director Reich Armaments; Heinz Kammer, Dr. Hans Luschen, Director of Reich Research; Rene Kolldehoff, Reimeck; Martin Brandt, Concierge (German); Paul Glawion, Concierge (Swiss); Emil Steinberger, Postal Clerk; Emily Jensen, Sandie Lawrence, Ursula Warel, Jane Faithe and Wendy Baldock, Dancers; Ursula Hamann, Pan-Am Lady. Other credited cast listed alphabetically: Hammam Shafie, Assassin (uncredited).

CHAPTER 12

Neighbors

The Difficult Becomes the Impossible

A number of films have sought to gain extra notoriety through the gimmick casting of its two shared leads taking unlikely parts — in effect switching roles — to play against type and against audience expectations. *The King of Marvin Gardens* (1972) is a perfect example, with Bruce Dern playing what would typically be a "Jack Nicholson role" and vice versa.

Somewhat mistakenly, Avildsen's *Neighbors* has always been lumped into this category. While it's true that loud, large funnyman John Belushi did play against type in the film as a muted, button-down character, the other toplining star — Dan Aykroyd — gave an obnoxious, sleazy performance that was right in line with the *Saturday Night Live* parts he was known for at the time: Irwin "Bag O'Glass" Mainway, E. Buzz Miller. It was hardly a switch for him. But regardless of the casting, *Neighbors* fought a couple of uphill battles that would ensure tremendous flaws in the resulting film.

The process began when producers Richard D. Zanuck and David Brown teamed with literary agent Irving "Swifty" Lazar to acquire the motion picture rights to Thomas Berger's 1980 novel version of *Neighbors*. The novel tells the story of a drab Johnny Punchclock named Earl Keese, whose world of routine is turned upside down when a bizarre couple — an in-your-face, habitually lying male and his seductress wife — moves in next door to Keese and his wife. With its title and logline, the novel sets up expectations in the reader that the story will be a satire of "Pleasant Valley Sunday"–style suburban life. Even Roger Ebert, when reviewing Avildsen's film adaptation of the novel, tried to read that into the material, by implying that the story lampoons middle-class America's "tendency to be rigidly polite in the face of absolutely unacceptable behavior."[1] But the story actually makes little effort to satirize identifiable incidents from typical neighborly relations, as its characters often act on absurd, non-relatable motivations. What's more, the story isn't even set in standard suburbia, but rather a two-housed, isolated cul-de-sac that civilization seems to have forgotten. Thus, Berger's work was difficult — difficult to categorize and (unless the reader has a unique sense of humor) potentially difficult to find funny.

In any case, the novel had fans in the industry besides just Zanuck, Brown and Lazar: John Avildsen also inquired about the motion picture rights, and when he got in touch with the three men who owned them, he became attached to the project as director. TV and big-screen comedy writer Larry Gelbert (*Your Show of Shows, A Funny Thing Happened on the Way to the Forum*) was assigned to write the adaptation. Upon meeting Avildsen for the first time, he made it clear that he did not collaborate. Gelbert turned in his draft by the end of 1980. Aykroyd and the director spent a week rewriting the script before shooting began.

According to Belushi's biography *Wired: The Short Life and Fast Times of John Belushi*,[2] there were several early misgivings about Avildsen's suitability for a full-blown comedic film. When Zanuck's wife Lilli attended the producers' first meeting with the director, she noticed a preponderance of "No Smoking" signs around Avildsen's office and wondered whether someone with such a "rigid" personality could effectively direct a comedy. When Gelbart asked Avildsen for an example of a funny film, Avildsen responded with *The Blues Brothers*, which the screenwriter found to be less than droll and which led him to believe he would not be on the same comedic wavelength as the director. Gelbert apparently asked for Avildsen to be replaced.[3]

But Avildsen had a strong affinity for the material; in an interview for the book *The Directors: Take Two*, he spoke of being "very taken by" Berger's "terrific novel." He had the original intent of casting a certain comic as the central character. He explained this initial vision in *The Directors: Take Two*: "My first choice for the role of Earl was Rodney Dangerfield because the character got no respect. Nobody was interested in working with Rodney. He hadn't made any movies. I had worked with him for a week and he did a great screen test."[4]

Avildsen's recollection in an interview for *Film Directors on Directing* has him working with Dangerfield for "a few weeks" and noting that the actor was the correct age for the part, and able to play the role straight and remove it from his stand-up persona.[5] Other parties had different ideas about casting. Sherry Lansing was then the president of 20th Century–Fox and her initial casting ideas were reportedly Dustin Hoffman, Richard Pryor, Gene Wilder, Bill Murray, Belushi and Aykroyd.[6]

After the project went into turnaround and ended up at Columbia Pictures, power agent Michael Ovitz, who represented Belushi, suggested the

rotund funnyman for the part of the obnoxious next-door homeowner, knowing that an Aykroyd casting often followed a Belushi casting. When Belushi
showed up for his first meeting with Avildsen, Belushi took a look at Avildsen's
"No Smoking" sign and immediately lit up as a joke. Belushi expected to be
offered the part of the boorish next-door neighbor (named Harry in the novel,
Vic in the screenplay), but the director suggested he play the unexpected role
of dumpy workaday everyman Earl Keese. It took a little convincing, but
Belushi warmed to the idea of playing against type, and he in turn convinced
Aykroyd to take the other part. Apparently, though, the actors continued to
switch parts and try out each role during early script read-throughs.

Fresh off her starmaking role in *Raging Bull* (opposite Belushi friend Robert
De Niro), Cathy Moriarty was cast as the seductive new neighbor. And Kathryn
Walker — whom Belushi knew through recently deceased *National Lampoon*
founder Doug Kenney — beat out Penny Marshall for the part of Earl's wife.

So Avildsen had his leads. Although the central character was going to
be played by someone other than his first choice Dangerfield, the casting
pleased him. According to *Wired*, he had been a fan of Belushi since *Lemmings*,
a stage parody of Woodstock, and he had been assured that the hard-living
actor could go drug-free during the production — and that, in fact, he had
gone drug-free on his previous film, *Continental Divide*.[7]

Dan Aykroyd, John Belushi and Cathy Moriarty in *Neighbors* (1981).

Despite such assurances, it turned out to be a production fraught with difficulties. As related in *Wired*, Belushi smoked marijuana during the first table read and was suspected of using harder drugs during several absences from that day's work. He threatened (idly, as it turned out) to quit the film if his favorite sound man William Kaplan wasn't hired. He bullied Avildsen into casting his 30-year-old friend as the film's 65-year-old tow-truck manager. He held up the first day of shooting by making a fuss — out of vanity — over the hair gray he needed in order to look the appropriate age. And one night he arrived on set in such an altered state that he couldn't get his mouth to articulate the lines of dialogue.[8]

During post-production he required speed to stay awake during looping, and he wasted many a person's time and energy by recording music for the film by his favorite punk band, Fear, which would go unused.

So Avildsen was directing a difficult star through difficult material, with principal photography going from April 20 to June 29, 1981, on Staten Island. The film version of the story has mild-mannered Earl (Belushi) coming home with wife Enid (Walker) one evening and discovering that new neighbors Vic (Aykroyd) and Ramona (Moriarty) have occupied the only other house on the cul-de-sac, the long-abandoned "Warren place," which sits next to a dangerously sparky power transmission tower. Dinner plans are made that night between the couples, and by the time the meal concludes — within mere hours of everyone having met — Ramona has:

• Shown Earl her naked body
• Tried to blackmail him for $1,500
• Accused him of rape
• Discussed his testicles at the dinner table; and
• Offered to spank his "little buns."

During this same time, Vic has:

• Scammed Earl out of $32
• Snooped into his personal finances
• Made innuendos about Enid
• Lied about the origins of their dinner; and
• Threatened to "pound" information out of Earl.

All the while, much to Earl's bewilderment and frustration, Enid has been siding with the new neighbors over her husband in these matters. Meanwhile, Earl's one act of retaliation is to push Vic's car into the nearby swamp. (It's one of the surreal touches of the film that these two houses are inexplicably surrounded by marshland.)

Earl's next twelve hours (and the viewer's next hour) is the same sort of waking nightmare. Earl's daughter comes home from college and gets worked into the mix (she, like her mother, is instantly enthralled by Vic and Ramona). Eventually, Earl comes to the conclusion that Vic and Ramona's lifestyle — full of bizarre logic, impulsiveness, deception and irresponsibility — is really a freer lifestyle, and he sheds the shackles of conventional living (wife, house and, presumably, his job) to join Vic and Ramona as they pile in the car and leave the cul-de-sac for good, heading somewhere else.

The big-screen *Neighbors* leaves the viewer with several possible interpretations as to the film's intent — and Avildsen's vision. Was it meant as a broadly comedic take on the *Cool Hand Luke–One Flew Over the Cuckoo's Nest* model, wherein a stranger comes into the humdrum lives of others and provides lasting inspiration before leaving? Or was the audience supposed to enjoy it, sympathetically, as a "last sane man" comedy (*à la* Bob Newhart's various sitcoms), wherein a rational protagonist must contend with the moronic incompetence and craziness that surrounds him? Or was it meant merely as an exercise in nightmarish absurdism and surrealism — the type that could be played for some darkly comedic laughs?

Avildsen's shadowy exterior visuals — as well as the fittingly nonsensical handling of the plot developments — would seem to indicate the latter, the nightmare. But the film's nightmarish quality is undermined by the comedically slanted Bill Conti orchestral score that made the final cut. Conti's score was not the initial music commissioned, and it does not reflect what seems to have been the original ideas about music's function in *Neighbors*— that music should help create the dark, surreal atmosphere, not hammer home gags and punchlines. When Avildsen first premiered his rough cut of the film to Columbia executives in August of 1981, the cut used a temp soundtrack of borrowed music from atmospheric old horror films like *King Kong* and *Creature from the Black Lagoon*. The screening was reportedly a knock-out success.[9]

Then Belushi friend and Blues Brothers Band saxophonist Tom Scott was hired to score the film. Scott delivered a score that seems to have been right in line with Avildsen's spooky vision — and right in line with what the material required. When finally released on CD in 2007 as a "rejected score," Scott's *Neighbors* music was called a "skilled and stylish score, melodic and dark, in a wonderfully gothic sense" in the Varese Sarabande liner notes. But when the movie tested poorly (according to *Wired*, the worst screening results that any Columbia executive had ever seen), studio head Frank Price ordered changes, including a new score. Avildsen remembers Lazar exiting a screening and saying, "It sounds like a score for a documentary about Auschwitz."

Several thousand dollars were allotted for a new score, and Conti — who had composed Oscar-nominated music for Avildsen's *Rocky*— was hired. The function of the new music, according to Belushi biographer Bob Woodward, was so "the film could be made to appear more in the mainstream of Belushi-Aykroyd comedy."[10] Obviously taking that as his directive, Conti crafted a broadly comedic score where "weird" moments were non-subtly accompanied by a theremin, Ramona's sultry entrances were accompanied by smoky "femme fatale" musical clichés, and every scene involving Enid's fascination with Native American culture (obviously meant as a subtle running joke) were now overplayed with beating Indian drums. The viewer was thumped over the head with music that only stopped short of penny whistles and "wah wah wah" trumpets. In a piece for *Film Score Monthly*, writer Scott Bettencourt called Conti's *Neighbors* score "the worst he ever wrote."[11] Any atmosphere created by Avildsen was now counteracted.

The music did not represent the only tinkering done with the film. Belushi-Aykroyd manager Bernie Brillstein relates, in his memoir *Where Did I Go Right? You're No One in Hollywood Unless Someone Wants You Dead*, that the two stars were terribly displeased with Avildsen's rough cuts and let him know about it.[12] According to *Wired*, the displeasure was expressed in a letter from Aykroyd and Belushi with such commands as "absolutely must be deleted" and "will remain," regarding specific moments in the film.[13] And for one test screening, Price added a prologue to the film that contained favorable blurbs of Berger's novel.

Perhaps the biggest change *Neighbors* saw during its post-production was a re-shoot of its ending in November 1981 on a California-built set recreation of Earl's living room. The re-shoot — done just over a month before the film's theatrical release — gave the film its more upbeat ending, one that departed from Berger's conclusion.

What results from this tampering is a muddled mess. The only element of *Neighbors* that really works is Aykroyd's performance as the bleach-blonde Vic, a sleazoid right down to his "used car salesman" wardrobe. The portrayal is obnoxious in a way that anticipates Jim Carrey's Ace Ventura persona by ten-plus years. Avildsen told interviewer John Andrew Gallagher that Aykroyd was "a real gentleman, a great pleasure to work with."[14] In the Belushi biography *Wired*, it is repeatedly implied that Aykroyd's stands against the director were more in support of his friend and co-star than they were problems he had with Avildsen.

Neighbors was released on December 18, 1981, to 1400 theaters in a "hit and run" strategy of booking the film onto an excessive number of screens (1000 theaters would have been the norm) in order for this star-studded picture to take in as much revenue as possible in a big opening, before word-of-mouth damaged its potential for a long theatrical run. Perhaps because of this measure, the film was a success.

In reflection, how does *Neighbors* fit into Avildsen's filmography? Like

Actor Dan Aykroyd and Avildsen share some laughs between takes on the set of _Neighbors_ (1981).

Save the Tiger, it had a setting of just over a day, leading his fans to believe that the director enjoyed directing stories taking place in a short time span. It also proved that Avildsen's projects could reference each other, as a bathroom primping scene in _Neighbors_ uses "Stayin' Alive," the signature song from a film Avildsen nearly directed, _Saturday Night Fever_.

Otherwise, though, _Neighbors_ sticks out like a sore thumb in Avildsen's oeuvre and can basically be described as ill-advised. After the film, Moriarty didn't act in another motion picture for half a decade. And the film prompted Belushi-Aykroyd manager Bernie Brillstein to suggest the two stars act in movies separately.[15] Belushi died in March of 1982 of a drug overdose, leaving _Neighbors_— however fitting or unfitting — his big-screen swan song.

Avildsen would rebound and prove himself yet again several years later with his first monster smash of the decade, 1984's _The Karate Kid_. And he has found the best possible spin when reflecting on _Neighbors_, speaking in interviews of its "endless life" on videotape (although as of this writing, the movie has yet to appear on DVD in its home country) and by noting that people continue to comment on the film.[16]

Production Notes

Directed by: John G. Avildsen. Writers: Novel, Thomas Berger; Screenplay, Larry Gelbart. Producers: Bernie Brillstein, executive producer; David Brown, producer; Irving Paul Lazar, executive producer; Richard D. Zanuck, producer. Original Music: Bill Conti. Cinematographer: Gerald Hirschfeld. Editor: Jane Kurson. Casting Director Kathy Talbert. Production Designer: Peter Larkin. Set Decorator: Thomas Tonery. Costume Designer: John Boxer. Make Up Department: Joseph Coscia, hair stylist; Michael Thomas, makeup artist. Production Manager: George Manasse. Second Unit Directors or Assistant Directors: Yudi Bennett, first assistant director; Francis Falvey, dga trainee; Paula Mazur, second assistant director; Mark McGann, second assistant director. Art Department: Richard Allen, construction supervisor; Kenneth Kammerer, set dresser; William B. Kane, property master; Ernest Southern, chargeman scenic artist. Sound Department: Dick Alexander, sound effects mixer; Les Fresholtz, dialogue mixer; Jerry Jacobson, sound editor; Les Lazarowitz, sound mixer; Todd A. Maitland, boom operator; Dan Sable, sound editor. Special Effects Department: Edward Drohan, special effects; Gary Zeller, special effects. Camera and Electrical Department: Donald Biller, second assistant camera; Kenneth Finlay, best boy;; Gil Geller, additional photographer Marc D. Hirschfeld, first assistant camera; Ronald Lautore, camera operator; James McGrath, key grip; Michael McGrath, dolly grip; Lorey Sebastian, still photographer; Louis Tobin, gaffer; John Thomas Kennedy, key rigging grip (uncredited); Michael Douglas Middleton, still photographer — props (uncredited). Costume and Wardrobe Department: Mark Klein, wardrobe — men; Rose Trimarco, wardrobe — women; Carol Anne Wegner, stand-by wardrobe. Editorial Department: John G. Avildsen, supervising editor; Paul Cavagnero, assistant editor; Chip Cronkite, assistant editor. Music Department: Stephen A. Hope, music editor; Peter Myers, orchestrator; Arthur Piantadosi, music mixer; Bruce Robb, music engineer: theme song; Bruce Robb, music mixer: theme song; Bruce Robb, music producer: theme song. Miscellaneous Crew: Ricky Jay Derby, production assistant; Joyce Wilson Fetherolf, assistant: John G. Avildsen; Jonathan Filley, location manager; Laurel Hargarten, production assistant; Michael Hourihan, teamster captain; Mary Kane, location services; Lynn Lewis Lovett, script supervisor; Vincent Martinez, location auditor; Nancy Wood Tuber, production office coordinator. Filming Location: Staten Island, New York City, New York, USA. Production Company: Columbia Pictures Corporation. Distributors: Columbia Pictures; RCA/Columbia Pictures Home Video (video).

Cast — in credits order: John Belushi, Earl Keese; Kathryn Walker, Enid Keese; Cathy Moriarty, Ramona; Dan Aykroyd, Vic; Igors Gavon, Chic; Dru-Ann Chuckran, Chic's Wife; Tim Kazurinsky, Pa Greavy; Tino Insana, Perry Greavy; P.L. Brown, Police Officer #1; Henry Judd Baker, Police Officer #2; Lauren-Marie Taylor, Elaine Keese; Sherman Lloyd, Fireman #1 (DOC); Bert Kittel, Fireman #2; J.B. Friend, Bernie Friedman, Edward Kotkin and Michael Manoogian, Additional Firemen; Dale Two Eagles, Mr. Thundersky.

CHAPTER 13

A Night in Heaven

If any subject matter can be considered dominant in Avildsen's mainstream studio career, it's the "David and Goliath" sports conflict. Likewise, if any topic emerges as a recurring pattern in the director's independent career, it's sex. Therefore, it's interesting to watch *A Night in Heaven*, a film he made for a small independent company (but distributed by Twentieth Century–Fox) about a certain aspect of the sex industry.

Although Avildsen's almost mutually exclusive directing careers were colliding in *Heaven*, the film is not a "lowbrow-sex-romp-meets-high-production-values" affair. The movie treats its story, set against the world of male strippers, with seriousness and thoughtfulness. That doesn't mean it necessarily worked for audiences or critics — or even as a film.

In fact, *A Night in Heaven* isn't even viewed positively by Avildsen: "*A Night in Heaven* was really terrible," Avildsen once said. "I knew it.... I have absolutely no defense for it. I'd almost be willing to give people their money back."[1]

> Gene Kirkwood, the man who brought me *Rocky*, brought *A Night in Heaven* to me. He took me to Orlando where these Chippendale-type clubs were just starting out, and women were going to see guys strip down to their jockey shorts. That was the premise of the movie, and the studio wanted us to use Chris Atkins, who had just made *Blue Lagoon*.[2]

"Male exotic dance" market leader Chippendales was founded in 1979, so by *Heaven*'s 1983 release, the phenomenon was still relatively new in the mainstream consciousness. Similarly trendy was heartthrob actor Atkins, who had burst onto the national scene with his performance in 1980's *The Blue Lagoon*. Atkins was signed by the producers before Avildsen joined the project.

More tried-and-true, on paper, was the female side of the equation: lead actress Lesley-Ann Warren and screenwriter Joan Tewkesbury. Warren began her on-screen career in the mid–1960s playing Cinderella on TV. By the time she starred in Avildsen's film, she had delivered performances that garnered one Oscar nomination (*Victor/Victoria*), two Golden Globe nominations, and one Golden Globe win. In landing the role of *Heaven*'s Faye Hanlon, Warren apparently beat out another Oscar-nominated actress, Carrie Snodgress, who ended up playing a waitress in the film. (The hard-luck Snodgress had previously come close to playing the Talia Shire role in *Rocky*.[3])

Neither Warren nor Snodgress were Avildsen's choice for the role. His preference was the then-unknown Judith Ivey. Ivey was new to the industry when Avildsen was preparing to start production in 1982. When the producers said no and she missed out on this role, she went to Broadway and won a Tony as Best Featured Actress in *Steaming*. She later won a second Tony for *Hurlyburly* in 1985 and became well-known to movie audiences for playing opposite Steve Martin in *The Lonely Guy* (1984). Despite her talent, Avildsen's choice was overruled because she wasn't known. "She would have been better than Warren," Avildsen said. "She was 31 years old, and she had no problem with nudity." Ivey's *Steaming* included nudity, while Warren objected to nudity in her love scenes with Atkins.

Joan Tewkesbury was already an award-winning screenwriter (Robert Altman's *Nashville*), and she also helmed directing projects for both screen and stage. Her research for *Heaven*, as with *Nashville*, reportedly involved spending a month in the film's locations.[4] Avildsen later said the script wasn't finished when he came aboard, but he had assurances that certain scenes would be added.[5] Specifically, Avildsen thought the movie was going to be a story of forgiveness for both a man and his wife; each engages in infidelity, both learn of the other's infidelity, and they forgive each other and start over. "I thought that would be a refreshing change," Avildsen said.

However, the screenplay never shaped up to Avildsen's satisfaction, and muddled scripting would be what Avildsen would later blame for what he considered the film's storytelling failure.[6] Avildsen said that Tewkesberry was never able to write the final scene; the wife never does learn about her husband's infidelity. "It was more of the same," Avildsen said. "I regretted that it didn't turn out the other way."

Did the director sense these problems from the very beginning? If so, why did he take on the project? When doing press conferences for 1989's *Lean on Me*, Avildesen explained his reasoning for accepting *A Night in Heaven*:

> Everyone thinks people in my business sit around with an invisible money supply, and, therefore, you can just choose when [a good prospect] comes by. I've got a mortgage and all the other stuff. When *Heaven* came around, I'd had three flops in a row.[7]

The story, as filmed, has community college speech professor Faye Hanlon (Warren) giving a failing grade to good-looking, lackadaisical student

Rick Monroe (Atkins), who seems to think he can get by on a "wink and a smile." After work, Faye has been having an unusually active nightlife to accommodate her visiting sister, Patsy (Deborah Rush), who is enjoying cutting loose and generally having time away from her emotionally cold husband. While at a strip club, Faye discovers that her slacker student has been dancing as "Ricky Rocket" on a strip circuit in the towns surrounding Orlando, Florida.

The astronaut shtick of Ricky Rocket's strip routine is an appropriate theme considering the story's location of Titusville, Florida — near the Kennedy Space Center. One critic remarked that a backdrop of rockets gave the story a lot of "space-phallic symbolic rivalry that is supposed to be terribly profound."[8]

Meanwhile, Faye's husband Whitney (Robert Logan) has been spending more time around the house since he lost his job as an aerospace engineer at NASA. He was given the ultimatum of working on missile silos or losing his job. After choosing the latter (he didn't want to design things that would be used "to blow things up"), he only half-heartedly pursued other design opportunities — for such things as a recumbent ("reclining") bicycle and video games.

Despite her husband having extra time potentially to check her whereabouts, Faye begins an affair with the substantially younger Ricky. After Faye's sister leaves town with an extra night left on the hotel room, the pair make use of it for a rendezvous, and that's where Whitney catches Ricky, shortly after the act. After intimidating Ricky with bluffed violence that leaves the dancer naked in a lake, Whitney (who's been having an affair himself) returns home. When Faye arrives, they begin to heal their marriage — with Faye never knowing about Whitney's infidelity.

A Night in Heaven leaves a number of elements underdeveloped, some of which will be apparent from any plot synopsis, others of which are reduced to such minor moments as to not even warrant mention in most story recaps. The glaringly under-explored aspect of the main plot is the relationship between Faye and Whitney. What is so unfulfilling about the marriage that drives Faye to look outside it? The viewer never gets a satisfying answer. The *New York Times* review speculates that Faye proceeds with the affair "out of boredom as much as anything else"[9] and the film critic for the *Boca Raton News* notes that whatever disintegration is occurring in their marriage is happening "almost imperceptibly."[10]

It's to the film's credit that *Heaven* avoids the cliché of the slovenly, abusive husband. Whitney is instead a kind, handsome, intelligent man as portrayed by the likable Logan. This unexpected portrayal of the husband — however refreshing it may be — doesn't aid in explaining the motivations of

On the set of *A Night in Heaven* (1983) Christopher Atkins, Avildsen, Lesley Ann Warren, and producer Gene Kirkwood discuss the scene.

Faye, who is ostensibly the central character (although strangely, we spend the first several scenes of the film with Whitney, before we ever meet Faye). Whitney is far from neglectful of his wife; he even tries to persuade her, during their first shared scene, to skip school and spend the day with him.

Also underdeveloped is Whitney's state of mind while out of work. He seems vaguely glum about the situation, and he seems reluctant to market his revolutionary bicycle design. But those are the only insights the audience is given. A job interview scene, where Whitney tries to find work with a video-game designer, is wasted as a cheap throwaway joke when an prepubescent computer whiz gets preferential treatment (and even has a manager). The character of Whitney was enough of a blank slate to allow for critics to project a whole range of descriptions on him, from "career-obsessed"[11] to "slightly bonkers."[12]

Myriad characters don't even qualify for their own subplots. Faye's sister, after setting the plot in motion with her need to party, has only a single obligatory scene where she explains about her inattentive husband. Ricky's sister appears in one scene and has dialogue, only to vanish for the remainder of the film. The character "Slick" (Sandra Beall) is so nebulous — is she is Ricky's manager or girlfriend?— that it's not clear until a shower scene in the film's final act.

There's also a NASA janitor (Deney Terrio) who, late in the film, becomes another male stripper. This skimpy subplot was likely added to include more scenes of male stripping, of which there are scarcely any in the third act, after Faye's affair is in full swing. After all, promotion for the film promised something that looked like an exposé or possibly a day-in-the-life-of look at the industry of male exotic dancers. As one reviewer wrote,

> "[T]his movie has surprisingly few scenes set in the club where [Ricky] dances. Ladies coming to this film for extended scenes of nude males gyrating on the dance floor will be disappointed."[13]

The production did however get a hot dance name in Terrio. In addition to playing the janitor, he also served as its dance choreographer. It was a task he had already handled for *Saturday Night Fever,* which is where Avildsen and Terrio first met. Terrio's role on *Saturday Night Fever* was that of dance instructor for John Travolta. The choreographer, a celebrity in the dance world, hosted TV's *Dance Fever.*

More substantial is the role of Ricky's mom (Snodgress), who happens to be a waitress at the lobby diner of the hotel at which the affair occurs. This character has been interpreted as representing the working class, as Ricky makes an issue of the fact that he's stripping in order to get through school, which in turn will provide him with enough income to allow the hard-working, middle-aged single-mom waitress to retire. Because of the sympathetic mother character, it's implied that Ricky's motivations for the affair are to earn a passing grade from Faye. One reviewer recognized these ultimate goals as "Ricky's class ambitions."[14]

The mother aside, however, the secondary characters are given the short shrift, as is the explanation for Faye's dalliance. For these reasons, the story perhaps would have worked better as a television mini-series. Relationships could have been better explained, even explored. As it was, though, at a tight 83 minutes, *A Night in Heaven* made the papers as "the third successive John Avildsen film that's undergone extensive editing just prior to release."[15] Many critics gave the screenwriter the benefit of the doubt: "Joan Tewkesbury is credited with having written the original screenplay, but whether what is on the screen is what she wrote is anybody's guess," wrote Canby. "I'd prefer to think that her work has been mutilated to attain its present look."[16] Similarly, Henderson wrote, "Tewkesbury's script gets trampled by the incessant accent on smoldering passion and teary pangs of guilt."[17] Meanwhile, director and editor Avildsen seemed to take much of the blame for the film. "Avildsen pulls the strings with hammy abandon" was typical of the criticism.[18]

Ironically, the film's chief failing, according to Avildsen, was due to an unfulfilled promise by Tewkesbury, and it had to do with yet another underdeveloped aspect of Whitney's story. The film contains a scene of Whitney re-connecting with an old female friend, and it ends ambiguously without revealing whether this re-connection becomes physical. Avildsen apparently wanted it to be clear that it did.

> I saw that it could be a story about forgiveness where both the husband and wife discovered the other's infidelity.... The script wasn't finished but the writer assured me that she would write this scene where each would discuss the other's infidelity, and there would be forgiveness. As luck would have it, she never did write the scene.[19], The movie turned out to be about this guy who catches his wife screwing around on him, but she never catches him doing the same. So he forgives her and he keeps his secret. And that's how it ends. So you just sat there saying, well what was that all about? Well, it was about a movie that never had a movie written for it.

Also drubbed was Atkins, who was described in one paper as "the sublimely untalented Christopher Atkins, who ruins scene after scene through his inability to convey a single convincing emotion."[20] In his defense, Atkins was hired as young sex-symbol beefcake (for which there are usually low expectations of thespic skill)—and one who was already well associated with nudity through his role in 1980's *The Blue Lagoon* and through a nude pictorial in a 1982 issue of *Playgirl*. *Heaven* was the actor's third big-screen role, and one that Atkins called his first "real shot at acting." Perhaps for this "real shot," the actor was willing to break his reported promise to his mother that he would never appear nude in another film after *The Blue Lagoon*.[21]

The actor survived both the critics' remarks and his mother's possible disappointment to land a role on the popular '80s prime-time soap opera *Dallas*.

Despite the garbled storytelling and Atkins' performance, *A Night in Heaven* achieves several moments of technical and visual brilliance, including a memorable shot during Ricky's first striptease where his head is perfectly framed by a radiating neon halo. The movie also makes good pre-hit use of the songs "Heaven" (Bryan Adams) and "Obsession" (Holly Knight and Michael Des Barres, later by Animotion).

The film flopped commercially and didn't make much of a cultural splash. But curiously, the same year's *Mr. Mom* featured a scene with an astronaut striptease — very similar to *Heaven*'s Ricky Rocket routine — that almost plays like a spoof. This coincidence begs the question of whether the filmmakers of *Mr. Mom*—which was also distributed by Twentieth Century–Fox—had access to a script or rough cut of *A Night in Heaven*. So maybe the film had one fan, but it certainly wasn't Avildsen.

Production Notes

Directed by: John G. Avildsen. Writer: Joan Tewkesbury. Producers: Gene Kirkwood, producer; Howard W. Koch, Jr., producer; Barry Rosenbush, associate producer. Original Music: Jan Hammer, David Wakeling. Cinematographer: David L. Quaid. Editor: John G. Avildsen. Production Designer: Anna Hill Johnstone. Costume Designer: Anna Hill Johnstone. Production Manager: Kerry Orent, post-production supervisor. Second Unit Directors or Assistant Directors: Alan Hopkins, assistant director; Robert E. Warren, assistant director. Sound Department: Anthony J. Ciccolini III, supervising sound editor; Tom Fleischman, sound re-recording mixer; Joseph Gutowski, apprentice sound editor; Neil L. Kaufman, sound editor; Les Lazarowitz, sound mixer; Hal Levinsohn, sound editor. Camera and Electrical Department: Garrett Brown, Steadicam operator. Casting Department: Dee Miller, location casting. Editorial Department: Chip Cronkite, assistant editor; Jim Finn, negative cutter. Music Department: Michael Chapman, song producer. Miscellaneous Crew: Joyce Wilson Fetherolf, assistant: John G. Avildsen; Dan Perri, title designer: main titles; James W. Skotchdopole, production assistant; Cynthia Streit, production coordinator; Deney Terrio, choreographer. Filming Location: Titusville, Florida, USA. Distributors: Twentieth Century–Fox Film Corporation (1983) (USA) (theatrical); 20th Century–Fox Home Entertainment (1985) (USA) (VHS); Anchor Bay Entertainment (2005) (USA) (DVD).

Cast — in credits order: Christopher Atkins, Rick Monroe (Ricky The Rocket); Lesley Ann Warren, Faye Hanlon; Robert Logan, Whitney Hanlon; Deborah Rush, Patsy; Deney Terrio, Tony; Sandra Beall, Slick; Alix Elias, Shirley; Carrie Snodgress, Mrs. Johnson; Amy Lyndon, Eve; Fred Buch, Jack Hobbs; Karen Margaret Cole, Louise; Don Cox, Revere; Veronica Gamba, Tammy; Joseph Gian, Pete Bryant; Bill Hindman, Russel; Linda Lee Cadwell, Ivy; Rosemary McVeigh, Alison Hale. Other credited cast listed alphabetically; John Archie, Mr. Raymer; Judy Arman, Patsy's Girl; Anthony G. Avildsen, Scooter; Danny Belden, Odyssey Dancer; Tina Belden, Odyssey Dancer; Harold Bergman, Mr. Sladkis; Spatz Donovan, Heaven M.C.; Dan Fitzgerald, Guard; Andy Garcia, T.J. The Bartender; Robert Goodman, Mr. Disick; Eric D. Henderson, Odyssey Dancer; Will Knickerbocker, Larry; Gail Merrill, Grace; Sherry Moreland, Teacher; Brian Mozzillo, Odyssey Dancer; Tiffany Myles, Bridesmaid; Craig Nedrow, Man Mountain Dean; Charles F. Pastore, Odyssey Dancer; Cindy Perlman, Linda; Hope Pomerance, Patsy's Girl; Sally Ricca, Bridesmaid; Brian Smith, Osgood; Scott Stone, Mr. Lee; Mary Teahan, Patsy's Girl; Pam Tendal, Bridesmaid; Butch Warren, Mr. Orihan; Bobbie Wolf, Teacher.

CHAPTER 14

The Karate Kid

Martial arts movies had their its first burst of pop-culture mania in the United States in the early 1970s, initiated by Bruce Lee's mainstream success and furthered by subsequent hits on screens both big (for example, *Five Fingers of Death*) and small (*Kung Fu*).

In the 1980s, martial arts again became a cultural phenomenon, but this time, it was sparked by the first two entries in *The Karate Kid* franchise and was maintained without support from any other mainstream hits.[1] Sure, there were other martial arts–themed movies and television programs, but none qualified as a crossover hit like *The Karate Kid* standard. For instance, the ninja-centric show *The Master* (1984) was canceled after half a season, and *Sidekicks* (1986–1987) didn't last much longer. (Both series, by the way, kept the age-disparity dynamic popularized in *The Karate Kid*.)

The point here is that if a 1970s youth signed up for martial-arts instruction, he could have been inspired by Bruce, "Grasshopper," or any number of big-screen chopsockers. But if a 1980s youngster signed up for classes at his neighborhood dojo, he almost certainly was motivated after seeing *Karate Kid*'s Daniel LaRusso.

If *The Karate Kid* sparked martial-arts popularity anew in the 1980s, it also took advantage of an existing '80s cinematic movement: teen orientation. The teen movie was one of the most commercially viable genres at the time, starting with comedy hits like *Fast Times at Ridgemont High* (1982) and *Valley Girl* (1983). By the mid–80s, teen movies were still going strong, but they were being mixed with other genres, as *Back to the Future* did with science fiction.

Mixing the teen movie with martial-arts cinema was a potential gold mine considering chopsocky's past popularity and teen flick's then-current vogue. So it's easy to see how *The Karate Kid* would be a hot property even in its early stages, before John Avildsen became involved. Hollywood heavyweight Clint Eastwood reportedly considered directing the picture. Sondra Locke, former co-star of Eastwood and his partner for 13 years, reported that the tough-guy actor-director had agreed to direct the film if Columbia would cast his sixteen-year-old son Kyle in the lead role.[2] Another source reported that Eastwood strongly lobbied for Kyle to get the role, with his name mentioned as a possible director.[3] Kyle Eastwood did audition for the role but Columbia decided not to use him. Eastwood chose not to do the film, and Avildsen was approached about the job.

When the studio first pitched the movie to him, Avildsen scoffed at the idea of working on a movie called *The Karate Kid*. ("I could just hear people calling it *The KaRocky Kid*," he said.) He had cause for concern. The movie has several plot similarities to *Rocky*: an unknown Italian-American underdog enters a fight, gets injured during the bout, but emerges a hero. The plots were so similar that Greydanus described it as one of "the Rocky clones."[4]

But *The Karate Kid* had different characters and a different underlying theme. *Rocky* was dominated by the title character: the dominating presence in *The Karate Kid* was a supporting character. The Karate Kid (Ralph Macchio) played second banana to his mentor Kesuke Miyagi, played by Pat Morita.[5] The film seems to be well aware of the elder's key role, as the final image is not of the titular karate kid, but rather a freeze frame and fade out on a Miyagi close-up.

That final shot was a change made in post-production. The original script called for the story to continue in the parking lot outside of the arena following the championship fight. However, Avildsen shot the fight scene on New Year's Eve in 1983. Once he had the final shot of Daniel and his Championship Cub being carried off by the fans, he thought that was a more appropriate ending. He called the producer, who agreed to cut the final scene. Avildsen then did a rough edit of the film and showed it to 100-plus workers at the studio. When he asked for comments, one woman raised her hand and said she thought the film should end with Miyagi and Daniel together.

Avildsen agreed, recalling that the original script had Miyagi and Daniel walking away together. Avildsen called Weintraub and asked for permission to shoot another scene featuring only Morita and a handful of extras. He offered to pay for the reshoot himself. If his idea played better before test audiences, Weintraub would repay him that expense. Weintraub agreed, and Avildsen got his shot of Miyagi's face filled with love and pride watching Daniel being carried off. That approach won over the test audiences, and thus the new end for the film reached audiences around the world.

The plot is essentially a combination of *Rocky* and teenage alienation. Jersey-born Daniel LaRusso moves to Reseda, California, with his mother when she gets a job offer. However, when she arrives, the management job she expected is not available. The single mom has to take a gig as a hostess at a restaurant to pay the family bills.

Daniel quickly feels out of place. Although he makes fast friends with the kids in his apartment complex, he doesn't fit in the local teen cliques at school, and he alienates the local surfer crowd even further when he asks one of their girls (Elisabeth Shue) for a date.

That sets up some bullying from the local in-group, a number of fair-haired boys who belong to the local karate school. Six of the bullies corner Daniel to teach him that Italian-American boys should stay away from California girls — especially ex-girlfriends of these karate students known as the Cobras.

The cavalry arrives in the person of Japanese gardener Mr. Miyagi, a character named after an early karate "sensei" from Okinawa. The original Miyagi is credited with creating "Goju Ryu," his own style of karate. The term "Goju Ryu" means "hard and soft style" in English, and reflects the approach that Miyagi teaches in the film.

Miyagi becomes Daniel's karate mentor, but turns out to be an unconventional one. Instead of directly teaching the youngster how to fight, Miyagi assigns him chores such as painting fences and waxing a yellow classic automobile ("wax-on, wax-off," Miyagi patiently instructs).

Meanwhile, Miyagi demonstrates his own proficiency by trying to catch flies with chop sticks, but never succeeds. Daniel tries the same stunt and grabs a fly (actually a dead fly on the end of a black thread) in his first try. "Beginner luck," Miyagi explains.

In one instance, Myagi chops the tops off of three beer bottles with his hand. But even the demonstrations seem to have limited instructional utility. After seeing Miyagi smoothly decapitate the three beer bottles, Daniel asks, "How did you do that? How did you do that?" "Don't know," Miyagi replies. "First time."

This cryptic teaching technique further frustrates Daniel. "When do I learn how to punch?" he finally asks Miyagi.

Miyagi's response doesn't make him feel any better. "Better learn balance," the instructor says. "Balance is key. Balance good, karate good. Everything good. Balance bad, better pack up, go home. Understand?"

Daniel didn't seem to understand at first, but the critics caught on. Hakari wrote, "Miyagi's self-defense–oriented martial-arts philosophy mirrors Yoda's teaching that a Jedi uses the Force for knowledge and defense, never for attack."[6] As *Variety* summarized it, "Daniel wants Miyagi to teach him how to defend himself, but the old man resists until Daniel learns that karate is a discipline of the heart and mind, of the spirit, not of vengeance and revenge."[7]

Perhaps not, but gradually, Daniel acquires the skills to become adept in the martial arts, setting up a scene where the underdog will challenge the bullies for the local All Valley Karate Championship. Kresse, the evil karate teacher, has one of his students deliberately attempt to break Daniel's knee. This leaves Daniel unable to continue. As a gong sounds, Miyagi claps his hands and rubs them together, part of a ritual therapy to mend Daniel's knee. Daniel must fight in the final round while standing on only one foot.

Part of the plot involved Miyagi teaching Daniel the crane kick. This one-legged karate stance became a cultural phenomenon, being imitated on the street, TV and the movies. "Crane Kick" produces hundreds of Google images of people around the world doing the crane kick. As his enemy approaches, ready to deliver a final blow to him, Daniel hops on his one good leg and kicks this adversary with his one good foot. The bully is floored and the good guy wins.

Sounds simple enough, except for the strange instruction and the unusual final karate blow. But it worked. Critics and audiences loved it. And the crane kick became an iconic symbol of the film.

The film grossed a surprising $91 million at the box office, nearly $200 million in today's dollars. Teenagers, inspired by the film, flocked to martial arts schools.[8] One critic recalled his own teenage years and wrote, "Did every one of us know how to do Ralph Macchio's victory kick at the end of *The Karate Kid*?"[9]

Critics were surprised and impressed. Greydanus described it as "formulaic, manipulative, hokey — and thoroughly rousing."[10] Their reaction was perhaps best expressed by Ebert:

> I didn't want to see this movie. I took one look at the title and figured it was either (a) a sequel to *Toenails of Vengeance*, or (b) an adventure pitting Ricky Schroder against the Megaloth Man. I was completely wrong. *The Karate Kid* was one of the nice surprises of 1984 — an exciting, sweet-tempered, heart-warming story with one of the most interesting friendships in a long time.... *The Karate Kid* is a sleeper with a title that gives you the wrong idea: It's one of 1984's best movies.[11]

Other critics saw deeper elements. Chee noted:

> This fine coming-of-age drama set the standard for the genre when it was made, and still holds up well.... The message of the film is clear, that the development of maturity and self-confidence is more important than the learning of fighting skills, but the message is not so heavy-handed that it put kids off. Instead, the film provides an inspirational story that motivates the audience to find the same qualities in themselves.[12]

A. J. Hakari had a similar reaction: "Surprisingly, *The Karate Kid* packs more of an earnest punch than a good chunk of today's inspirational dramas, a solid teen flick that teaches the virtues of patience and respect without clumsily wielding its commentary like a four-year-old with a sledgehammer."[13] He showered similar praise on both Macchio and Morita:

> *The Karate Kid* works mostly due to the worthy emotional investment put into the characters and competent acting. Ralph Macchio does a solid job of playing a good kid with a few rough edges, a teen with problems that, for once, comes across as sympathetic and likable rather than whiny and annoying. But his Daniel-san wouldn't be the same if it weren't for Pat Morita doing as terrific a job as he did in the near-iconic role of Mr. Miyagi.[14]

Clee noted, "The message of the film is clear, that the development of maturity and self-confidence is more important than the learning of fighting skills, but the message is not so heavy-handed that it put kids off."[15]

Some, though, were not kind. *Variety* called it "a *Rocky* for kids." Canby described it as "popcorn soaked in hot margarine — not great as a steady diet but harmless as a short-term binge."[16] Rayns said it "borrows its formula from both East and West with good humor, and is completely free of intelligence, discrimination and originality. No wonder it was a hit."[17]

But most critics saw it as a surprise hit that worked against clichés, and the passage of time has generally sided with the positive reviews. Daniel Griffin viewed the movie a second time 15 years after he first saw it as a teenager. "I ended up catching myself surprised how engaging the material is, and how timeless so much of this film has become," he wrote,[18] and also mused on "the character of Miyagi, who has since become one of the most lasting of American cinematic icons."[19] Ebert named it one of the best films of 1984.[20] According to Greydanus, it's "sincerity and emotional poignance have a way of steam-rolling over gaps in plausibility and logic."[21] Griffin added, "[W]hile the film plays out typically, it does not feel cliched or recycled, primarily because of the way that the film carefully establishes unlikely personalities to inhabit these familiar roles.... Most of the characters work against the expectations of what could otherwise have been predictable material."[22]

Much of the critical acclaim went to Morita, not Avildsen. Chee wrote that Morita "is outstanding as the humorous but intelligent old Japanese handyman." Ebert wrote, "It's refreshing to see a completely original character like this old man,"[23] and later added that Miyagi was "one of the genuinely interesting characters of recent movies."[24] *Variety* noted, "Morita is simply terrific, bringing the appropriate authority and wisdom to the part." Similarly, Hakari wrote it was a near-iconic role, adding, "Morita's performance here is pitch-perfect, playing Miyagi rather subtlely as a man who has buried a troubled past in years of self-discipline and has at last found a release in passing on these ways to a young dude from Jersey."[25]

Greydanus noted, "If the *Karate Kid* film itself embraces the two-fisted cliché that the way to win a bully's respect is by licking him good, the idea of violence as a last resort still comes across with tolerable cogency."[26]

Morita began his career as a stand-up comedian and spent much of his early life as a character actor, often playing roles that depicted Orientals in demeaning ways. He broke out of that mold in 1975 by playing Arnold, the restaurant owner on TV's *Happy Days*. His work in *The Karate Kid*, though, overshadowed his other roles. Morita was Avildsen's first choice for the role. Avildsen didn't know he was a comedian, and was impressed by his reading for the role. "I was knocked out," Avildsen said. "This guy was terrific."

Unfortunately, producer Jerry Weintraub first rejected Morita, thinking the actor's comic role on *Happy Days* would color audience reaction. Morita grew a beard and did his own screen test using a Japanese accent. Morita's wife Evelyn later recalled, "When Jerry saw it, he said, 'That's what I want, a goddamn actor,' not realizing it was Pat."[27] Weintaub billed the actor as "Noriyuki (Pat) Morita," to make him sound more ethnic. Morita later said he used the "Noriyuki" name because it was "the only name my parents gave me."[28]

Weintraub, in his autobiography, credits Avildsen with insisting that Morita get the role. He recalled that the test scene had Miyagi nursing Daniel, who had been injured. While watching the shooting of the scene, Weintraub later wrote he "started to cry, I mean, real goddamn tears." The next day, as he and Avildsen watched the footage, he told Avildsen, "You were right, so very right."[29]

Once on the set, Morita seems to have had an influence on the script. The famous "catching flies with chopsticks" scene, for example, was inspired by a similar scene in *Miyamoto Musashi kanketsuhen: kettô Ganryûjima*, a 1956 Japanese film directed by Hiroshi Inagaki. Morita made it such a memorable moment that 25 years later, when President Barack Obama caught and killed a fly during an interview, at least one commentator compared his feat to Morita's chopstick scene, quoting Miyagi's line: "Man who catch fly with chopstick accomplish anything."[30]

Morita seemed to have a similar impact on his infamous drinking scene. The song that he sings in the scene is a Japanese folk song from his childhood. The scene lets the audience into Miyagi's inner thoughts, including the Congressional Medal of Honor that he won in Italy during World War II while his wife was incarcerated in a U.S. concentration camp for Nissei. She and her child die in childbirth in the camp while Miyagi is fighting for his country. Daniel learns about the deaths and Miyagi's medal when he finds a telegram notifying the sensei of the death of his wife and child. The studio originally wanted to cut that scene, arguing that it slowed down the plot, but Avildsen credits it with getting Morita the Oscar nomination.

The critics had mixed reactions to the other cast members. Most liked the title performance of Ralph Macchio, who got the role despite being 22 years old when filming started in 1983. He immediately took a six-week crash course in karate to prepare for the work. Macchio's performance remains his most memorable role, one that Greydanus described as "still his signature role."[31] As Roger Ebert wrote:

> Macchio is an unusual, interesting choice for Daniel. He's not the basic handsome Hollywood teenager but a thin, tall, intense kid with a way of seeming to talk to himself. His delivery always sounds natural, even off-hand; he never seems to be reading a line.[32]

Clee wrote that Macchio "does a fine job as the put-upon lad who has much to learn about himself."[33] Macchio took more from the film than just a paycheck and international recognition. He got to keep that classic yellow car — a 1946 Ford convertible — that he spent so much time waxing. The Ford was chosen by Avildsen, and he selected a car that was the same model and year as the one his father gave to his sister for her 20th birthday in 1946. In the movie, Mr. Miyagi offers the car to Daniel as a birthday gift. In real life, producer Weintaub gave the car to Macchio after the film was completed.

The Daniel LaRusso character — thanks in part to Macchio's winning performance — is one of the film's major breaks from formula and cliché. For

Avildsen lining up a shot of Ralph Macchio in *The Karate Kid* (1984).

increased conflict, it would have been tempting to make LaRusso a complete outsider, who succeeds despite being ostracized by his peers. However, LaRusso is merely scrawny and lower-income; those are his only disadvantages. In his favor is a witty, personable, extroverted personality that instantly charms the kids in his apartment building and the prettiest girl in school.

Elisabeth Shue, enrolled at Harvard when casting began, interrupted her studies to make her movie debut in the female lead. She didn't seem to impress a lot of the reviewers. Ebert described her as "your standard girl from the right side of town and has the usual snobbish parents."[34]

The strongest negative comments were reserved for Martin Kove, who played the amoral karate instructor. Chuck Norris was reportedly the first choice for the role, turning it down because it was an unfavorable portrayal of a karate professional.[35] Avildsen has no memory of Norris ever being considered. Further, Norris denied being offered the role, but has confirmed that — had he been offered it — he would have turned it down for those reasons. One of Norris' students did get in the film: Pat Johnson provided karate instruction to the actors during filming and appears as the referee in the final match.

One other person auditioned for the role but was not seriously considered. Steven Seagal was a unknown actor at the time, with no film credits. His first movie, *Above the Law*, wouldn't be released until three years later. But he was super-agent Mike Ovitz's personal karate instructor at the time. Ovitz, who co-founded Creative Artists Agency, arranged for Seagal to get an audition with Avildsen. Avildsen was unimpressed. Seagal came in at seven P.M. wearing a cape and talking about the CIA and other national secrets. "I thought the guy was from another planet," Avildsen said.

Avildsen's first choice for the role was Perry King, but King turned it down for a television pilot. Still, Avildsen was pleased with Kove's performance, but many critics disagreed. Griffin, for example, wrote:

> The militant sensei is played by Martin Kove in such hammy overdrive that his archetype nearly established a household name of its own, as the malicious drill instructor-turned-coach.... Of all the key players, his role seems the most forced and unnatural; it's like he wandered in from a *Kickboxer* sequel.... In a more routine film with similarly cliched characters, in which we are encouraged to suspend our disbelief, Kove would be the highlight. Here, he is merely a distraction from the more convincing proceedings.[36]

Perhaps such mundane performances made Morita's stand out even more. Either way, Morita's performance garnered him an Oscar nomination for Best Supporting Actor. He lost out to Haing S. Ngor, who won for his work in *The Killing Fields*. In retrospect, though, Morita's role was more memorable. As Molloy noted, Morita's role in the 1984 film "would define his career and spawn countless affectionate imitations."[37] Roger Ebert agreed, writing that "the movie really belongs to Pat Morita."

Griffin had similar praise for Morita's performance:

> He works beyond the predictable requirements of his role and emerges as a character who puts the wise sensei into a human context. "Catch fly with chopstick" becomes not just the action of a conventional sage with a moral to every story, but also the declaration of a patient, witty man who enjoys amusing himself with trivial delights. That Miyagi can be both of these things reveals the insight that elevates *The Karate Kid* from a routine high school sports picture to an enduring reflection of friendship and the spirit of endurance.[38]

Praise for the performance went beyond the karate scenes. As Ebert wrote:

> In a couple of scenes where he has to face down a hostile karate coach, Miyagi's words are so carefully chosen they don't give the other guy any excuse to get violent; Miyagi uses the language as carefully as his hands or arms to ward off blows and gain an advantage.[39]

Avildsen believes that writer Robert Mark Kamen deserves credit for much of the success of the movie. Kamen was a black-belt karate expert himself, a factor that contributed to the realism of the film. (He worked with Avildsen again on *The Power of One*.) As Avildsen said, "The script is greatly responsible for the success of the movie."

Much of the film shoot followed a chronological order. The first scene shot in California was a beach scene where Daniel is playing soccer and meets Elisabeth Shue's character. The opening shot of the movie, in which Daniel and his mother leave their home in Jersey, wasn't easy. Avildsen, being his own cameraman, finally climbed to the top of a Hoboken, New Jersey, water tower to get the angle he wanted. He and his two-man crew returned to California in a series of short plane hops, stopping along the way to get shots to represent the cross-country trip for the two sojourners. The scene where Daniel pushes his mother's malfunctioning car was shot in Sedona, Arizona, using doubles for the two actors.

There were some problems, including one shot that took 35 takes to get right. The meticulous Avildsen wasn't happy with any of the first 34 takes in which the camera, at the end of a long crane, followed Daniel, Ali and Mr. Miyagi as they exited the locker room at the tournament to reveal a panoramic view of the gymnasium. The long, continuous shot is one of the most impressive in the film.

And accidents happened. The most memorable came in the bullying scene, when Daniel receives a final spin kick before Miyagi arrives to save him. That kick really hit and injured Macchio.

Copyright problems were also an issue. The title *The Karate Kid* had previously been used by DC Comics for a character in its "Legion of Super-heroes." The comic publisher gave special permission for use of the title, and received a special "thank you" in the end credits.

The *Rocky* comparisons could not be avoided; after all, the movie ends with the same type of fight scene. Further, one song in the film, "You're the Best," was originally written for use in *Rocky III* two years earlier, but was dropped in favor of "Eye of the Tiger" by Survivor. *The Karate Kid* producers kept the original lyrics of the song, including the phrase "History repeats itself"—which made no sense in *The Karate Kid* but fit well with the *Rocky* sequels.

Still, as Ebert noted, "the heart of this movie isn't in the fight sequences, it's in the relationships."[40] Those relationships made it so successful that *The Karate Kid* led to three sequels, *The Karate Kid II, The Karate Kid III,* and *The Next Karate Kid.* There was also a Karate Kid musical (*Genzlinger*, 2004),[41] an animated series, and a clunker called *The Karate Dog* (2004) in which Morita spoofs his own role.[42] In 2004, clips from the movie were included in a program at Lincoln Center. The impact of the film even reached the university classroom, with some religion classes introducing the "Miyagi Method" for religious education.[43]

Respect for the movie and its director continues today. When Will Smith co-produced a 2010 remake starring his son Jaden Smith, he asked Avildsen to review the film before its release. Other fans post their comments on YouTube and other sites, including one United Kingdom viewer who studies Eastern philosophy and signed in as "Jac98865" in 2012. The 33-year-old professional noted that he first saw the film when he was seven and has seen in "countless times" since then. He concluded by calling the movie "the most inspirational film of my life" and added that his interest in Eastern philosophy could be traced back to the film.

Fans of the movie can now view audition tapes, rehearsal videos and deleted scenes that Avildsen has posted on YouTube. Avildsen shot this material with his home video camera during rehearsals. One reviewer compared the material to the commentary provided on a 2005 Special Edition DVD released by Sony, concluding that "nothing on the DVD compares to the trove of archival footage that director John Avildsen has posted on his YouTube channel." Writer John Swansburg adds that the footage "will change the way you think about the movie—even if, like me, you've already thought about it a lot."[44]

One of those clips shows that the announcer's (Bruce Malmuth) original lines as Daniel prepares to compete again after being injured. In the final movie, Malmuth asks incredulously, "Daniel LaRusso's gonna fight?, Daniel

LaRusso's gonna fight?" In the rehearsal video, the line is, "Hold on, hold on, hold on, hold on, hold on, Isn't this what it's all about?" [45]

The Karate Kid was Avildsen's first hit after *Rocky.* Unlike the *Rocky* series, in which Avildsen chose not to continue as the director after the first film, Avildsen stayed with this series through its three-film run. That helped make the *Karate Kid* series the most successful of Avildsen's career. The wild success of the 1984 original also proved that Avildsen was a relevant, hit-making director across multiple decades, and not just a director continuing to find work in Hollywood despite being past his 1970s glory days.

Production Notes

Directed by: John G. Avildsen. Writer: Robert Mark Kamen. Producers: R.J. Louis, executive producer; Bud S. Smith, associate producer; Jerry Weintraub, producer. Original Music: Bill Conti. Cinematographer: James Crabe (director of photography). Editors: John G. Avildsen, Walt Mulconery, Bud Smith. Casting Directors: Pennie DuPont, Caro Jones, Bonnie Timmermann. Production Designer: William J. Cassidy. Set Decorator: John H. Anderson. Costume Designers: Richard Bruno, Aida Swinson. Make Up Department: E. Thomas Case, makeup artist; Cheri Ruff, hair stylist. Production Manager: Howard Pine, unit production manager. Second Unit Directors or Assistant Directors: Peter Choi, trainee assistant director; Clifford C. Coleman, first assistant director; Hope R. Goodwin, second assistant director. Art Department: Craig B. Ayers, Sr., greensman; Sam Gordon, property master; William F. Matthews, set designer; Michael Muscarella, construction coordinator. Sound Department: Norval D. Crutcher, sound effects editor; Samuel C. Crutcher, sound effects editor; Thomas Cunliffe, boom operator; Don Digirolamo, sound re-recording mixer; Robert J. Glass, sound re-recording mixer; Dean Hodges, sound mixer; J. Paul Huntsman, post-production dialogue; Robert Knudsen, sound re-recording mixer; Clive Taylor, sound recordist; Glenn T. Morgan, assistant sound editor (uncredited). Special Effects Department: Frank Toro, special effects. Stunts: John Atkinson, stunts; Clarke Coleman, stunts; David Crockett, stunts; Fumio Demura, stunts; Pat Green, stunts; Gary Hillenbeck, stunts; Douglas Ivan, stunts; Buck McDancer, stunts; Bob Nichimura, stunts; Alan Oliney, stunt coordinator; Patrick Romano, stunts; Ronnie Rondell, stunts; Spike Silver, stunts; Lance Turner, stunts; Scott Wilder, stunts; Luke LaFontaine, stunts (uncredited). Camera and Electrical Department: Peter J. Breen, dolly grip; Malcolm Bryce, electrician; Allen D. Easton, first assistant camera; Brad Edmiston, first assistant camera; Joel Kirschner, second assistant camera; John London, key grip; Ross A. Maehl, gaffer; Tom D. May, best boy grip; Ralph Nelson Jr, still photographer; Pat Ralston, best boy; Stephen St. John, Steadicam operator; Jonathan West, camera operator; Don Zobel, best boy. Editorial Department: Richard Alderete, associate editor; Seth Flaum, associate editor; M. Scott Smith, associate editor. Music Department: Brooks Arthur, music supervisor; Stephen A. Hope, music editor; Russ Regan, music supervisor; Dan Wallin, score mixer; Gheorghe Zamfir, musician: pan flute; Angela Morley, orchestrator (uncredited); Celia Weiner, music editor (uncredited). Transportation Department: Alan Falco, transportation coordinator. Miscellaneous Crew: Richard Davis, location manager; Pete Emmet, unit publicist; Alvin Greenman, script supervisor; Jeannie Jeha, production coordinator; Pat E. Johnson, martial arts choreographer; Patrick Romano, instructor: bicycle riding. Filming Locations: Los Angeles, California, USA; Malibu, California, USA; Matadome, California State University Northridge; Northridge, Los Angeles, California, USA; Oak Creek Canyon, Sedona, Arizona, USA; Phoenix, Arizona, USA; Reseda, Los Angeles, California, USA; Woodlands Hills, Los Angeles, California, USA. Production Companies: Columbia Pictures Corporation, Jerry Weintraub Productions, Delphi Films. Distributors: Columbia Pictures (1984) (USA) (theatrical); RCA/Columbia Pictures Home Video (1985) (USA) (video) (laserdisc); National Broadcasting Company (NBC) (1987) (USA) (TV); Columbia TriStar Home Video (1997) (USA) (VHS); Columbia TriStar Home Video (1998) (USA) (DVD); Sony Pictures Home Entertainment (2005) (USA) (DVD) (special edition); Sony Pictures Home Entertainment (2010) (USA) (DVD) (Blu-ray).

Cast — in credits order: Ralph Macchio, Daniel Larusso; Noriyuki "Pat" Morita, Mr. Kesuke Miyagi; Elisabeth Shue, Ali Mills; Martin Kove, John Kreese; Randee Heller, Lucille Larusso; William Zabka, Johnny Lawrence; Ron Thomas, Bobby Brown; Rob Garrison, Tommy; Chad McQueen, Dutch; Tony O'Dell, Jimmy; Israel Juarbe, Freddy Fernandez; William Bassett, Mr. Mills; Larry B. Scott, Jerry; Juli Fields, Susan; Dana Andersen, Barbara; Frank Burt Avalon, Chucky; Jeff Fishman, Billy; Ken Daly, Chris; Tom Fridley, Alan; Pat E. Johnson, Referee; Bruce Malmuth, Ring Announcer; Darryl Vidal, Vidal — Johnny's Semi-final Opponent. Double for Miyagi doing the crane kick at the beach.; Frances Bay, Lady with Dog; Christopher Kriesa, Tournament Official; Bernard Kuby, Mr. Harris, History Teacher; Joan Lemmo, Restaurant Manager; Helen J. Siff, Cashier; Larry Drake, Yahoo #1 at Beach; David Abbott, Yahoo #2 at Beach; Molly Basler, Cheerleading Coach; Brian Davis, Boy in Bathroom; David De Lange, Waiter; Erik Felix, Karate Student; Peter Jason, Soccer Coach; Todd Lookinland, Chicken Boy; Clarence McGee, Jr., Referee #2; William Norren, Doctor; Sam Scarber, Referee #3; Scott Strader, Eddie, Ali's Friend in the Corvette. Other credited cast listed alphabetically: Chris Casamassa, Tournament Guest (uncredited); Tom Levy, Cheering Kid (uncredited); Andrew Shue, Member of Cobra Kai (uncredited).

CHAPTER 15

The Karate Kid Part II

Let the Sequels Begin

The success continued with *The Karate Kid Part II*. The story picks up at the end of the original movie and quickly sends the mentor-student duo of Miyagi and Daniel to Okinawa where Miyagi "has to face up to a matter of honor that he had left unfinished."[1]

Before shooting started, Avildsen, his son Jonathan and co-producer Bill Cassidy traveled to Okinawa to check on the feasibility of shooting there. They decided that wouldn't work, so Hawaii was chosen as a substitute, with location shots done on the island of Oahu.

Cassidy was a close friend of Avildsen's. They met in 1958 at D'Arcy's in New York where Cassidy was an art director and Avildsen was a copywriter. Cassidy also served as production designer on the film. He served a similar role on other Avildsen films, starting with *Rocky*, until he died after finishing *8 Seconds* (1994).

The cast was mostly familiar. Elisabeth Shue was out of sight as Daniel's girlfriend, dumped from the film because her agent wanted a bigger fee than the producers wanted to pay. But Pat Morita (again billed as Noriyuki "Pat" Morita) was back as Miyagi. Ralph Macchio revived his role as Daniel LaRusso, and Martin Kove returned as the evil karate instructor John Kreese. Even Pat E. Johnson, the karate instructor who had a brief role as a referee in the original, returned, again playing a referee.

The sequel essentially stayed true to the approach of the original, probably because writer Robert Mark Kamen — who created the characters — provided the script for *Part II* also. There is a repeat of Miyagi's non-traditional teaching techniques, and the paradoxical emphasis on nonviolence in an action film continued.

This time, the stakes were higher (a life-and-death battle, rather than a tournament) and the audience learns more about the mysterious Miyagi. Trailers let fans know, "This time, the combat is real."

As a work of art, *Part II* was more like a serial than a sequel. It begins with Daniel having won the local championship. In fact, the opening scene was originally written as the end of the first movie. It was omitted in favor of an alternative ending with a final shot focusing on Miyagi as Daniel is carried away.

The evil dojo master Kreese kicks Daniel's opponent off the karate team, as punishment for his loss to our hero. When the kid protests, evil dojo master gets the youngster into a headlock.

Miyagi steps in to save the day. Kreese tries to hit Miyagi twice, but the agile Miyagi avoids both blows and Kreese instead breaks two car windows. Miyagi then appears ready to land a fatal blow to the bully, but pulls up at the last minute and merely humiliates him by grabbing and honking his nose.

Skip ahead six months and life has turned sour for Daniel. He and Ali made it to the senior prom, but Ali dumped him shortly afterwards (after all, they needed some way to explain the absence of Shue). Then Daniel finds that his mother is moving again, heading off to Fresno for a job there.

Miyagi puts Daniel to work, adding a new room to the mentor's house, to get his mind off his problems. Not only does it restore Daniel's ego, but the new addition also becomes his new home. Miyagi reveals that he has arranged for Daniel to live with him while his mother is in Fresno.

But Daniel gets to spend little time in his new room. Miyagi soon receives a letter and learns that his father is dying back in his native Okinawa. The mentor immediately packs to visit his dying father, intending to make the trip alone. But Daniel packs to go with him, using some of his college savings to pay for the trip.

Miyagi quickly runs into Sato (Danny Kamekona), karate expert who hates Miyagi because of an old love triangle — the problem that led Miyagi to leave Okinawa originally. The fact that the object of their affection still seems to have some emotions for Miyagi, doesn't help. The situation seems to be setting up a fight to the death with Sato — decades after the original triangle.

Signs of the coming conflict are apparent early. After Daniel and Miyagi land at the Okinawa airport, Daniel spots a poster advertising Sato's karate school. The poster depicts Sato breaking a log with his bare hands. "You think you could break a log like that?" Daniel asks Miyagi.

"Don't know," Miyagi replies. "Never been attacked by tree."

Miyagi provides no indication that the poster depicts his long-time rival. To make matters worse, Sato is now a rich and ruthless businessman who has amassed his wealth at the expense of the locals in Tome, Miyagi's native home.

Sato has made much of his money in the fishing industry, using large boats that have depleted the fish population near the coastal village.

Daniel rambles around the area behaving like the species that the folks of Okinawa call a "henna gaijin" (silly foreigner). He makes a new set of friends after meeting a young Okinawan girl, Kumiko (Tamlyn Tomika), who causes him to forget about Ali.

But that pesky matter of Okinawa honor keeps causing problems for both Daniel and Miyagi. Daniel raises the wrath of Chozen, Sato's nephew, while Sato goes after Miyagi on a village street, ready to attack. They are interrupted by news that Miyagi's father wants to see both of the combatants. The dying patriarch wants to end the feud before he dies.

Miyagi is willing, but not Sato. He refuses to leave Miyagi alone. Miyagi reluctantly agrees to fight, but only if Sato will sign a deed giving the village back to the villagers.

That set-up is interrupted by a typhoon that hits the village. Most of the villagers, plus Daniel and Miyagi, gather at a local storm shelter. As they enter, Daniel sees Sato's dojo collapse from the storm, while Chozen escapes from the wreckage. Daniel and Miyagi rush to the collapsed building, find Sato trapped inside, rescue him from beneath a large beam, and take him to the shelter.

Hero Daniel spots another person in trouble: a little girl, crying and clinging to the warning bell in a tower. Daniel rushes to the rescue again, but finds he can't save the girl by himself. Sato orders nephew Chozen to go and help. Chozen refuses to do so and runs away. Sato, denouncing his nephew, disregards his own injuries and goes to help Daniel. Together they save the child and bring her back to the shelter.

The typhoon serves a symbolic role of washing away the clutter in the mind of Sato. He returns the next day with the deed to the village and ready to rebuild the locals' homes and shops. He publicly apologizes to the villagers for his years of hatred, and asks their forgiveness. And in true Okinawa tradition, they forgive him and hold an o-Bon dance in his honor.

The fight between Sato and Miyagi is now off, but there's still that pesky nephew Yuji. He kidnaps Kumiko at the dance and challenges Daniel to a fight to the death. Their battle is on a platform surrounded by water. Daniel comes out the winner. He first relies on the same crane technique that won him the championship in the original movie.

His choice of the kick is understandable. After all, in the original film, Miyagi had told Daniel that there was no defense against the crane kick ("If do right, no can defense"). Apparently, Okinawa karate masters had a defense after all. Daniel tries the kick, but Yuji blocks it.

Daniel must learn a new move to win this fight: the Swinging Drum

Kick. It requires understanding another karate principle, and Miyagi gives him a toy drum to help him learn the move. "I don't get it," Daniel says, after seeing the drum. "Practice, you will," Miyagi replies.

The early practice sessions don't go well. In Daniel's first full practice of the new move, he merely succeeds in ripping his own shirt off his body. He sheepishly returns to Miyagi and says, "That was pretty stupid, wasn't it?"

Miyagi smiles and says, "Miyagi say that to father when same thing happen. Father agree, was stupid. Father was right." Daniel eventually understands the principle and uses it to defeat Yuji — but doesn't kill him.

In some ways, this movie was more successful than the original. The first was such a mega-hit in 1984 that filming on the sequel began the following year. *The Karate Kid II* reached theaters on June 20, 1986, and took in more than $115 million. Armstrong wrote, "The fact that it cleared over $115 million domestically, compared to the $90 million taken in by the original, indicates the appetite for escapism that prompted two more similar sequels."[2]

The film also drew 1987 Oscar attention for its use of pop music. The film's major song, Peter Cetera's "Glory of Love," was a No. 1 hit and garnered an Academy Award nomination for Best Song. "Glory of Love," written by David Foster (music) and Diane Nini (lyrics), was honored by ASCAP in the

Avildsen and actor Pat Morita on the set of *The Karate Kid Part II* (1986).

"Most Performed Songs from Motion Pictures" category. Conti teamed with
Carly Simon and Jacob Brackman to write "Two Looking at One," which was
recorded by Simon.

Avildsen also effectively used music to tie the sequel to the original. After
they arrive in Okinawa, Chozen and a friend drive Daniel and Miyagi from
the airport while a song plays on the radio. The tune, "Fascination," was heard
over a dance scene in the original. The choice of that song was no accident;
"Fascination" was a major hit in 1957 — staying on the charts for 29 weeks —
for Jane Morgan. Morgan was the wife of producer Jerry Weintraub.

That connection also led to Avildsen meeting future president George
H.W. Bush. Jane Morgan was a longtime friend of Barbara Bush; when the
political couple visited the Weintraubs, they introduced them to Avildsen.

The strength of *Karate Kid, Part II* was its script and its main characters.
Peretta noted:

> The sequel retains the strengths of its predecessor, the gawky charm of
> Ralph Macchio (is he really 24?) as the cute boy-next-door turned hero,
> and Noriyuki "Pat" Morita as his ever-smart, ever-wisecracking Oriental
> mentor Miyagi.... The plotline is classic Western morality-play stuff, with
> the goodies and baddies clearly delineated, but the set pieces are well con-
> structed, and the whole thing is beautifully staged and shot.[3]

Morita and Macchio stayed in character and yet also let their characters
grow as compared to the original film. The script deserves credit for not fully
repeating the plot of the first. While both lead to a climactic fight, the motivations are different.

The film serves an important purpose by filling in the gaps in Miyagi's
biography, both in terms of his background and motivations. Moving the
locale to Okinawa also provided for explorations of different themes.

The writing remains witty despite the predictable plot. When Daniel
gloats over his victory, and plans a career path in karate tournaments, he asks
Miyagi for advice. Miyagi's suggestion: "Early retirement."

A scene in which Daniel and Ali break up (she tells him it's because she's
traveling to Europe for the summer) was written but never shot. In the final
version, we learn that the two parted ways after Ali borrowed his car and
wrecked it. The information that Ali had fallen for a college football player
is made in a reference by Daniel when bemoaning the fate of his car.

The film version has Daniel recounting the story to Miyagi while his car
sputters, with Daniel also telling his mentor that his mother has taken a job
in Fresno. A bit of Eastern mysticism creeps back into the plot, as Miyagi
twists something under the hood and the car starts running smoothly.

There is also plenty of pseudo–Eastern wisdom dispensed by Miyagi.
The karate master explains that he doesn't kill his opponent because "for man

with no forgiveness in heart, life worse punishment than death."

In another scene, Daniel gives Miyagi a rosewood display case for his Congressional Medal of Honor, but Miyagi refuses to use it. Daniel says, "Well, you know, winning the Medal of Honor and all, it says something about you. Like, you're brave. And all that stuff."

Miyagi disagrees, puts his hand on Daniel's chest, and says, "*This* say you brave." Then, pointing toward the medals, adds, "This say you *lucky*."

In another instance, Miyagi advises Daniel to "never put passion before principle. Even if win, you lose."

Daniel seems to be gaining insight by the time he asks Miyagi about the fight-to-the-death challenge from Sato and Chozen. "How do you know who wins?" he asks.

"The one who still alive," Miyagi replies.

"You make it sound like the one who's still alive doesn't always win, either," Daniel adds.

Miyagi nods, and says. "You catch on fast, Daniel-san."

On the set of *The Karate Kid*, from left: Avildsen, Pat Morita, Barbara Bush, Jerry Weintraub, President George H.W. Bush and Ralph Macchio (photograph by Ralph Nelson, SMPSP, courtesy Jerry Weintraub).

TV buffs will spot Clarence Gilyard and B.D. Wong in brief scenes. Gilyard, who played Ranger Conrad McMasters on *Walker, Texas Ranger*, appears in an ice-breaking scene. Wong, who became a regular playing Dr. George Huang on *Law & Order: Special Victims Unit*, is credited as Bradd Wong and has a cameo as a kid who runs up to Daniel and Kumiko.

Some critics were lukewarm about the effort. Armstrong described it as "basically more of the same from director John G. Avildsen, a sequel that studies the high points of the original so closely that it could be considered a remake set in a different location."[4] But, in fairness to Avildsen, the film took a more philosophical turn than the original and also explored the cultural backgrounds of the characters..

It was, after all, the only one of the four Karate Kid films in which Daniel fights for a cause (the people in the village), not for some personal honor or self-respect. And it succeeded in doing this at a high level. Even Armstrong noted, "*The Karate Kid Part II* does manage to duplicate the original's winning vibe, including prompting pleased moviegoers to karate chop the air on their way out of the theater, in turn expelling their adrenaline."[5]

The film was a blockbuster success. Avildsen, who had a dual role as director and one of the editors, had hit gold on two movies in a row. He was on a roll.

Production Notes

Directed by: John G. Avildsen. Writers: Robert Mark Kamen Characters created by; Robert Mark Kamen Written by. Producers: William J. Cassidy, associate producer; Susan E. Ekins, associate producer; R.J. Louis, executive producer; Karen Trudy Rosenfelt, associate producer; Jerry Weintraub, producer. Original Music: Bill Conti. Cinematographer: James Crabe. Editors: John G. Avildsen, David Garfield, Jane Kurson. Casting Directors: Caro Jones. Production Designer: William J. Cassidy. Art Director: William F. Matthews. Set Decorator: Lee Poll. Costume Designer: Mary Malin. Make Up Department: John Elliott, key makeup artist; Stephen Elsbree, hair stylist; James R. Kail, makeup artist; Cheri Ruff, key hair stylist. Production Manager: Howard Pine, unit production manager. Second Unit Directors or Assistant Directors: Clifford C. Coleman, first assistant director; Christine Larson, second second assistant director; Dennis Maguire, second assistant director. Art Department: Giovanni Casalenuovo, painter; Sam Gordon, property master; Bobby Ikeda, set dresser; Jim Teagarden, set designer; Michael Van Dyke, construction foreman: Hawaii; Robert Van Dyke, propmaker foreman; Hendrik Wynands, construction coordinator; Michael Denering, scenic artist (uncredited). Sound Department: Jim Bullock, foley editor; Blake R. Cornett, first assistant sound editor; Don Digirolamo, sound re-recording mixer; Doreen A. Dixon, supervising adr editor; Robert Glass, sound re-recording mixer; Joseph Holsen, sound editor; Jay Kamen, adr editor; Robert Knudson, sound re-recording mixer; Tom C. McCarthy, supervising sound editor; Greg Orloff, foley mixer; William J. Randall, Jr., sound mixer; William M. Randall, Jr., cable person; Dennis C. Salcedo, cable person — supplemental unit; David Stafford, boom operator; Martha Burns Holsen, sound editor (uncredited); Carolyn Tapp, foley recordist (uncredited). Special Effects Department: Dennis Dion, special effects foreman; Walter Dion, Paul Haines and Al Wininger, special effects. Visual Effects Department: Syd Dutton, special visual effects; Bill Taylor, special visual effects. Stunts: Linda Arvidson, Erik Felix, Mike Hassett, Roger Ito, Lori Lynn Ross and Bill Ryusaki, stunts; Pat E. Johnson, stunt coordinator (uncredited); Nijel, assistant fight coordinator (uncredited). Camera and Electrical Department: Craig Denault, camera operator; Alan R. Disler and Brad Edmiston, first assistants camera; O.T. Henderson, dolly grip; John Lubin, best boy; John Lubin, grip; Ross A. Maehl, gaffer; Ralph Nelson, Jr., still photographer; James M. Sheppherd, key grip; Stephen St. John, Steadicam operator; Stephen St. John, camera operator; Ron Veto, key grip: stunt unit; Phil Walker, best boy; Mario Zavala, second assistant camera.Costume and Wardrobe Department: Eddie Marks, costume supervisor — men; Elizabeth Pine, costume supervisor. Editorial Department: Timothy Alverson, first assistant editor; Reid Burns, color timer; Karen Kory, assistant film editor. Music Department: Brooks Arthur, music supervisor; Jack Eskew, orchestrator; Stephen A. Hope, music editor; Dan Wallin, score mixer; Masakazu Yoshizawa, musician; Julie Giroux, orchestrator (uncredited). Transportation Department: Alan Falco, transportation coordinator; Harry Ueshiro, transportation coordinator. Miscellaneous Crew: Peter Benoit, unit publicist; William "Pete" Corral, location manager; Paul De Rolf and Jose De Vega, choreographers; Jennifer Erskine, assistant to Jerry Weintraub; Joyce Fetherolf, assistant to director; Zenko Heshiki, technical advisor; Adam Hill, breakaway statue caster: Paramount Studios; Jeannie Jeha, production coordinator; Pat E. Johnson, martial arts choreographer; Daniel Malmuth, assistant to director; Marshall Schlom, script supervisor; Douglas Seelig, assistant to director; Stephanie Spangler, location scout; Yasukazu Takushi, technical advisor; Jamie Weintraub, assistant to Jerry Weintraub; Jody Weintraub, assistant to Jerry Weintraub; Julie Weintraub, assistant to Jerry Weintraub. Filming Locations: O'ahu, Hawaii, USA; Los Angeles, California, USA. Production Companies: Columbia Pictures Corporation; Delphi V Productions. Distributors: Columbia Pictures (1986) (USA) (theatrical); National Broadcasting Company (NBC) (1988) (USA) (TV) (broadcast premiere); Sony Pictures Home Entertainment (2010) (USA) (DVD) (Blu-ray).

Cast — in credits order: Noriyuki "Pat" Morita, Mr. Kesuke Miyagi; Ralph Macchio, Daniel LaRusso; Pat E. Johnson, Referee; Bruce Malmuth, Announcer; Eddie Smith, Bystander; Martin Kove, John Kreese; Garth Johnson, Autograph Fan #1; Brett Johnson, Autograph Fan #2; Will Hunt, Postman; Evan Malmuth, Cab Driver; Lee Arnone, Stewardess #1; Sarah Kendall, Stewardess #2; Yuji Okumoto, Chozen; Joey Miyashima, Toshio; Danny Kamekona, Sato; Raymond Ma, Cab Driver in Okinawa; George O'Hanlon, Jr., Soldier; Tamlyn Tomita, Kumiko; Nobu McCarthy, Yukie; Charlie Tanimoto, Miyagi's Father; Tsuruko Ohye, Village Woman; Arsenio "Sonny" Trinidad, Ichiro; Marc Hayashi, Taro; Robert Fernandez, Watchman; Natalie N. Hashimoto, Kumiko's Street Friend; Diana Mar, Girl in Video Store; Bradd Wong, Boy on Street; Clarence Gilyard, Jr., G.I. #1; Michael Morgan, G.I. #2; Jack Eiseman, G.I. #3; Jeffrey Rogers, G.I. #4; Aaron Seville, G.I. #5; Wes Chong, Sato's Houseman; Traci Toguchi, Girl Bell Ringer; William Zabka, Johnny Lawrence — returning as The Cobras; Chad McQueen, Dutch — returning as The Cobras; Tony O'Dell, Jimmy — returning as The Cobras; Ron Thomas, Bobby Brown — returning as The Cobras; Rob Garrison, Tommy — returning as The Cobras.

CHAPTER 16

Happy New Year

Sometimes a good picture simply gets overlooked. Avildsen's 1987 film *Happy New Year* falls into that category. It had the Oscar-winning director at the helm, hired by Columbia Pictures because, as Avildsen said, "They wanted to keep me busy so I'd be available to do *Karate Kid 3*." His friend Jerry Weintraub was the producer. James Crabe, Avildsen's favorite cameraman, was the director of photography. The cast included top-notch actors Peter Falk and Charles Durning. The musical score was provided by *Rocky* composer Bill Conti. There were a lot of things going for it.

"It appealed to me because it seemed to be about forgiveness," Avildsen later said, "and Peter Falk is terrific, so I figured we could come up with a good script using the same basic story and update it, setting it in America."[1]

But talk about being overlooked! It got little recognition at the time of its release, and little since. Even today, DVDs of the film are not available. Avildsen explained the problem by once saying that *Happy New Year* "was released by the CIA. It was a secret release!"[2]

Despite good initial reviews, *Happy New Year* was caught in a regime change at Columbia Pictures and new head David Puttman didn't like it. He quickly relegated it to video release with little support for movie-house distribution. "It was released primarily to qualify for video sales," Avildsen has said. "When it was released for about a minute and a half, it got some very good reviews that surprised everybody."[3]

Happy New Year was based on the 1973 French movie *La Bonne Annee*, directed by Claude Lelouch and starring Lino Ventura. In Avildsen's movie, Lelouch has a cameo as a man whose pocket is picked on the train in the opening scenes.

The plot features a pair of con artists (Falk and Durning) who develop a plan to rob a Palm Beach, Florida, jewelry store during the Christmas holidays. Mickey Rooney was Avildsen's first choice for the sidekick role, but Falk vetoed that. Durning got the job instead and "did a marvelous job," Avildsen said.

Multiple scripts were commissioned, included versions by Norman Wexler (*Joe, Serpico, Saturday Night Fever*) and Herb Gardner (*A Thousand Clowns, I'm Not Rappaport*). "We had three terrific scripts written by three very good writers," Avildsen recalled. "[Falk] unfortunately rejected all of them. He really wanted a translation of that French movie, which basically is what we got. We tried to jazz it up a bit, but it's not one of my favorites."[4] The problem, Avildsen told the authors, "was Falk wanted to be Leno Ventura." The script used was a simple translation of the French version. The writer is credited as "Warren Lane," but that's actually a common alias used in Hollywood when the writer doesn't want his name attached to the film.

Falk's influence on the script is apparent. *Happy New Year* is essentially a Peter Falk film rather than a John Avildsen film. Avildsen directed it, and his influence is present in the shot sequence and cinematography, but Falk still dominates as con man Nick. Falk was justifiably proud of the film, calling it his best comedy performance to that point.[5]

Nick (Falk) is the master of planning and disguise. He and Charlie (Durning) buy a hot Rolls-Royce with $40,000. ("How many miles on it?" Charlie asks the fence. "How many you want?" he replies.) The Rolls adds credibility to Falk's posing as a rich old man who enters the jewelry store ("Harry Winston, Rare Jewels of the World").

The duo cases the shop, noting when the manager (British actor Tom Courtenay) and employees arrive, when the doors are opened, when alarms are set, and when the store closes. Nick does most of the watching, using binoculars, but his observations are interrupted when he spots the owner of the antique shop next door, an attractive woman named Carolyn (Wendy Hughes).

Nick immediately starts a side plan to meet and court this vision of loveliness. Charlie senses a problem. "Nick has real good power of concentration," he says to himself in a voiceover. "The problem is, you never know what he's going to be concentratin' on."

The next day, Nick enters the store disguised as an old man, searching for a gift for his ill wife. It is one of two impressive disguises (the other, an elderly woman) that Falk uses in the film. The extraordinary makeup work took more than three hours each day, and garnered an Oscar nomination for Robert Laden. The original French film just had one make-up character, the old man. According to Falk, the studio added the idea of the sister for more "zip" because the film needed something extra. Falk based his woman character on his mother, inspired by having dinner with Elaine May before shooting started.[6] "I so enjoyed playing my mother that when I was actually acting I forgot all that crap on my face," Falk later said.[7]

Producer Jerry Weintraub's family also had an impact. Weintraub's parents visited the Florida set and Avildsen suggested that his mother be an extra for a jewelry store scene. Falk chimed in with his support of the idea. Rose Weintraub appeared as a customer, walking with the store manager (Courtenay). Avildsen also suggested that Weintraub direct the scene, and Weintraub agreed. The simple scene, in which she was supposed to walk in front of the camera, took several shots. Rose started ad libbing in the first take and looked directly into the camera in another. Weintraub continued working with her while Avildsen, Falk and the rest of the crew laughed. It finally got on film, and the scene was included in the final cut.[8]

Falk's character is in the store and spots a pair of ruby earrings, priced at $49,999. At first he complains about the price. "Why would you want a price with so many nines?" he asks the store manager. But he eventually makes the purchase for "his wife."

Later that evening, Nick and Charlie (without disguises) are dining in a restaurant when they spot Carolyn eating. The restaurant owner approaches Carolyn about ordering some antiques. Carolyn laughingly refuses to do so until the owner first sells her a Louis XVI table that sits in the dining area. The owner refuses.

Nick overhears the conversation. After Carolyn leaves, he approaches the restaurant owner about purchasing the table too. She explains that it's a family heirloom and she will not sell. "So I have no chance?" Nick asks. "None," she replies.

Cut to the next morning, with Nick walking out of the restaurant carrying the table. A Durning voiceover lets the viewer know that he paid $7,000 for the heirloom, which he immediately takes to Carolyn's antique shop.

Carolyn is startled to see the table and even more surprised when Nick offers to sell it to her. He bought it, he explains, for $8,000 as a gift for a lady, but she left that morning.

Carolyn tells him that the table would complete a set, matched with a pair of chairs that she already owns. Nick offers to complete the set for $9,000, but she declines, saying the price is too high. He asks if she will take it on consignment, for $9,000, and she agrees.

Nick returns to the jewelry store the next day, this time disguised as an elderly woman. She wants to return the earrings purchased the day before by "her brother," and find another gift that her brother's "wife" would like better. She selects a diamond bracelet, priced at $60,000. "Round numbers this time," Nick observes, in a momentary slip of his new persona. "Oh, your brother told you," the manager replies.

Nick, still dressed as an older woman, exits the store and stops to speak to Carolyn. He compliments her on her appearance and demeanor, grabs her arm, and wishes her Merry Christmas.

Nick and Charlie, drive through the streets of Palm Beach and then to

Tom Courtney and Peter Falk in *Happy New Year* (1973).

a pier where they jump into a cigarette-style motorboat. They check their time and agree that it is acceptable. To be safe, however, Nick plans to stay behind and delay any efforts to catch Charlie, thus giving him more time to escape. Charlie has only one regret, noting that he'd prefer if Nick came with him rather than staying behind. That statement is important to a subsequent plot element.

The next day Nick, disguised as the old man, stops at the antique shop and asks about the Louis XVI table. Carolyn gives him a price for the set, saying she would prefer to not break up the "family." Nick turns to walk away, and she offers to sell just the table for $10,000. "It's a shame to break up a family," Nick says at first, but he finally agrees.

Carolyn later calls Nick, telling him she's found a buyer for his table. The only problem: The most she could get for it was eight thousand. Nick invites her to dinner to discuss the proposal.

At dinner she repeats the offer and also volunteers to pay for dinner since Nick would lose a thousand dollars on the deal. She starts to write a check for $8,000, but is interrupted by Nick who says, "Wanna make that out to cash?"

At that point, the restaurant owner joins them. They discuss the table, and Carolyn is surprised to learn the Nick paid only seven thousand. "I'm the one who loses a thousand dollars," she says, as they both laugh.

As they leave the restaurant, Carolyn says she must return to her apartment above her antique shop. "You look like anything but a married woman," Nick says.

"How am I supposed to take that?" she responds, noting that it's Christmas Eve. Nick, still optimistic, invites her to his hotel.

She jokingly answers that he went too far, and adds, "Why don't we just drop it and maybe pick it up later?" They shake hands and say good night. Back at the hotel, Charlie complains that Nick is paying too much attention to the woman.

The next day Charlie, disguised as a chauffeur, arrives at the antique shop to pick up the table. He gives Carolyn the money and, when she goes to get a receipt, he puts an envelope on the table and leaves. The message says she may keep the table with the chairs, thus keeping the "family" together. She looks out the window, sees the old man in the Rolls, and waves to him.

On Christmas Day, Nick and Charlie are in their hotel room exchanging gifts. Nick gives Charlie a gadget to blow open a safe. Charlie gives Nick an antique pistol. The two stand and hug. That night, the duo visits the local Catholic church, where they sit in the pews as the choir signs "Silent Night." Nick spots Carolyn in another pew, and they both smile.

In the next scene, Nick and Charlie have joined Carolyn for Christmas dinner. Several others are gathered around the large table, including Carolyn's significant other. Carolyn's boyfriend is an art curator who quizzes Nick on art exhibitions.

Nick pleads ignorance, saying he's never seen any of the exhibits or art pieces mentioned by the man. "How do you choose an exhibition?" the boyfriends asks. "The same way I choose a woman," Nick replies. "I take a risk."

The tension in the room mounts, and Nick and Charlie rise and leave. The other guests quickly leave too. Only Carolyn and her boyfriend remain. She asks him to leave too, saying, "This was not Christmas. It was a courtroom."

Charlie is actually pleased with the way things went, believing that Nick will forget about "Carol and her fancy friends and get back to work." He's wrong. The phone rings, and it's Carolyn calling for Nick to say, "I should have spent Christmas with you and you alone."

The film cuts to Nick walking up the stairs to Carolyn's apartment. The camera stays outside but watches them through a window as they dance to the song "I Only Have Eyes for You." The next day, Charlie asks Nick if Carolyn is "worth it." "I wish she were," Nick replies.

Nick returns to the jewelry store, disguised this time as the elderly woman. Her brother's wife, she explained, didn't like the diamond necklace she had purchased. "It has to be something very beautiful, because this present is her last present," Nick explains, referring to his "wife's" supposedly terminal illness.

The elderly woman asks to take photos of other necklaces so she can show them to her brother's wife. That would allow her to go to the hospital and show her the pictures. Her brother will be by later to purchase the one she likes.

The manager reluctantly agrees, but reminds his customer that her brother must be back to the store by 7:30 that evening.

He doesn't make it. The shop closes, three saleswomen leave, and the manager sets the night alarms. As he walks out, Nick — disguised as the old man — arrives in the Rolls Royce. He shows the manager the photo of the necklace his wife chose — the "most expensive one."

The manager says Nick has arrived too late. To purchase the necklace, he'll have to come back the next day. Nick insists, adding that "the doctor says it may be her last night."

The manager agrees, returns to the shop, turns off the alarm system, and gets the necklace out of the vault. He turns the alarm system back on and returns to the front door to let Nick into the shop.

Nick prepares to write a check, but the manager stops him, saying that he can't accept a check. Nick argues that they've accepted checks from him before with no problem. True, the manager answers, but he is required to call the bank for any check over ten thousand dollars. Since the bank is closed, he can't do that or accept the check. Nick has an easy answer: What if he pays in cash?

Nick goes to the door, calls to Charlie, and asks him to bring in the two briefcases in the car. He opens one case and gives the manager $170,000 in cash, asking him to count it himself. Charlie pretends to leave, but ducks into another room to hide.

After collecting the money, the manager lets Nick out and disconnects the alarm to the vault. Charlie comes out from hiding, points a gun at him, and orders him to put money and jewels into a bag.

Charlie opens the front door so Nick can enter again, while he leaves to start his drive to the motorboat. Thus the importance of Charlie's early statement about wanting Nick to join him on the getaway. Instead of leaving, Nick handcuffs the manager to a chair. He holds a gun on the manager for the time it will take Charlie to reach the boat.

When enough time has passed, Nick tries to leave the shop, but he can't open the front door. At first he pushes the manager around, asking how to get it open. The manager explains that when the door to the safe stays open for more than two minutes, the front door automatically locks and the police are alerted.

By now, the police have surrounded the shop. Nick picks up the phone and calls his lawyer, asking for advice, while he takes off his disguise. When he hangs up, he uncuffs the manager and they go out together.

A policeman (Bruce Malmuth) arrests him, saying, "Lighten up. You'll be out in ten to 15 years." This brief appearance by Malmuth continued a tradition of Malmuth working with Avildsen. He was the ring announcer in *The Karate Kid* and a burger joint operator in *Lean on Me*. He made his directorial debut in Sylvester Stallone's *Nighthawks* in 1981, after Avildsen recommended him for the job.

Following the policeman's comment, Nick's first thought is that Carolyn may have turned him in. Not so. She hires lawyers and stands by him in court. She visits him in jail, complaining, "I can't touch the man I love."

When Nick is extradited to a prison in New York, Carolyn moves there to be near him. On one of their visits, Nick notices that she's changed her hair style. "When a woman changes her hair, it usually means she's changing men," Nick says.

Charlie, meanwhile, lays low. Nick refuses to name his accomplice or give any information about him. Somewhat surprisingly, Nick and two other inmates receive conditional New Year's paroles. Nick believes his release is part of a plan to recover the loot from the Palm Beach heist.

When he's outside, Nick tries to call Charlie but gets a bad connection. Then he stops at a florist, buys flowers, and goes to his New York apartment where Carolyn has been living. He's followed all the way by two policemen in an unmarked car.

Nick enters the apartment and the phone rings. He picks it up and hears Carolyn trying to call "Steve." He hangs up slowly.

Steve enters the apartment, while Nick hides. When Steve goes to another room, Nick slips out. He walks to a bar that's hosting a New Year's Eve party. The Temptations are on the stage, singing "I Only Have Eyes for You." The two cops enter behind him and take seats in the room where they can watch Nick.

Nick spots Frank, the bar's owner, and approaches him. Nick explains that he's being followed and the police will think that Frank is his partner. Nick asks Frank to let them think that for a couple of days before explaining that he was in New York when the Palm Beach robbery occurred.

Nick leaves, and Charlie enters the bar. Nick spots Charlie through the window, goes to a pay phone, and calls from outside. He asks to speak to Charlie, saying that Louis XVI is calling.

The duo reunites in the alley behind the bar. While driving, they discuss Carolyn. Nick says she has a boyfriend. Charlie defends her, saying, "She always has a guy." They arrive at Charlie's hideout and retrieve the loot. Nick's share is $1.6 million, a little less than he expected, but he's happy with it.

Charlie drives Nick to the airport, where he's planning to catch a plane to Rio. As they drive, Charlie argues that Carolyn still loves him. Nick doesn't respond. When he gets out at the airport, Charlie asks about Carolyn: "What should I tell her?" "Nothing," Nick responds.

As Nick walks through the airport, Charlie (in a voiceover) comments about Nick having a "sack full of loot, but running from the best thing that ever happened to him."

Cut to Carolyn in the apartment when the phone rings. "Hurry, I'm waiting for you," she says.

Cut to Nick in the airport, putting his bag of loot in a locker.

Cut back to the apartment. Steve is dressing quickly to leave. She gets his key, tells him, "I never lied to you," and kisses him goodbye.

An overhead shot shows a taxi stopping in front of the building. Carolyn runs to the window, sees Nick, and runs down to let him in.

Nick enters the apartment but says nothing. Carolyn knows why.

"It was my way of staying alive," she says.

When he doesn't respond, she adds, "I love you and nothing else matters." Music starts playing, the everpresent "I Only Have Eyes for You."

Cut to the final scene, with Nick, Carolyn and Charlie on the way to Rio. They're celebrating the New Year as they travel. The only odd element: Nick is in disguise again, dancing with Carolyn while in his elderly woman disguise. Even at the end of the movie, Nick is not what he appears to be.

The film received mixed reviews. *New York Times* critic Vincent Canby noted that the plot "didn't look very original or very funny back in 1973 when the original French film, opened in New York. The curious thing about the American remake, is that although it's no better, it's certainly not worse."[9] Canby went on to praise the cast: "Though the story now seems just that much more tired than it did then, the new film has the advantage of good comic performances by [Falk, Durning, and Hughes]."[10] Gene Siskel really liked the film, describing it as "a fine little comedy caper."[11]

Could it have been a success? Avildsen thought so, had it not been for "how out to lunch they [Columbia Pictures] were in hustling this movie."[12]

"In the advertising for the film, they say, 'See what happens when two guys go to West Palm Beach'!" Avildsen continued. "Nothing happens when two guys go to West Palm Beach and nothing happened with the film either."[13]

Falk blamed the problem on a transition of leadership at Columbia. Guy MacElwaine (Falk's one-time agent) was replaced by David Puttnam, who seemed to have no budget for promoting his predecessor's film. It was released in only 25 cities "with a virtually non-existent advertising campaign."[14]

Despite the criticisms, it remained a favorite of Falk's, who summed it up by saying, "It's not easy to find, but I recommend it."[15] Even with poor marketing, the film garnered an Oscar nomination for makeup. Other than that, it remains Avildsen's forgotten movie.

Production Notes

Directed by: John G. Avildsen. Writers: Film "La bonne annee"; Claude Lelouch. Screenplay: Warren Lane. Producers: William J. Cassidy, associate producer; Allan Ruban, executive producer; Jerry Weintraub, producer. Original Music: Bill Conti. Cinematographer: James Crabe (director of photography). Editor: Jane Kurson. Casting Director: Bonnie Timmermann. Production Designer: William J. Cassidy. Art Director: William F. Matthews. Set Decorator: Don K. Ivey. Costume Designer: Jodie Lynn Tillen. Make Up Department: Frank Bianco, hair stylist; Elvira C. Garofalo, makeup artist; Peter Garofalo, makeup artist; Diane Johnson, hair stylist; Robert Laden, special prosthesis makeup. Production Manager: Allan Ruban, unit production manager. Second Unit Directors or Assistant Directors: James Chory, second assistant director; Clifford C. Coleman, first assistant director; Bruce Malmuth, second unit director. Art Department: John Balling, scenic artist; Eugene Bright and Michael Bright, construction carpenters; Harold Collins, Jr., construction coordinator; Daniel Duarte, shop person; Jose Duarte, scenic artist; Richard Helfritz, leadman; Scott Jacobson, greensman; James Latham, construction foreman; James Robinson II, assistant prop man; Nicholas J. Romanac, prop master; D. Rex Downham, greensman (uncredited). Sound Department: J.H. Arrufat, supervising sound editor; Destiny Borden, assistant sound editor; Don Digirolamo, sound re-recording mixer; Doreen A. Dixon, supervising adr editor; Robert Glass, sound re-recording mixer; Buzz Knudson, sound re-recording mixer; Tom C. McCarthy, supervising sound editor; Rick Roberts, cable man; James Sabat, sound mixer; Lou Sabat, boom man; Vanessa Theme Ament, foley artist. Special Effects Department: J.B. Jones, special effects. Stunts: Chick Bernhardt, stunt double; Camera and Electrical Department: Bert Bertolami, best boy grip; Jerry Bertolami, dolly grip; Thomas Cocheo, rigging grip; Robert De Stolfe, still photographer; Robert Heine, second assistant camera; Edward Knott III, key grip; Ross Maehl, chief lighting technician; William McConnell, first assistant camera; Jonathan McGowan, first assistant camera; Michael McGowan, camera operator; Robert Ulland, Steadicam operator; Robert Ulland, second assistant camera; Phil Walker, rigging lighting technician. Casting Department: Deborah Aquila, casting assistant; Enid Howell, extra casting. Costume and Wardrobe Department: Linda Benedict, wardrobe assistant; Mary Lou Byrd, wardrobe supervisor; Vivian Cocheo, wardrobe supervisor — men. Editorial Department: Timothy Alverson, assistant editor; Gaston Santiso, apprentice editor; Jonathan Shaw, assistant editor; Penelope Shaw, assistant editor. Music Department: Jack Eskew, orchestrator; Stephen A. Hope, music editor; Dan Wallin, music scoring mixer. Transportation Department: Huey Laborde, transportation captain; William Rogers, transportation coordinator. Miscellaneous Crew: Jean Bass, first aid; Mark Bass, production assistant; Helen Caldwell, assistant — Peter Falk; Jan Foreman, assistant production auditor; Jack Cowden, script supervisor; Dan Curry, title designer; Susan Ekins, assistant — Jerry Weintraub; Pete Emmet, unit publicist; Jennifer Erskine, assistant — Jerry Weintraub; Joyce Fetherolf, assistant — John G. Avildsen; Luke Halpin, marine coordinator; Joel Hatch, production assistant; Rob Kobrin, assistant — John G. Avildsen; Kip Langello, production assistant; Carol Lees, production associate; Daniel Malmuth, assistant — John G. Avildsen; Margaret A. Mitchell, production auditor; Bruce Pflueger, production assistant; Chuck Porretto, production assistant; Bill Randall, production assistant; Celia Randolph, assistant production coordinator; Charles Ruban, assistant location manager; Douglas Seelig, assistant — John G. Avildsen; Jeffrey Stacey, location manager; Cyndy Streit, production coordinator; Marcia

Tangen, first aid; Sherry Thorup, assistant location manager; Harry Winston, jewels. Production Companies: Columbia Pictures Corporation; Delphi IV Productions. Distributors: Columbia Pictures (19.87) (USA) (theatrical). RCA/Columbia Pictures Home Video (1987) (USA) (VHS).

Cast — in credits order: Peter Falk, Nick; Charles Durning, Charlie; Claude Lelouch, Man on Train; Gary Maas, Fence; Jack Hrkach, Bellboy; Tom Courtenay, Edward Saunders; Earleen Carey, Winston Sales Girl; Debbie Garrett, Winston Sales Girl; Karina Etcheverry, Winston Sales Girl; Ted Bartsch, Doorman; Wendy Hughes, Carolyn; Tracy Brooks Swope, Nina; Joan Copeland, Sunny Felix; Cloyce Morrow, Dinner Guest; Anthony Heald, Dinner Guest; Peter Sellars, Dinner Guest; Daniel Gerroll, Curator; Bruce Malmuth, Police Lieutenant; Gary Richardson, Sargeant; D.L. Blakely, Guard; Clarence Thomas, Warden; Pinky Pincus, Joe; Gary Cox, Young Con; Yoshiko Minami, Oriental Housekeeper; Dian Piccolo, Julie; Ray Jason, Young Con's Father; Jackie Davis, Cabbie #1; Fritz Bronner, Steve; Reuben Rabasa, Maitre D'; Richard Street, Temptation; Ron Tyson, Temptation; Otis Williams, Temptation; Ali Woodson, Temptation; David English, Temptation; Sal Carollo, Frankie G.; Don Kalpakis, Bartender; Bruce Kirby, Taxi Driver; Ellen Simmons, Proprietress; Dan Fitzgerald, Airline Ticket Clerk. Other credited cast listed alphabetically: Steven Elwell, Baritone Sax Player on Corner.

CHAPTER 17

For Keeps

By the end of the 1980s, Avildsen had proven himself in step with yet another decade's worth of cinematic zeitgeist. He had directed one of the 1980s' biggest hits, *The Karate Kid*, and successfully expanded it into a franchise. He directed a star vehicle for two of the 1980s' biggest comedic talents (Dan Aykroyd and John Belushi in *Neighbors*) and tackled cultural trends like male strip clubs (*A Night in Heaven*), and was soon to confront the pressing social issue of inner-city school failure (*Lean on Me*). So it seemed fitting that at least one of his '80s films would star a member of the so-called "Brat Pack" — the decade's reigning collective of young actors, which included, among others, Molly Ringwald, Emilio Estevez, Judd Nelson, and Andrew McCarthy (who were experiencing, as they transitioned awkwardly into adult roles, their own stardom wind-downs coincidental to the decade's close). Avildsen had already worked with Ralph Macchio, considered a peripheral Brat Packer. But in *For Keeps*, he got to work with the "queen of the teens," Molly Ringwald.

In reality, the motivations behind making the film and working with Ringwald doesn't fit any film historian's desire to package a director's oeuvre neatly into decades. As Avildsen explained in an interview with John Andrew Gallagher:

> The opportunity to do a love story [is what attracted me to *For Keeps*]. I always liked Molly Ringwald. The story itself seemed to be about something that's unusual. I had to do something because there was going to be a cut-off period when people stopped making movies in anticipation of the Directors Guild strike that never happened. So those were the factors.[1]

Ringwald, who had just begun moving away from high-school comedies with 1987's *The Pick-Up Artist*, was attracted to the project mainly because of the material, which centers on an unplanned pregnancy between two teen unmarrieds: "I thought that it dealt with the subject in a very interesting way, with a lot of humor, with a lot of romance, but still managed to paint a realistic picture," she said.[2]

It was reportedly a story idea that began with producer-writer Jerry Belson (*The Odd Couple, The Dick Van Dyke Show*), who didn't have time to draft it up as a script. So the team of Tim Kazurinsky and Denise DeClue, who had just had a hit with the Brat Pack film *About Last Night,* were hired to create a screenplay. Kazurinsky had been a writer and performer both with Chicago's Second City and on *Saturday Night Live,* and he had previously worked with Avildsen as an actor on *Neighbors* (in a small part, at John Belushi's insistence). DeClue and Kazurinsky began researching teen pregnancy, which included article-reading and the interviewing of teen moms. The writing duo invariably heard, "I never thought it would happen to me."[3]

Shooting took place in late spring and early summer of 1987 under the working title *Maybe Baby.* Other locations — Winnipeg according to the Internet, and Monrovia and Pasadena, California, according to one review[4] — doubled as the film's main setting of Kenosha, Wisconsin. The scenes set at the University of Wisconsin were actually shot there.

Also starring was unknown actor Randall Batinkoff, who plays *For Keeps'* male lead, Stan Bobrucz. Stan, a high school senior bound for CalTech's architecture program (on a full scholarship), is fully supportive of girlfriend Darcy Elliot's (Ringwald) ambitions in journalism. She plans on attending the University of Wisconsin. With some wool pulled over their respective parents' eyes, the couple even manages a weekend getaway to the University of Wisconsin, and that's when their trouble begins.

In a sequence that features footage of spermatozoa swimming into ova for the miraculous act of fertilization, we realize that Darcy has been impregnated by Stan (most of the story's set-up occurred in a prologue sequence). This micro-photography in the opening credits seemed to catch the ire of almost every critic, as it seemed to strike an awkward jokiness in *For Keeps* that got the subject matter off to a less-than-serious start. Thus Armstrong wrote:

> *For Keeps* cannot shake its very strange tone. It's not often, for example, that a mainstream movie gives you a visual ride up the vaginal canal, and follows that up with microscopic evidence of conception. *For Keeps* does it just for chuckles under the opening titles.[5]

Similarly, Healy wrote:

> We in the audience have already seen the sperm swimming vigorously to its meeting with the ovum during the film's credits.... Those of us who saw John Avildsen's other film *Rocky* might recall the boxer running ecstatically up the steps to leap about in triumph at the top. Such memories should be suppressed in the interest of keeping a straight face while witnessing the miracle of life.[6]

Avildsen said the sequence was never intended to be humorous. In fact, the sperm sequence was the only scene not shot specifically for the movie. That scene was purchased from *Nova*, the PBS documentary series. Avildsen considered the footage "something of a find." It marked the first time that such a scene was used in the movies.

For Keeps proceeds from this credits sequence with a continued mix of drama and humor. Stan and Darcy reveal the pregnancy to their families during Thanksgiving dinner ("I'm pregnant. Can you pass the turnips?"), and Darcy's single mom (Mirian Flynn)immediately advocates abortion. Darcy's mother is given the backstory of having been abandoned by Darcy's father, so that informs her outlook. Stan's parents (Kenneth Mars, Conchata Ferrell) are part of the "family values" set that advises having the child and then giving it up for adoption.

The birth of the baby marked another cinematic milestone. The scene was an actual childbirth filmed as it happened. An employee at Columbia was pregnant, and her child was due while the film was being shot. The producers obtained permission to film the birth from her, her doctor, and the hospital. One room at the hospital was designated for the shoot, and a dolly set-up was in place prior to birth. Once the birth became imminent, the crew rushed to the hospital and captured the event on film.

Neither side wants the kids to keep the baby, and Stan's working-class

Miriam Flynn, Molly Ringwald and Kenneth Mars in *For Keeps* (1988).

father eloquently assesses his son's parenting readiness: "You had a gerbil last year, you forgot to feed it, it died."

When Darcy and Stan decide to keep the child, they are cut off financially and cease contact with their folks. They rent a slummy apartment and get married in a ceremony their parents don't attend.

From this point, the complications mount for the young family: hospital bills, post-partum depression, night school, cut-off utilities, and difficult manual labor (tarring roofs — a "real shit job," as Stan puts it). The teen father's transformation from promising architect (who hides his CalTech scholarship confirmation from Darcy) to boozing, angry blue-collar family man is presented gradually, and with great realism — thanks to the script, Avildsen's direction, and Batinkoff's performance. This metamorphosis is one of the film's strongest points.

At this point in the story, some critics noted that Avildsen was in familiar "underdog" territory: "Once the 'issues' have been swept away, director Avildsen can get down to his real agenda: *For Keeps* turns into a conventional 'go-for-it' movie, much in the manner of Avildsen's *Rocky* and *The Karate Kid*, designed to communicate the joy of triumph over unimaginable odds."[7] Another derided, "Apparently, he thought he was making *The Kenosha Kids*."[8]

In an interview with *The Forerunner*, the director seemed to inadvertently confirm this "patented Avildsen approach" to the material, telling the publication's staff that the script was attractive because it concerned two teens' relationship in the face of obstacles that threaten to tear them apart. He added, "You want them to work out their problems and stay together."[9]

When Darcy learns that Stan passed up the CalTech scholarship because the college had no married housing, she selflessly divorces her husband to free him from his family obligations. Stan, in turn, selflessly reconfigures his college career so that both he and Darcy can attend the local college and take advantage of their full scholarships, married housing and child-care co-ops. This provides a convenient (er, too convenient, perhaps) escape route for the young family.

Avildsen edited the film in New York instead of Los Angeles, because of a union rule in the L.A. local that didn't allow editors to hold any other title on the movie. Avildsen had actually applied for the editor's union membership in L.A. and was declined on those grounds. He later recalled:

> I think they're afraid all the directors will cut their own pictures. I don't think that's a concern that has any reality. It's not that it's so difficult, but I think most directors don't want to bother, and they're used to working with an editor and often have one they enjoy working with. I always did it myself because I started that way, and also figure that no one will stay up as late as I will covering my blunders. The cutting process is the last chance to save the movie, so I've always done it myself.[10]

The film was released to mixed reviews, and sometimes a message was perceived in the film. The Christian publication *The Forerunner* embraced *For Keeps* for its supposedly "strong pro-life message." *Morning Call* critic Paul Willistein thought it intentionally baited pro-choice groups and cheered anti-abortionists.[11]

Other critics didn't seem to infer any advocacy out of the film, and neither did Ringwald: "I don't consider it an anti-abortion film or a pro-life film in any way at all. I think it's about two kids who make a choice. Whether it's the right choice remains to be seen. These kids have no money, and they've lost a lot. They've grown up so much in one year, a crash course in life — too much for any kid, really."[12]

Ringwald had a point. Except for the unrealistically tidy and happy ending, the film portrays teen parenthood as tremendous toil and grief. Nonetheless, Illinois officials criticized the film upon its January release for glamorizing teen pregnancy. In March, it was announced that Ringwald would donate her time to record public-service radio announcements for the state's Parents Too Soon program, aimed at preventing teen motherhood.[13]

There was also a contingent of critics who seemed to resent *any* humor in the movie at all. One wrote, "Frankly, there's nothing funny about teen pregnancy,"[14] while the headline of another announced, "movie makes light of serious teen subject."[15] These were typically the reviewers who took exception to the tone set by the credits sequence.

No matter the critical reaction, there was a certain relevance to the film. It was mentioned in two *New York Times* cultural trend pieces ("Teen-Age Sex: New Codes Amid the Old Anxiety" and "Film View: '80s Movies Take the Easy Route"). And Avildsen's film was part of a subgenre of baby movies popular at the time, like *Baby Boom* and *Three Men and a Baby* (both 1987). Even Ringwald's frequent director, John Hughes, was making a competing film, *She's Having a Baby*, which opened the month after *For Keeps*.

Although Avildsen was now in his fifties, the director was continuing to be highly relevant.

Production Notes

Directed by: John G. Avildsen. Writers: Denise DeClue, Tim Kazurinsky. Producers: Jerry Belson, producer; William Cassidy, associate producer; Walter Coblenz, producer; Cindy Pierson, associate producer; Douglas Seelig, associate producer. Original Music: Bill Conti. Cinematographer: James Crabe. Editor: John G. Avildsen. Production Designer: William J. Cassidy. Set Decorator: Richard Goddard. Costume Designer: Colleen Atwood. Make Up Department: Susan Germaine, key hair stylist; Robert Jiras, key makeup artist; Tom Lucas, makeup artist; Allen Payne, hair stylist. Production Managers: Jack Terry, unit production manager; Ted Zachary, executive in charge of production (uncredited). Second Unit Directors or Assistant Directors: Alice Blanchard, second assistant director; Kalai Strode, second assistant director; Ron L. Wright, first assistant director. Art Department: Ronnie Chambers, lead man; Bernard Cutler, set designer; Bob Denne, paint foreman; Philip Hurst, greensman; Fred Paulsen, swing gang; Paul Rylander, assistant property master; John Schacht, lead man; Terry Lynn Shugrue, assistant property master; Steven Westlund, property master; Don Winter, construction coordinator. Sound Department: Marko A. Costanzo, foley artist; Lee Dichter, sound re-recording mixer; Ken Eluto, assistant sound editor; Kirk Francis, sound mixer; Chris Houghton, apprentice sound editor; Neil Kaufman, sound editor; Hudson B. Marquez, cable person; Jack M. Nietzsche, Jr., boom operator; Rose Rosenblatt, assistant adr editor; Dan Sable, supervising sound editor; Lynn Sable, assistant sound editor; Ann Stein, adr editor. Special Effects Department: Bob Stoker, Jr., special effects; Jerry D. Williams, special effects supervisor. Camera and Electrical Department: Debbie Arrowood, camera loader; Michael A. Benson, camera operator; Brad Edmiston, first assistant camera; Ron Grover, still photographer; Frank J. Keever, key grip; Bill Kenney, dolly grip; Ross A. Maehl, gaffer; Randy Nolen, Steadicam operator; Andy Padilla, best boy grip; Aaron Pazanti, first assistant camera; Warren Roth, video assistant; Bob Samuels, second assistant camera; Jim Thibo, camera loader; Paul Threlkeld, dolly grip; Philip D. Walker, best boy electric. Casting Department: Bess Gilbert, extras casting; Pat McCorkle, casting — New York; Tomorrow Michaels, extras casting assistant. Costume and Wardrobe Department: Robert Chase and Anthony J. Scarano, costume supervisors — men; Maritza L. Garcia, costume supervisor — women. Editorial Department: Scott Arundale, William Joseph Kruzykowski, James H. Nau, Jerry C. Rogers, Mitchel Stanley, assistant editors; Debra C. Victoroff, apprentice editor; Susan Sklar Friedman, apprentice editor (uncredited). Music Department: Stephen A. Hope, music consultant. Transportation Department: Fritz Braden, transportation coordinator; Mike Padovich, transportation captain. Miscellaneous Crew: Anthony Avildsen, production assistant; Frawley Becker, location manager; Bee Beckman, production secretary; Larry Bibi, production assistant; Brian Brosnan, location manager; Mary Connor, assistant — Mr. Avildsen; Keith Crossley, assistant — Mr. Avildsen; Joyce Wilson Fetherolf, assistant — John G. Avildsen; Sonny Filippini, script supervisor; Lawrence Greenberg, production assistant; Mark Hatfield, production assistant; Robin Hinz, production coordinator; Lynette Katselas, dialogue coach; Sharon Langley, accounting clerk; Toni St. Clair Lilly, assistant — Mr. Coblenz; Evan Malmuth, production assistant; Marila Meggett, assistant production accountant; Gloria Milone, assistant — Mr. Belson; Susan Murray, first aid; Cynthia Quan, production accountant; Yvonne Ramond, assistant — Mr. Coblenz; Reid Rosefelt, unit publicist; David Salven, Jr., location manager; Mike Sexton, production assistant; Andy Spilkoman, production assistant; Linn Zuckerman, craft service. Thanks: Tracy Swope Avildsen, Sandra Jansen, Anne Klein, Annette Lowrie, Mark Lowrie, Cliff Notes, Ed Orshan. Filming Locations: Madison, Wisconsin, USA; Winnipeg, Manitoba, Canada. Production Companies: ML Delphi Premier Productions; TriStar Pictures. Distributor: TriStar Pictures.

Cast — in credits order: Molly Ringwald, Darcy Elliot Bobrucz; Randall Batinkoff, Stan Bobrucz; Kenneth Mars, Mr. Bobrucz; Miriam Flynn, Donna Elliot; Conchata Ferrell, Mrs. Bobrucz; Sharon Brown, Lila; John Zarchen, Chris; Pauly Shore, Retro; Michelle Downey, Michaela; Patricia Barry, Adoption Official; Janet MacLachlan, Miss Giles; Jaclyn Bernstein, Mary Bobrucz; Matthew Licht, Lou Bobrucz; Renée Estevez, Marnie; Darcy DeMoss, Elaine; Leslie Bega, Carlita; Helen Siff, Landlady; Anne Curry, Push Nurse; John DiSanti, Mr. Kolby; Robert Nadder, Night School Teacher; Shane McCabe, Amorous Porker; Jack Ong, Reverend Kim; Sean Frye, Wee Willy; Allison Roth, Ambrosia; Trevor Edmond, Ace; Patricia Patts, Desdemona; Brandon Douglas, Trapper; Kimberly Bailey, Baby Cakes; Darnell Rose, Erin; J.W. Fails, High Flyer; Monika Khoury, Angel; Kelly

McMahan, Pediatric Nurse; Candy Peak, Nurse; Robert Ruth, Prom Photographer; Dr. Barry Herman, Doctor; Jeff Marshall, Michaela's Boyfriend; Peggy Walton-Walker, Bookkeeper; Bonnie Hellman, Mrs. Sitwell; Larry Drake, Night Clerk; Robin Morse, Beth; Steve Eckholdt, Ronald; Marty Zagon, Manager of Quickie Nickie's; Annie Oringer, Anastasia; Pamela Harris, Beverly; Hailey Ellen Agnew, Baby Thea; Rae Worland, Student; David De Lange, Uniformed Official; Roger Hampton, Roofer; Tino Insana, Capt. O'Connell; Steven Barr, Sgt. Blaine. Other credited cast listed alphabetically: Nancy Abramson, Nurse; Sandra Jansen, Nurse.

CHAPTER 18

Lean on Me

Good Guys Don't Always Win

In 1988, New York theatrical producer Norman Twain saw an NBC News report on Joe Clark, the high school principal of Eastside High School in Paterson, New Jersey. By then, "Crazy Joe" (as he was known in some circles) had been making headlines along the East Coast for his "tough love" approach to public education. Clark walked the halls of Eastside High with a bullhorn and a baseball bat, sometimes encouraging his students to do better or bullying them when they failed.

Somewhat surprisingly to his critics, Clark's unorthodox style seemed to work. Twain, believing he knew a good story when he saw, drove to Paterson and signed a deal for the movie rights to his story. Michael Schiffer was signed to write the screenplay, and Twain sent an early draft to Avildsen along with a video of Clark speaking at Eastside's graduation.

The tape convinced Avildsen to take the job. "I was hooked because he was such a charismatic character," he said.

Avildsen traveled to Paterson to become more familiar with his subject. "I hung out at Eastside quite a bit," Avildsen said. "I got to know Joe, who was really an inspiring teacher, and what he was doing with those kids was terrific. He'd walk down the halls and would toss 25-cent words at the kids, and they'd have to define them. It was really inspiring. The kids loved him."

But it would take the right actor to translate that charisma to the screen. Avildsen chose Morgan Freeman, who had recently been nominated for an Oscar for his performance in *Street Smart*. "I met Morgan Freeman and had recently seen *Street Smart*," Avildsen said. "I was totally blown away with his performance, and I thought he would be the perfect actor to play Joe Clark."

Twain also liked Freeman for the role. His first choice was apparently Sidney Poitier, but Poitier turned it down — reportedly because he disagreed with Clark's political ideology. Twain had also considered approaching Bill Cosby, Eddie Murphy, and Danny Glover about the film. Twain later said, "I never thought of anyone to play him but Morgan Freeman."[1]

"Morgan Freeman is an absolute gem," Avildsen added. "He's a gentleman, a consummate actor, a very bright man. I was fortunate to have him as the actor. I did a subsequent picture with him, *The Power of One*, in Africa. He has no ego, no attitude. He's there to do the job, he listens, he has great ideas. He's a really nice person."

Joe Clark didn't really know who Freeman was, but he also approved, saying, "My youngest daughter had seen him on *Sesame Street* and liked him."[2]

At the time, Freeman had gained industry respect for his award-winning stage role in *Driving Miss Daisy*. He had also been nominated for an Academy Award and a Golden Globe for his performance in *Street Smart*. He had just completed another film for Warners, *Clean and Sober*, so Twain knew he was available.

Much of the movie was shot on location at Eastside High, despite the production company's objection. "They didn't want to shoot there for some reason I couldn't understand," Avildsen said. "I spent a lot of time looking at schools all over New York and other places. Finally, I told them, 'Nothing's going to be good. Why go anywhere else besides the place where it's happening, and they'll have us.' They finally saw the wisdom of that, and that's where we shot it."

Eastside also had the mood. "Joe was always there to keep us on course," Avildsen said. "School was going on while we were making the movie, and Joe was speaking over the loudspeaker and carrying on with his bullhorn. Occasionally we'd run into him in the halls, so Morgan was constantly being inspired by the real guy. It was a joy."

It also worked out well for Freeman, who could learn more about his character on a daily basis. "That's how I shaped my character," Freeman said. "I shaped it around Joe himself."

Freeman admitted that he shared much of Clark's philosophy. "You have to have discipline at school," he said. "Once you lose it, you've lost the whole ballgame. And that's why, on the job, Joe's a tyrant."[3]

When he needed a boost, Freeman said he would simply go to Clark and hold his hand. "Joe Clark has a lot of power and energy," Freeman said. "He came to work geared for the day. By nature, I'm a little more laid back than that. To get that kind of energy that Joe works through the day with, I would go and hold his hand and talk to him."

Freeman credited Avildsen for letting him approach the role in that manner. "I will give John credit in his ability to do that. We had to discuss it early on. But he did give me that latitude."

Lean on Me (1989). Morgan Freeman (as Principal Joe Clark), and the real Joe Clark.

Freeman also noted that Clark "understood the importance of hard work, a proper behavior, of a supportive environment that is conducive to learning. So I did not have to articulate too much. I could just tell from the expression on his face that he had an incredible degree of understanding of what he was about."[4]

While Freeman studied his character, Avildsen focused on translating the script to screen while filming in the hot New Jersey summer. "My vision was the script which Michael Schiffer wrote and what an inspiring character Joe Clark was," Avildsen said. "That was my vision, to tell Joe Clark's story in an emotionally moving, entertaining way."

"School was in session while we were shooting, so he was there all the time," Avildsen said. "He was a pleasure and never got in the way. He was a source of inspiration for Morgan Freeman. He was terrific and very hospitable and made it very easy for us."

Still, Freeman said that Clark's presence on the set added to the pressure on him to perform well. "Because when you don't get it right, you can't convince yourself that this will slide by," he said. "If you're going to play John Adams or Abraham Lincoln, or somebody dead like that, who knows?"[5]

Avildsen lining up a shot in *Lean on Me* (1989).

Despite his proximity to the set, Clark never made it on-screen in the film. "He looked a lot like Morgan," Avildsen said. "If we'd put him in there, we would have had to write in that he had a twin brother. A couple of members of the school board, the actual school board, were in the movie though, but that's all."

While Clark was a real person, the script developed to tell his story was fiction. "I'm sure Joe got payment for his story," Avildsen said. "I don't know how much it was, but he probably also had to sign an agreement that upon accepting the money, that was the end of the dialogue. He couldn't approve the script. The studios are reluctant to make a deal with you where you have approval, because then you've got too much power. When you make a deal with the devil, you sell your soul. Just hope you get the right devil. And Joe was very pleased with it."

Maybe, but he was also suspicious. Universal Studios had purchased the rights to his story five years before Twain approached him about a deal for Warner Bros. He remained skeptical during the filming process. "I'd become accustomed to promises being made and declarations declared and ultimately nothing emanating from it," he said. "So I said to myself pessimistically that nothing will ever come of this new attempt either.... Only when I saw the cameras in the building with John Avildsen, Morgan Freeman and everybody else, did I say, 'Yes, a movie is really being made.'"[6]

This time it did come together, even if it was a work of fiction. Clark approved, despite the fictional approach, "Because I go by instinct. And because I believed in Norman Twain's honesty and integrity, and because I had a very good rapport with the writer and the director."[7]

His faith in Twain came from a pre-production promise that "nothing in the picture would be untrue without his approval," while everything that was true, "even if it embarrassed him, had to stay."[8]

Avildsen made some changes in Schiffer's original script. "Before you shoot the script, you usually noodle with it a lot," he said. "We personalized the kids a bit more, got some of the kids' back stories going more. We tried to give each of them more of a sense of character so that you could get a little bit more of a glimpse into them." Some of the changes were based on real incidents.[9]

When Avildsen started shooting, he used a detailed storyboard similar to the ones that had irritated Burt Reynolds so much in *W.W. and the Dixie Dancekings*. Instead of drawings, though, he used a video camera to establish his shot sequence:

> I would rehearse the movie at the school with a little video camera. Then I would cut that together and see if I liked it and make storyboards from the video so that everybody would know what we were going to do that partic-

ular day *vis a vis* the ten different scenes that we had to do. We had to do this before lunch, and this after lunch, and we get the sunset, etc., so that by the time I came to do it, it was pretty well organized on the page and in my head what we were going to do.

Victor Hammer handled the cinematography duties, the first of several films in which he worked with Avildsen. Avildsen's previous cameraman, James Crabe, died in 1989 after the completion of *For Keeps*. Hammer would later work with Avildsen on *Rocky V, 8 Seconds* and other projects.

The film opens in the 1960s with Clark as a teacher at Eastside High. After a run-in with his principal, he gets transferred. The story picks up twenty years later with Clark teaching in another public school, a neat, well-run one in a nice neighborhood.

Those same twenty years had not been good to Eastside High. Clark's forming stamping grounds is now a troubled inner-city school with a large minority student body. Students attend school amid an atmosphere of violence and drug deals. Not surprisingly, they don't learn much.

Clark is hired to clean up the situation, and he moves quickly. First, he calls a school-wide assembly in which he expels the known drug users and troublemakers. Second, he arms himself with a baseball bat and bullhorn and patrols the school's hallways. A few other reforms are tossed in — painting over graffiti, teaching the students the school song, and trying to instill some pride in learning. He makes some progress, but along the way he alienates almost as many people as he helps.

Among his enemies are the local school board and some of the teachers, all of whom object to his roughshod treatment of them. These people eventually band together, forming a coalition that tries to push him out of power.

Clark's only chance of staying in control is to show some real results, i.e., a passing grade for the school on the state's standardized test. As test time approaches, he lets teachers teach the material while he focuses on motivation — convincing the students they're smart enough to do well.

The showdown comes in a nighttime meeting of the school board, which convenes to fire the controversial principal. Meanwhile, the students organize and march on the meeting to protest the planned dismissal. As tensions build, and Clark confronts the crowd to urge them to go home, the test results arrive. The school has passed the test. Clark gets to keep his job.

During the entire process, Clark (as played by Freeman) remains the center of attention. Most critics focused on that performance while denigrating other aspects of the movie. Roger Ebert said Freeman was "riveting in the central role, making up for the script's shortcomings and Avildsen's all-too-familiar approach."[10] Another wrote, "Freeman gives a vigorous performance as a controversial New Jersey high school principal who cleans up his school and wins the hearts of his students in this formulaic but energetic and engaging version of a true story."

But Freeman's strong portrayal also brought criticism of the character he depicted. Ebert chastised the film for two scenes, one in which Clark suspended a teacher for stooping to pick up a scrap of paper while he was talking and another in which he insults a teacher in front of students. Ebert described the film version of Clark as someone who "behaves in an erratic and irrational way, and conducts himself like an autocratic dictator." Thus while praising Freeman's performance, he criticizes its impact; it is, he says, "a performance that is powerful and consistent and thus all the more troubling. Although he has taught in schools for more than twenty years, he has never really fit in anywhere. He has an unshakable belief in his own opinions, no interest in anyone else's, and a personality so abrasive it's no wonder his wife left him and he has only one friend. As an administrator, he shoots first and doesn't ask questions afterwards: He's sort of the Dirty Harry of the Paterson, N.J., educational system."[11]

Clark, Ebert said, was portrayed as a "character who is so troubled, obsessed, and angry that the film is never able to say quite what it thinks of him." He continues:

> As the movie progresses, we wait for Joe Clark to undergo a personality change, to soften, to grow, to start learning to respect the right of other people to have an opinion. But with the exception of one half-hearted apology, Clark never does change. He is an arrogant bully, a martinet who demands instant, unquestioning obedience. Yes, he does clean up Eastside High. And, yes, the students are able to pass a state proficiency exam, so that the school can remain under local control and not be taken over by the state. But we never see how this is done.[12]

Ebert also criticized Avildsen, writing that the director was "so concerned to show us the hell of Eastside High that he goes overboard; the corridors look like a cross between a prison riot and a Hell's Angels rally."[13] He continued,

> The movie's most bizarre scene has Clark onstage at a pre-exam pep rally, ranting and raving and leading the school song, as if the test were a football game. But you can't pass a test simply because your spirits are high. And I am not convinced that any kind of meaningful learning can take place under the reign of public humiliation enforced by Clark. Discipline is not the same thing as intimidation.[14]

Richard Schickel noted that the thesis of the movie rested in Norman Mailer's observation that tough guys are often decent guys at heart. "Since John Avildsen, is obviously not attracted to depressing subjects, you know up front that *Lean on Me* will lean heavily on Mailer's theorem in telling the Joe Clark story," Schickel wrote.[15] Ultimately, Schickel argued, the approach dooms the film. "After the cheers die and the tears dry comes the realization that *Lean on Me* is serving up empty emotional calories. They don't leave you sick, just hungry for an honest meal."[16]

Similarly, Ebert wrote, "*Lean on Me* wants to be taken as a serious, even noble, film about an admirable man. And yet it never honestly looks at Joe Clark for what he really is — a grown-up example of the very troublemakers he hates so much, still unable even in adulthood to doubt his right to do what he wants, when he wants, as he wants. How can he teach when he's unteachable? His values have little to do with learning how to learn."[17]

Ebert's criticism continued:

> Is it true that tough schools need mad-dog teachers? One of the sneaky, uneasy feelings I got while watching *Lean on Me* is that the movie makes a subtle appeal to those who are afraid of unruly, loud, violent, black teenagers. As Joe Clark takes a baseball bat and begins to whip them into shape (at one point even physically fighting a student), the audience is cheered, not because education is being served, but because Clark is a combination of Dirty Harry and Billy Jack, enforcing the law on his own terms.[18]

Despite the criticism, Avildsen has fond memories of the film:

> This movie has a minimal amount of regrets, or things you'd like to change. They're never finished. At certain points, they take it away from you. You could always do more. You could always make it a little shorter, make it a little better, use a different music cue. But at a certain point the people who finance them say, "Okay, time's up. That's it. Next." But in this case, there were very few of those.
>
> It's easier to know who the good guys and the bad guys are. In our lives, we're always trying to psych things out in those terms, but often in reality it's not so clear. The supposed bad guy may have a good reason. And the good guy may have a different agenda, and maybe he isn't so good. Who's the good guy and who's the bad guy is a fascinating story, but it also demands very good writing to tell a story like that. It's much easier to tell the good guy-bad guy story. I think that's a good idea for a one- or two-minute movie.

Critics were particular impressed with Freeman's work. Karney wrote that he "gave an impressive performance."[19] One YouTube reviewer wondered "why Morgan Freeman didn't win or was nominated for another Oscar," adding that his performance in *Lean on Me* "was just as superb as *Driving Miss Daisy.*" [20]

Avildsen praised the work of cast member Beverly Todd, who played Clark's main opposer, Ms. Levias. "Beverly was a very gracious lady and not at all strident like this gal that she played," Avildsen said. "That's the marvelous things about actors. They pretend so successfully we think that they are who they play. But that happens to me, too. I'll see a movie and I'll forget. If the actor's really good, you'll forget that they're acting and figure that the actor is just a crumb instead of playing a crumb."

Avildsen disagrees with those who compare the film to his Oscar winner. "I don't think Rocky and Joe Clark are the same person," Avildsen said. "They both have an uphill battle, and they both triumph. But to say they're both the same person is giving Rocky a lot of credit."

But the underdog theme is dominant in both, something Avildsen admits. "That's one of the things we tried to reinforce in the script. Certainly the two stories are about overcoming adversity, which isn't a new idea. It's been around a long time."

Not surprisingly, the movie was a box-office disappointment. It was hindered, apparently, by the problems of marketing an essentially black movie to a broader audience.[21] Some of the critics didn't like it either. Jon Young, for example, said that Freeman "brings bravado to his role . . , but the film, is shallow, simpleminded, and depressing."[22] Hyman said it was "inspiring but superficial," promoting "simplistic solutions."[23]

Avildsen's only disappointment is that it had little long-term social impact. "I wish I could tell you that the students in Newark saw the movie, became A students, and suddenly crime went down and everything was great. I haven't heard that," he said. "Hopefully it inspired some people."

He also noted that it did little to help Joe Clark either. "Joe Clark was being talked about as being Secretary of Education for a while," Avildsen said. "Then his enemies got jealous and they framed him. He was out in California doing a promotion for the movie, and some dance students showed up at Eastside High in scanty costumes and his enemies pointed the finger at him. He got into trouble and we lost a great educator. Now he's head of a mini-prison school for kids who've gotten into trouble in New Jersey.

"The same thing happened to Serpico. Serpico was a good cop who is driven out. And Joe is certainly the perfect person to be a principal, because of his rapport with the students and his passion. But I haven't heard that the movie caused the sun to come out."

Clark, though, still liked the film and Freeman's portrayal of him. "I wanted a true depiction of me," he said. "Now I admit some situations call for a Mother Teresa. But I'm more of a Dirty Harry kind of guy. So when I'm portrayed as being ornery, obdurate, rebellious, irascible and especially adversarial, it's absolutely right."

In many ways, it seems, Avildsen got this one right.

Production Notes

Directed by: John G. Avildsen. Writers (WGA): Written by: Michael Schiffer. Producers: John G. Avildsen, executive producer; Michael Schiffer, associate producer; Doug Seelig, associate producer; Norman Twain, producer. Original Music: Bill Conti. Cinematographer: Victor Hammer. Editors: John G. Avildsen, John Carter. Casting Directors: Mary Colquhoun, Stanley Soble. Production Designer: Doug Kraner. Art Director: Tim Galvin. Set Decorator: Caryl Heller. Costume Designer: Jennifer von Mayrhauser. Make Up Department: Annie M. DeMille, hair stylist; Toy Van Lierop, makeup department head. Production Managers: Joseph P. Kane, unit production manager. Second Unit Directors or Assistant Directors: Randy N. Barbee, Nelson Cabrera and Joseph Ray, second assistant directors; Dwight Williams, first assistant director. Art Department: Carlos Quiles, construction coordinator; Jimmy Raitt, property master; John Michael Reefer, assistant property master; Manny Sanchez, carpenter; Dick Tice, lead man. Sound Department: Wayne Artman, sound re-recording mixer; Tom Beckert, sound re-recording mixer; Allan Byer, production sound mixer; Tom E. Dahl, sound re-recording mixer; Chris Jargo, dialogue editor; Elliott Koretz, sound editor; Kim Maitland, boom operator; Tom C. McCarthy, supervising sound editor; Terence J. O'Mara, boom operator; Troy Porter, adr mixer; Michael Stone, sound mixer; Bill Voigtlander, adr editor; Burton Weinstein, supervising sound editor; Glenn T. Morgan, assistant sound editor (uncredited). Stunts: John Cintron, Robert Figueroa, Mark Fischer, Sean Madjette, Mallie Moody, Craig Watson, Greg Wilson; Harry Madsen, stunt coordinator. Camera and Electrical Department: Bobby Brown, second assistant camera—"a" camera; Michael Burke, gaffer; Rusty Engels, best boy; Brian Fitzsimons, best boy; Dennis Gamiello, key grip; Alec Hirschfeld, camera operator; Marc Hirschfeld, first assistant camera; Michael L. Kiddon, first assistant camera; Anastas N. Michos, camera operator; Kathina Szeto, second assistant camera; Barry Wetcher, still photographer. Casting Department: Scott McKinley, casting assistant; Hedy Stempler, casting assistant (uncredited). Costume and Wardrobe Department: Andrea Ross, wardrobe supervisor. Editorial Department: Trevor Jolly, assistant editor; William Kruzykowski, assistant editor; Hope Moskowitz, assistant editor. Music Department: Brooks Arthur and Glen Ballard, music producers; George Craig and Stephen A. Hope, music editors; John Rotondi, scoring engineer— Y4; Dan Wallin, score mixer; Celia Weiner, music editor (uncredited). Transportation Department: Joseph Fanning, transportation coordinator. Miscellaneous Crew: Mary Fellows, production assistant; John Gregg, craft service; Ira Hurvitz, script supervisor; Solomon J. LeFlore, production financing; Dale M. Pierce, assistant production coordinator; Angela Salgado, key production assistant; Art Smith, Jr., location assistant; David Ticotin, location manager; David H. Venghaus, Jr., production assistant. Filming Locations: Paterson, New Jersey, USA; The Academy of the Most Blessed Sacrament, Franklin Lakes, New Jersey, USA (school where Joe Clark taught). Production Company: Warner Bros. Pictures. Distributors: Warner Bros. Pictures (1989) (USA) (theatrical); American Broadcasting Company (ABC) (1993) (USA) (TV) (broadcast premiere).

Cast—in credits order: Morgan Freeman, Principal Joe Clark; Beverly Todd, Ms. Levias; Robert Guillaume, Dr. Frank Napier; Alan North, Mayor Don Bottman; Lynne Thigpen, Leonna Barrett; Robin Bartlett, Mrs. Elliott; Michael Beach, Mr. Darnell; Ethan Phillips, Mr. Rosenberg; Sandra Reaves-Phillips, Mrs. Powers; Sloane Shelton, Mrs. Hamilton; Jermaine "Huggy" Hopkins, Thomas Sams; Karen Malina White, Kaneesha Carter; Karina Arroyave, Maria; Ivonne Coll, Mrs. Santos; Regina Taylor, Mrs. Carter; Michael P. Moran, Mr. O'Malley; John Ring, Fire Chief Gaines; Tyrone Jackson, Clarence; Alex Romaguera, Kid Ray; Tony Todd, Mr. William Wright; Mike Starr, Mr. Zirella; Michael Best, Stephen Capers, Jr., Dwayne Jones and Kenneth Kelly, The Eastside "Songbirds"; Yvette Hawkins, Mrs. Arthur; Nicole Quinn, Lillian; Elsie Hilario, Louisa; Michael

A. Joseph, Brian Banes; Richard Grusin, Mr. Danley; Jim Moody, Mr. Lott; Veniece Ross, Sally; Raffll Gonzffllez, Ramon; Luz Tolentino, Conchita; Andre Howell, Reggie; Nancy Gathers, Tanya; Corey Ginn, Charles Yale; Marina Durell, Miss Ruiz; Nathalee Fairmon, Nathalee; Hershel Slappy, Reverend Slappy; Todd Alexander, Derrick; Anthony Figueroa, Hoodlum at Microphone; Delilah Cotto, Chita; Frances Sousa, Francesca; Lynda La Vergne, Student; Robert Kamlot, Photographer; Linda M. Salgado, Linda; Markus Toure Boddie, Markus; Ashon Curvy, Ashon; Michael Imperioli, George; Marcella Lowery, Mrs. Richards; Jennifer McComb, Ellen; Knowl Johnson, Tommy; Anthony G. Avildsen, Anthony; Pat McNamara, Police Officer; Harry Madsen, Teacher in Cafeteria; Heather Rose Dominic, Stacey; Mario Biazzo, Student in Cafeteria; Kisean Blount, Girl in Cafeteria; Bruce Malmuth, Burger Joint Manager; Frank Firrito, Manuel Carneiro and Steve Adrianzen, White Boy/Singers. Other credited cast listed alphabetically: Steven Lee, Richard Armand. Rest of cast: Ahmed Best, Extra (uncredited); Monique Dupree, Student (uncredited); Steven Lezak, Man in Crowd/Fighter (uncredited); Gwyn English Nielsen, Background Teacher (uncredited); Gloria Sauve, Reporter (uncredited); Michelle L. Wease, Girl with Big Hair Under Clock Before Test (uncredited).

CHAPTER 19

The Karate Kid Part III

Sometimes there can be too much of a good thing. In the case of *The Karate Kid* series, you could start to see the wheels fall off with the third film. The formula was familiar — same cast, same producers, same writer and same director. It was just too familiar, adding dollars at the box office but little to the story. As Roger Ebert wrote in 1989, "The problem with most movie sequels is that they don't continue the original story, they repeat it."[1] That was the problem with *The Karate Kid Part III*. As Ebert added, "*The Karate Kid Part III* was made in 1989, but all of the original thinking on this movie took place five years ago."[2]

Actually, there was more original thinking about this movie. Avildsen's vision of *The Karate Kid Part III* was a retrospective look at Miyagi's ancestor, the original Mr. Miyagi who was a fisherman in the Okinawan village. Mr. Miyagi made a reference to his ancestor in *The Karate Kid Part II* when he tells Daniel the story.

Avildsen wanted to explore that connection by going back in time. The story he proposed has Miyagi and Daniel travel back in time to when the original Miyagi is out fishing. He drinks some strong sake and falls asleep. When he wakes up, he's off the coast of China. Ten years later, he returns to Okinawa and his Chinese wife, having learned karate while in China, and the Miyagi saga begins.

Coca-Cola, which owned a major share of Columbia Pictures at the time, liked the idea. Avildsen's plan called for the movie to be shot in China, and that fit with Coca-Cola's goal of expanding their market to China. But the idea was vetoed by the producer, who thought it would be too expensive. So, instead, "we made a boring remake of the first one," Avildsen said.

Ralph Macchio and Pat Morita returned as the dual leads, and Martin Kove reprised his role of the arrogant karate instructor John Kreese, but this time it was only a minor character. The newcomer was making his movie debut playing Kreese's friend from their Vietnam War days. Griffith took over

179

most of Kove's function, because Kove dropped out of a major role in the film so he could work on a pilot for a TV show. That turned out to be a mistake, since nothing ever came of the TV show.

Sean Kanan played Mike Barnes, aka the "bad boy of karate," Daniel's new opponent, and Robyn Lively played Jessica Andrews, Daniel's new girlfriend. The latter was necessary because Yukie, Daniel's soulmate in *The Karate Kid Part II*, had stayed behind in Okinawa when the dynamic duo returned to California.

Jerry Weintraub returned as the producer, but he had help this time from Doug Seeling, Karen Trudy Rosenfelt, and Sheldon Schrager. The script came from the typewriter of Robert Mark Kamen, who had also written the scripts for the first two entries in the series. Bill Conti, best known for his work on *Rocky*, handled the music score.

The setting is Los Angeles, about one year after the original movie, with Miyagi and Daniel returning from Okinawa. Much of the film was shot in the city. The home of villain Terry Silver is actually the Ennis-Brown House, a 1924 construction designed by Frank Lloyd Wright. The house has also appeared in the Vincent Price film *House on Haunted Hill* (1959) and several other movies (e.g., *The Day of the Locust*, 1975, and *Blade Runner*, 1982). Television fans might have spotted it in the *Buffy the Vampire Slayer* series.

Upon returning from Okinawa, Miyagi finds his job as a handyman is gone. Daniel steps up to help his mentor, using his college money to lease a building so Miyagi can open a bonsai tree shop.

Daniel decides not to defend his karate championship, preferring to work in the bonsai shop. He meets a girl, Jessica (Robyn Lively) in the pottery shop across the street, and friendship starts to blossom faster than the bonsai trees. There's the implication that a romance will also develop, although we later discover that was doomed because she already had a boyfriend.

The story returns to karate when Daniel has to defend his All-Valley Championship title. Let's just say that what happens is predictable.

The character with the real problem this time is John Kreese, the karate teacher played by Martin Kove. Kreese lost his karate school, Cobra Kai dojo, when it folded from lack of business after Daniel beat his star student. A new All-Valley Championship offers Kreese a chance to regain his standing in the karate community.

Meanwhile, Kreese finds an ally, Vietnam veteran Terry Silver (Thomas Ian Griffith). Silver is also *The Karate Kid Part III*'s new villain, a businessman whose company Dynatox Industries specializes in dumping toxic waste. Black wrote, "Silver's role is essentially to be evil and train Daniel to the point of physical and psychological pain."[3]

Ebert was disappointed with the new character: "Formula movies like this are only as good as their villains, and I would have liked to know more about the weirdness that glows in their eyes. But the movie doesn't care: They're not in the movie as characters, but as little pop-up cartoon characters to further the plot."[4]

Kreese and Terry map out their revenge on Daniel, stalking and harassing him until he finally signs up for the tournament. Daniel's new opponent is Mike Barnes (Sean Kanan). Barnes seems to be the toughest foe yet: He has the mentality to stoop to a variety of tactics to win and an arsenal of moves that are new to Daniel.

No problem. Daniel can simply call on old mentor Miyagi to get the extra training needed to be competitive. Right? Not really. Miyagi isn't interested. "Karate to defend life and honor means something," Miyagi says. "To defend a plastic trophy means nothing." Short of a trainer, Daniel looks for an alternative and finds Vietnam vet Terry, unaware of his ties to Kreese.

Naturally, things don't go well and Daniel eventually catches on to Terry's real intention. That's enough to bring Miyagi back into the plot and to set Daniel up with a new training location. Under Miyagi's tutelage, Daniel gets ready for the bout.

The championship opens with a show of false piety. Villain Silver starts the festivities with a speech about sportsmanship. Behind the scenes, though, he has developed an unscrupulous strategy for the contest: Barnes will hit Daniel with a legal blow to score a point, then follow that with an illegal blow to lose a point. That approach will allow Barnes to savagely beat Daniel, while keeping the score tied at 0–0. That tied score will require a "sudden death" round where Barnes can deliver a finishing move on Daniel.

Barnes follows orders, scoring a point and then kicking Daniel in the groin to revert the score to 0–0. He then scores another point with a blow to Daniel's ribs, but loses it by hitting Daniel after the round is over. He repeats that process for the rest of the bout, pounding Daniel while keeping the score tied. Daniel takes the punishment for a while, but eventually tells Miyagi that he wants to forfeit the match. Miyagi reminds Daniel to focus on his best moves. Really. That's the magical instruction in this movie: Concentrate.

Both of the earlier versions had a signature move that led to victory — the crane kick in the original film, and the drum technique in *The Karate Kid Part II*. In *The Karate Kid Part III*, the signature concept is focus or, in Miyagi's terms, "kata." And, not surprisingly, it works. When the combatants move into the sudden death round, Daniel gets in his only blow of the contest — first flipping Barnes and then punching him to the mat for the win. Kreese and Silver try to leave quickly, Daniel and Miyagi hug each other, and the Cobra Kai students in the audience take off their dojo shirts and throw them away. Ah, too bad. Looks like Kreese will lose his school after all.

The critics were not impressed. Leonard Maltin was the harshest, rating it a "bomb" and describing it as "an utterly stupid movie that was hopeless." Ebert wrote, "Avildsen and writer Robert Mark Kamen have exhausted themselves with these particular characters. It's time to move on."[5] Critic Paul Brenner simply described it as a "shopworn formula."[6] Adrienne Miller said the film was "so painfully bad — you can't look away."[7] Eyre described it as "possibly one of the worst films ever made," and added, "Use this DVD as a coaster, but don't waste your valuable time watching it."[8] Heckman said, "I can't believe that people actually liked this film."[9] Roger Bagula wrote, "After *Part II* this movie is kind of a mockery of the Karate Kid [and] it pretty much gave American Karate a bad name."[10] Eyre noted that the characters had become more stereotypical: "Kreese's character, which was very interesting in the first film, has been debased to scary B-movie proportions."[11] Weinberg added, "The best thing I can say about *Part III* is that it's a clear indication that *some* time and effort when into *Part II*."[12]

According to critic Ben Black, "*The Karate Kid Part III* is by far the worst in quality of the trilogy, but by far the most fun to watch. The best parts come from the corny lines and inane plot workings. Just have fun with this one — it's so bad it's great!"[13] Ebert also complained about the shift in themes that the movie had taken: "The first movie made at least a bow in the direction of a nonviolent philosophy. No more. This movie depends as much on a violent showdown as *Rocky*."[14]

Public response was a little more positive — particularly at the box office. The movie took in nearly $39 million in the United States and garnered another $19 million on the rental market. Audiences took the opportunity to relive the glory days of the series while Miyagi and Daniel work some of their familiar magic. This attitude was captured by one reviewer who wrote, "The acting could have been a bit less cartoonish in some parts from the two-dimensional bad guys, but it was the relationship between Miyagi and Daniel, and Daniel and his new female friend, which held the movie together. It comes together perfectly, for what it is, a *KK* movie."[15]

Still, most critics saw problems with the films. There were even editing mistakes, something rare for an Avildsen film. During the training sequence, two shots of "Bad Boy" Barnes breaking bricks with his hands are the same clips repeated. In another scene, Miyagi throws Barnes through the front door of the Cobra Kai. The camera angle is a little off, and viewers can see a blue table used by actor Sean Kanan to jump off and into the door. A similar problem occurred with a scene in the Cobra Kai when Daniel tries to kick a leg from under a wooden dummy. He can't break the solid wooden leg. Silver follows with his own kick that knocks breaks the dummy's leg, but a crack in the leg is clearly visible in the second scene before the kick. When Daniel goes to the Cobra Kai dojo to talk to Silver, the scene is set at night but daylight streams in from the shutters of the windows.

Ralph Macchio was beginning to get too old for the role (he was 27 when filming started). As Miller wrote, "Ralph Macchio looks so uninspired and he gained a lot of weight, poor kid."[16] Another reviewer wrote, "You get the feeling he doesn't know any real karate and you actually feel sorry for him being stuck in this awful plot and having to get beat up in the final match to keep his title."[17] Another noted that Daniel was "getting older but seldom wiser,"[18] while Ebert wrote, "Daniel (Ralph Macchio) is no longer an interesting kid, but simply a series of predictable attitudes."[19]

Still, *The Karate Kid* remains Macchio's signature role more than 20 years after he last played the character. Fans still identify him with the role, and he has learned to take pride it the identification. "Years ago I might have eye-rolled," he said. "But now I walk tall with it."[20]

The criticisms were not limited to Macchio. Miller wrote, "Pat Morita's deadpan expressions have always been funny but some of his magic is gone as well. The acting from those dumb karate teachers is so horrible and even Robyn Lively seems stiff."[21]

Others didn't even think it was fun to watch. Weinberg wrote, "There are only so many times we can see Daniel whimpering at the mistakes he's made while Miyagi stands around tossing out vague platitudes and wizened smiles.... [T]his time it all feels cynical and hollow, which is *not* the vibe we still get from Part 1."[22]

Ebert had a similar reaction: "I think I have the message by now. It was contained in *The Karate Kid* (1984), which was a wonderful movie, and then it was recycled in *The Karate Kid Part II.* Now we have *The Karate Kid Part III,* and still the message is the same. This material is wearing out its welcome."[23]

Some critics mistakenly assumed that *The Karate Kid Part III* was so bad that it would be the end of the series. In 2001, Haflidason wrote, "Any warmth of the previous two films is lost in this sequel, as the desperate continuation of the *Karate Kid* franchise shudders to a pathetic halt."[24] Not so fast, Sensei. *The Next Karate Kid* was waiting in the future. In fact, several incarnations of the series lay ahead. Hilary Swank had the title role in *The Next Karate Kid,* with Morita providing her the same mentoring style that he provided for Ralph Macchio in the original film.[25] That was followed by an animated series and a dud called *The Karate Dog* (2004) in which Morita spoofs his own role. The plot of the latter, as Griffin wrote, "finally killed poor Miyagi off. It was a mercy killing." Griffin added, "I suppose it's telling that Miyagi became such an engrained martial arts icon that he was ultimately spoofing himself, for better or for worse."[26]

By then, however, Avildsen was out of the picture. He dropped out of *The Next Karate Kid*, leaving the director chair open to Christopher Cain. Still, as Greydanus observed, "As with the *Rocky* films, the *Karate Kid* sequels increasingly went off the rails, and are thoroughly disposable; the original, though, is a keeper."[27]

That original film would be Avildsen's gift to the series.

Production Notes

Directed by: John G. Avildsen. Writers (WGA): Characters, Robert Mark Kamen; Written by, Robert Mark Kamen. Producers: Karen Trudy Rosenfelt, co-producer; Sheldon Schrager, executive producer;Douglas Seelig, associate producer; Jerry Weintraub, producer. Original Music: Bill Conti. Cinematographer: Stephen Yaconelli (director of photography). Editors: John G. Avildsen, John Carter Casting Director: Caro Jones. Production Designer: William F. Matthews. Art Director: Christopher Burian-Mohr. Set Decorator: Catherine Mann. Make Up Department: Del Acevedo, key makeup artist; Ron Berkeley, makeup artist; Shanon Ely, hair stylist; Cheri Ruff, key hair stylist. Production Managers: Lester Wm. Berke, unit production manager; Linda Landry-Nelson, production manager: Introvision. Second Unit Directors or Assistant Directors: Clifford C. Coleman, first assistant director; Hope R. Goodwin, second assistant director; David N. Schrager, second second assistant director. Art Department: Elijah Bryant, swing gang; Richard Evans, property assistant; Joseph C. Fama, construction foreman; Sam Gordon, property master; Dick Lasley, illustrator; Richard Leon, property assistant; Michael Muscarella, construction coordinator; Terry Shugrue, swing gang; Carl J. Stensel, set designer; Jerry Wax, lead man; Ronnie Sue Wexler, swing gang; Robert Wittenberg, construction painter. Sound Department: Eddie Becker, foley editor; William C. Carruth, adr editor; Don Digirolamo, sound re-recording mixer; Dean Drabin, foley mixer; Jack Dronsky, adr assistant; Susan Dudeck, foley editor; Robert Glass, sound re-recording mixer; Scott A. Hecker, supervising sound editor; Robert Knudson, sound re-recording mixer; Robert Mackston, dialogue editor; Dan O'Connell, foley artist; Kay Rose, adr editor; Victoria Rose Sampson, supervising adr editor; Clem Sheaffer, cable person; Mary Ruth Smith, adr editor; Alicia Stevenson, foley artist; Barry Thomas, sound mixer; Joel Valentine, sound effects editor; Forest Williams, boom operator. Special Effects Department: Dennis Dion, special effects foreman; Walter Dion, special effects. Visual Effects Department: John Coates, producer: visual effects; Gene Dobrzyn, production coordinator: visual effects; Tim Donahue, art director: visual effects; John P. Mesa, visual effects cameraman; Bill Mesa, director of visual effects; Andrew Naud, producer: visual effects; David Stump, camera: visual effects; Marcus Tate, producer: visual effects; Chris Dawson, model maker (uncredited); Stephen Lebed, model maker (uncredited). Stunts: Clarke Coleman, Fumio Demura, Thomas De Wier, Carol Neilson, Debby Lynn Ross, Tony Snegoff, Pat E. Johnson, stunts choreographer; Billy Morts, stunt rigger (uncredited). Camera and Electrical Department: Ronald Batzdorff, still photographer; Michael Benson, camera operator; Jeffrey R. Clark, first assistant camera; Gary J. Dodd, best boy; Gary R. Dodd, grip; Jim Dunford, best boy; Jim Dunford, grip; Scott Fieldsteel, best boy; Jack N. Green, aerial camera operator; Frank Keever, key grip; William Kenney, dolly grip; Ross A. Maehl, gaffer; Stan McClain, aerial camera operator; Edward Morey III, camera operator; Ralph Nelson, Jr., still photographer; Jeffrey Norvet, first assistant camera; Joe A. Ponticelle, second assistant camera; David St. Onge, best boy; Elizabeth Ziegler, Steadicam operator. Costume and Wardrobe Department: Michael Chavez, key costumer; Tom Johnson, costume supervisor: men. Editorial Department: Douglas Brumer, assistant film editor; Gary Burritt, negative cutter; Phil Hetos, color timer; David Holden, additional editor; Jere Huggins, additional editor; David Jansen, apprentice film editor; Thomas G. Jingles, apprentice film editor; Trevor Jolly, first assistant editor; Frederika Kesten, apprentice film editor; Kevin Lindstrom, assistant film editor; Russell Paris, post-production coordinator; Mark Sadusky, assistant film editor; Rex Stewart, assistant film editor; Merry Tigar, apprentice film editor; Rick Tuber, assistant film editor; Stan Wohlberg, assistant film editor. Music Department: Brooks Arthur, music supervisor; Jack Eskew, orchestrator; Stephen A. Hope, music editor; Dan Wallin, score mixer; John Rotondi, scoring engineer: Y4 (uncredited); Celia Weiner, music editor (uncredited). Transportation Department: Richard C. Belyeu, transportation captain; James E. Foote, transportation coordinator. Miscellaneous Crew: Paula Abdul, choreographer; David Bandler, assistant — John G. Avildsen; James Barrett, advisor — bonsai plants; Howard Brandy, unit publicist; Jimmy Crabe, the Karate Kid family will miss our dear friend; Richard Davis, Jr., location manager; Patricia L. DeShields, production accountant; Thomas De Wier, rappelling advisor; Joyce Wilson Fetherolf, assistant — John G. Avildsen; Sonny P. Filippini, script supervisor; Craig Hosking, helicopter pilot; Pat E. Johnson, martial arts choreographer; Kathryn J. McDermott, assistant — Shel Schrager; Roy Nagatoshi, advisor — bonsai plants; Karyn Saffro, production associate; Joyce M. Warren, production coordinator; Jamie Weintraub, assistant — Jerry Weintraub; Jody Weintraub, assistant — Jerry Weintraub; Julie Weintraub, assistant — Jerry Weintraub; Sarah Weintraub, assistant — Jerry Weintraub; Anne Marie Yantos, production associate; Lynette Katselas, dialogue coach. Filming Location: Los Angeles, California, USA. Production Companies: Columbia Pictures Corporation; Weintraub International Group. Distributor: Columbia Pictures.

Cast — in credits order: Ralph Macchio, Daniel LaRusso; Noriyuki "Pat" Morita, Mr. Kesuke Miyagi; Robyn Lively, Jessica Andrews; Thomas Ian Griffith, Terry Silver; Martin Kove, John Kreese; Sean Kanan, Mike Barnes; Jonathan Avildsen, Snake; Randee Heller, Lucille; Christopher Paul Ford, Dennis; Pat E. Johnson, Referee; Rick Hurst, Announcer; Frances Bay, Mrs. Milo; Joseph V. Perry, Uncle Louie; Jan Triska, Milos; Diana Webster, Margaret; Patrick R. Posada, Man #1; C. Darnell Rose, Delivery Man; Glenn Medeiros, Himself; Gabe Jarret, Rudy; Doc Duhame, Security Guard; Randell Dennis Widner, Sparring Partner #1; Raymond S. Sua, Sparring Partner #2; Garth Johnson, Spectator #1; E. David Tetro, Spectator #2; Helen Lin, Tahitian Girl #1; Meilani Figalan, Tahitian Girl #2; Other credited cast listed alphabetically; Rob Garrison, Tommy (archive footage); Chad McQueen, Dutch (archive footage); Tony O'Dell, Jimmy (archive footage); William Zabka, Johnny (archive footage). Rest of cast: John Timothy Botka, Spectator (uncredited); Sandy Shimoda, Dancer (uncredited).

CHAPTER 20

Rocky V

The End of the Line?

General Douglas MacArthur was famous for closing out his military career with the classic quote, "Old soldiers never die, they just fade away." Too bad the same can't be said for some old boxers. Too many of them, it seems, just become punch drunk. And it's too bad that the *Rocky* series had to follow the latter tradition.

After bursting onto the scene with *Rocky* in 1976, Sylvester Stallone's Hollywood star was on the rise. He had used his writing of the script to bargain his way into a starring role in that film. As he became one of Hollywood's top attractions, he used that power to get more influence over his subsequent films. Unfortunately, except for his *Rambo* series, most of them were box-office disappointments. As Medavoy noted, his attempts to play another kind of character "were less than successful."[1]

But he still kept control of most of his movies. Among those were the *Rocky* sequels, a series of five films that were critically dubious but popular enough to gross more than a billion dollars.[2] As Nye noted, "Many critics moaned when Stallone announced a sequel was in the works. But movie fans didn't."[3]

Indeed, the times seemed right for an action-packed sequel. The high demand by the public for video cassettes forced the industry to produce to meet the new need. Further, the video industry gave the film industry new economic possibilities after the three-decade decline caused by television. Action-packed movies fulfilled the new demand.

With the video market on the rise, the distribution of American films exploded abroad. Everyone, from Koreans and Italians to French and Turkish, all were looking for films to rent in video stores. Long dialogues and "intellectual films" did not work for the foreign markets as they had to be translated and understood by other cultures. Action films offered a more interesting aspect to the distributors. Of course, the success of the genre was detrimental to other styles of filmmaking as well as to the foreign film industry.

The sequel trend has been commonplace throughout the history of motion pictures. During the first half of the 20th century, though, this trend was usually reserved for "B" and low-budget films. Over the past three decades, it became a common Hollywood practice which reached its peak in the '80s and '90s with the super "tech" hero embodied by stars such as Schwarzenegger, Stallone, Willis, Van Damme, and many famous and obscure others. The makeup of these characters is represented by male dominant distinctiveness who often strive for actions with superheroic flavors. Actions mixed with special effects became the essence of the genre, often ignoring the basic principles of story telling.

John McTiernan, who made films in the genre, explained that he tried "to gravitate towards movies that [he] likes to see, a sort of boys adventures — big boys, little boys."[4] Numerous elements seemed to have triggered that form of cinema in the early '80s. Producer Robert Chartoff, Stallone and Avildsen were part of that trend. As soon as *Rocky* was finished, Chartoff handed Stallone a notebook and a gold-plated pen and jokingly told him, "Now, write the sequel!"[5] Perhaps he realized that both Stallone and Avildsen had already considered that.

In fact, the two men had planned for sequels from the moment that filming first started. "When we started making *Rocky*, we had a sequel in mind," Avildsen said. "In fact, it was intended to be a trilogy."

A good idea, perhaps. But by the time shooting began on *Rocky II*, Avildsen had chosen not to work on the project. Nor did he participate in the next three sequels. Stallone took control and directed *Rocky II, III,* and *IV.*

Rocky II (1979) reunited the cast three years later. Carl Weathers returned as Apollo. This time Apollo seeks a rematch, an effort on his part to quiet those rumors started by some people who thought that Rocky should have been declared the winner of the first fight. A good idea for a plot, perhaps, and this time Horatio Alger does indeed triumph when Rocky wins.

In 1982's *Rocky III*, the villain was a verbose and obnoxious fighter named Clubber Lang, played by Mr. T of TV's *The A-Team.* Lane catches Rocky at a vulnerable time. Despondent over the death of his friend and trainer Mickey (Burgess Meredith), Rocky accepts Lane's challenge but doesn't have the heart to win the match. But Apollo Creed (Carl Weathers again) arrives to take over the training duties. Rocky is revitalized and wins the match. It was fun, but couldn't compare to the original.

There was little to say about *Rocky IV* (1985), a boring entry with a now-antiquated Cold War theme. Writer Stallone tried to wrench some emotion by having Apollo Creed killed by a superhuman Soviet boxer named Ivan Drago (Dolph Lundgren). Rocky defeats Drago and avenges Apollo on Christmas Day in Moscow, and the world is again safe for democracy. Nye described the entire debacle as "1940s comic book stuff,"[6] a critique that was overly kind.

The originality of plot and characters — so critical to the success and appeal of the original — are gradually lost as each subsequent story strays a little bit further from reality while making more overt efforts to tug at the audience's hearts. As Nye noted, "The *Rocky* films are contrived and are meant to touch your most basic emotions but they do it well. Stallone ... knew better than anyone how to milk this formula for all it was worth."[7]

By the end of *Rocky IV*, he had milked the cow once too often. *Rocky IV* was particularly embarrassing. After that debacle, Stallone tried to return the character to greatness with the same formula that worked in the original. He brought Avildsen back to direct the final sequel. Avildsen reluctantly agreed, lured to it because he liked the script (written by Stallone) and its emotional ending.

"I wasn't sure that Sylvester would want me back, because I hadn't worked on the three sequels in between," Avildsen recalled. "But they sent me the script, and it was a good one. Sylvester always was a good writer, and he had written a good script, with Rocky dying at the end."

The go-between who put Avildsen and Stallone together again was composer Bill Conti. Avildsen didn't approach Stallone about the project because of his uncertainty about whether Stallone would want him. But Conti provided Avildsen with the script and told him that Stallone wanted him to direct it.

Avildsen liked the script; its presentation of a Rocky with no money and down on his luck was similar to the concept of the original movie. Further, he would have more money for the project than he did for the original, or as Avildsen said, "This time we didn't go there with a non-union crew" to do the filming.

Critics were not thrilled to see Avildsen on the job. Jack Mathews of the *Los Angeles Times* complained that Avildsen's "earlier sequels warned against expecting too much."[8]

For the most part, though, Avildsen did his job. As Grant noted, "There is ... no need to speculate why Stallone had the talented John G. Avildsen ... return as director. The ever-so-brief ring scenes here have the nicely composed quality and raw power that could never have been captured with Stallone's heavy hands at the editing table."[9]

Expectations were low. When the film was released in 1990 — 15 years after the original — one critic wrote, "*Rocky V* arrives advertised as the last of the Rocky pictures, and I hope that's true, because the series has run out of steam. You can only make the same movie so many times." Another noted, "*Rocky II* ... was at least a legitimate sequel, and created the appealing character of Apollo Creed. But the later Rocky movies have been low on inspiration and eager to repeat the same formula, in which everything leads up to a climactic fight scene and a triumphant fade-out."

The plot was typical of Rocky Balboa's up-and-down fortunes, with some of the elements of the originally planned sequels added to the drama. As planned for the third sequel, Rocky's star has dimmed again. In *Rocky V*, Adrian's brother Paulie betrays Rocky by tricking him into signing a power of attorney. Rocky takes the fall as some unseen but evil accountant gets his hands on the document and uses it to rob the befuddled boxer. He and Adrian have to watch as their home and all their possessions are sold at auction. Even Rocky, Jr. (played by Stallone's real-life son Sage) loses his motorbike.

They move back into a tiny row house in the old neighborhood, where schoolyard bullies steal Rocky, Jr.'s jacket. He finds himself in his old Philadelphia neighborhood with no money and few friends.

He tries to seek redemption by opening Mickey's old gym and training young boxers. He does a pretty good job, particularly with a young kid named Tommy Gunn (honest, that's the character's name).

Tommy "The Duke" Morrison — an actual boxer — plays the young upstart. Morrison was a distant relative of John Wayne; thus, the nickname "The Duke." Avildsen elicits a solid performance from the amateur and viewers quickly figure out that this dumb palooka doesn't appreciate his luck. He abandons Rocky and signs with rival promoter George Washington Duke, a character inspired by Muhammad Ali's promoter, the flamboyant Don King. Duke's plan is to set up a title bout that will lure Rocky out of retirement. Another fight might take care of Rocky's financial problems, but it could also kill him. There was just too much brain damage, it turns out, after that patriotic fight in *Rocky IV*. The climactic scene is a street fight that Rocky finally wins, but there's not much to celebrate.[10]

The critics were brutal. "You pays your money, and you gets what you expects in this Stallone screenplay, but seriously, folks, the thrill is gone," one wrote. Noting the importance of a good villain to a good story, another wrote, "We know *Rocky V* is in trouble when one of the major villains doesn't even appear in the movie; he's an accountant who remains offscreen, never seen, while he strips the Balboa family of its assets." Another started the review by noting that at least "no one dies in this Rocky picture," a reference to the deaths of Mickey (Burgess Meredith's character) in *Rocky III* and Apollo Creed in *Rocky IV*.

The problem, they noted, was a premise that never quite meshed. "The back-to-basics approach, with original director Avildsen back at the helm, is sensible," one wrote, "since nothing could have topped the bone-crunching climax of *Rocky IV.* But whereas the first and far superior *Rocky* had real heart, this tries and fails to have brains."

Avildsen realized soon after he arrived on the set that the film was headed toward disaster. "I read the script, and it was a beautiful script, very touching death scene," Avildsen said. "Rocky will be riding in the ambulance and he will be dying in the arms of Adrian. Adrian will come out in the end and talk to the press, announcing Rocky's death and telling them, 'As long as people believe in themselves, Rocky's spirit will live forever.'"

Once the film got underway, though, and time for filming the climactic scene approached, the president of MGM got cold feet. "James Bond doesn't die," he said. "Why should Rocky die?" Further reflection and the possibility of making a *Rocky VI*" finally won the day. Rocky, the producers insisted to Avildsen, would not die. "So Rocky lived," Avildsen recalled. "But the movie died."

And Avildsen's career almost died with it. Not from the movie, but from the reputation he developed in Hollywood as a result. "I wish I had been pragmatic rather than idealistic," Avildsen said. "That would have been better for my career."

Incensed by the decision, Avildsen fought hard to keep the original scene. As the arguments grew, so did his reputation as a temperamental artist. And he lost the argument anyway. "It almost ruined by career," Avildsen admits. "It took me five years to get over it and another five years to get on with my life." He acknowledges that he brooded about the decision during the first half of that time; meanwhile, his temperamental reputation made it hard for him to find other work. He had forgotten the filmmaker's maxim: The goal is not to make one film; the goal is to keep on making films.

Ironically, the idea to kill off the character was Stallone's. After all, he had written the scene in his original script. Karney argued that the scene was a deliberate attempt on Stallone's part to get rid of the character because "Stallone has increasingly complained that he is trapped by his two most famous characters, ... typecast by studio and public alike as a bruiser."[11]

Irwin Winkler and Robert Chartoff, producers of the original *Rocky*, have since said that Stallone was manageable on the original movie only because he was a starving actor at the time.[12] Avildsen agreed with their assessment: "He was humble, willing to take advice, and easy to work with. When I came back for *Rocky V*, he was a star. I preferred the starving actor."

The non-starving Stallone would still have one more punch for his first major character. The sixth and (to date) final installment in the *Rocky* saga came in 2006 with the release of *Rocky Balboa.* Avildsen ran into Stallone at

Sylvester Stallone and Avildsen on the set of *Rocky V* (1990).

a restaurant prior to filming and approached him about possibly directing the new release. Stallone didn't bite, but gave him a general overview of the film.

When the movie opens, Adrian has died. Avildsen suggested that he not let her die off screen, but instead have her die in the boxer's arms at the beginning of the movie. "You'll have the audience in the palm of your hands for two hours," Avildsen added. But Stallone was not interested in that suggestion.

Avildsen also asked if Sly's real son Sage (who died at age 36 in 2012) would play his son in the movie. Stallone said he would not, because he had put on some weight. Avildsen praised Sage's work in *Rocky V*, calling it "terrific," and encouraged Stallone to reconsider. He wasn't interested in that either.

As for Avildsen's assessment of the ending of *Rocky Balboa*, his comment was similar to his opinion of *Rocky V*: "I thought it was good, except for the ending."

Production Notes

Directed by: John G. Avildsen. Writers (WGA): Written by Sylvester Stallone. Producers: Robert Chartoff, producer; Michael S. Glick, executive producer; Tony Munafo, associate producer; Irwin Winkler, producer; Suzanne DeLaurentiis, associate producer (uncredited). Original Music: Bill Conti. Cinematographer: Steven Poster (director of photography). Editors: John G. Avildsen, Robert A. Ferretti, Michael N. Knue. Casting Director: Caro Jones. Production Designer: William J. Cassidy. Art Director: William Durrell, Jr. Set Decorator: John Dywer. Make Up Department: Sugar Maryce Blymyer, hair stylist; Colleen Callaghan, hair stylist — New York; Jay Cannistraci, makeup artist — New York; Katalin Elek, makeup artist; Hiram Ortiz, hair consultant — Talia Shire; Frank Carrisosa, makeup artist; Carol Schwartz, makeup artist; Michael Westmore, special makeup; Zoltan Elek, makeup artist (uncredited). Production Manager: Michael S. Glick, unit production manager. Second Unit Directors or Assistant Directors: Clifford C. Coleman, first assistant director; Hope R. Goodwin, second assistant director; Richard "Dub" Wright, second second assistant director. Art Department: Sharlene Bright, stand-by painter; Gary L. Deaton, construction foreman; Bruce DiValerio, construction foreman; Audrey Johnson, assistant property master; Kent H. Johnson, property master; Chuck Sertin, set dresser; Barton M. Susman, lead man; Donald F. Winter, construction coordinator; Craig Baron, assistant property master (uncredited); William Boyd, mill foreman (uncredited); Kirk S. Heinlen, set dresser (uncredited); Kirk S. Heinlen, swing gang (uncredited); Edward T. Reiff, Jr., set constructor (uncredited); Randy Severino, set dresser (uncredited). Sound Department: David Behle, sound recordist; Stu Bernstein, sound effects editor; James Beshears, adr supervisor; Alan Bromberg, sound effects editor; Mark Cafolla, assistant sound editor; David B. Cohn, supervising sound editor; Simon Coke, sound effects editor; Samuel C. Crutcher, sound effects editor; Debra Dobb, sound recordist; Julia Evershade, sound effects editor; John P. Fasal, special sound effects; Gary Hecker, foley artist; Ronald S. Herbes, assistant sound editor; Joseph Holsen, sound effects editor; Doc Kane, foley mixer; Jack Keller, sound recordist; Robert J. Litt, sound re-recording mixer; Robert Martel, assistant sound editor; Matthew C. May, first assistant sound editor; Harry B. Miller III, sound effects editor; Bob O'Brien, sound effects editor; Judy Oseransky, assistant sound editor; Lauren J. Palmer, adr editor; Katie Rowe, foley artist; Greg P. Russell, sound re-recording mixer; Monique Salvato, assistant adr editor; Clement Sheaffer, cable person; Peter Michael Sullivan, sound effects editor; Barry Thomas, sound mixer; Renee Tondelli, adr editor; Elliot Tyson, sound re-recording mixer; Sherman Waze, sound effects editor; Forest Williams, boom operator; Steve Bartlett, sound (uncredited); Samuel C. Crutcher, sound editor/design (uncredited); Donald C. Rogers, technical director of sound (uncredited); Kaitlyn Walker, adr artist (uncredited). Special Effects Department: Lou Carlucci, special effects; Joe DiGaetano III, special effects coordinator; Dave Fletcher, special effects; Dennis Petersen, special effects. Stunts: Bobby Bass, stunt coordinator; Mark DeAlessandro, stunt double; Terry Funk, additional stunts; Curtis Lupo, stunt double. Camera and Electrical Department: Ben Beaird, key grip; Daniel Buck, gaffer; Marty Wayne Eichman, key grip; Sam Emerson, still photographer; Mike Fauntleroy, first assistant camera; Victor Hammer, additional photographer; Stephen V. Isbell, best boy grip; George Kohut, camera operator; Peter Kuttner, first assistant camera; Robert La Bonge, camera operator; Charles Lantz, dolly grip; Clayton Liotta, first assistant camera: New York; Anastas N. Michos, camera operator: New York; Andrew M. Nelson, best boy electric; James Plannette, chief lighting technician; Tim Prince, video technician; Kathina Szeto, second assistant camera; Byron White, best boy electric; Roy Bean, video technician (uncredited); Garrett Brown, Steadicam operator (uncredited); Daniel C. Cook, additional second assistant camera (uncredited); Damien Harrer, electrician (uncredited); Michael Leonard, additional first assistant camera (uncredited); Steven Mann, first assistant camera: camera tests (uncredited); Maricella Ramirez, assistant camera (uncredited); Mark Simon, assistant camera (uncredited). Casting Department: Tony Dinizo, location extras casting: Philadelphia; Meredith Jacobson, location extras casting: Philadelphia; Jack Jones, casting assistant; Diane Kirman, location extras casting: Philadelphia; Barbara Spitz, casting assistant. Costume and Wardrobe Department: Brad Anderson, costumer; Leah Brown, costumer; Carole Brown-James, costume supervisor; Ed Fincher, costumer; Barton Kent James, costume supervisor. Editorial Department: Douglas Brumer, Alessandra Carlino, Angela Jackson, Fran Kaplan and Neil Silver, assistant editors; Robert A. Ferretti, additional film editor; Phil Hetos, color timer; Trevor Jolly, additional film editor; Marypat Plottner, synching editor; Brian Ralph, negative cutter; Neil Eric Wenger, first assistant editor. Music Department: Ken Johnson and Steve Livingston, music editors; Chris McGeary, assistant music editor; Daniel J. Johnson, co-music editor (uncredited). Transportation Department: Gregory J. Cimino and Paul Cimino, transportation captains — Philadelphia; Linda Conrad, transportation dispatch; Lee Garibaldi, transportation captain; Tommy Tancharoen, transportation coordinator. Miscellaneous Crew: Lori A. Balton-Sharp, assistant location manager; Leslie Brander, and Richard Brander, dramatic coaches; Cathleen Clarke, production assistant; Marcia Coleman, first aid; Karen Day, production accountant; David Fulton, unit publicist; Clifford M. Hirsch, studio teacher; Lori Imbler, assistant: Robert Chartoff; Thomas F. Keniston, assistant production accountant; Jonathan B. Kuyper and Kacy L. Magedman, production assistants; Gregory Manson, assistant production accountant; James A. McPeak, craft service — Philadelphia; Barbara Millie, location liaison — Philadelphia; Susan Persily, assistant — Sylvester Stallone; Janice Polley, location manager; Missy Pray, assistant production coordinator; John Reul, production assistant; Carol Sagusti, assistant — Michael S. Glick; Michael Stermel, representative — Philadelphia Police; Laura "L.T." Tateishi, production coordinator; Steve Timinskas, production assistant; Angela Tortu, production assistant — Philadelphia; Maria Tortu, production assistant — Philadelphia; Michael Vieira, production assistant — Sylvester Stallone; Kathryn Weygand, script supervisor; Jeff Winn, craft service; Joyce Wilson Fetherolf, assistant — John G. Avildsen (uncredited); Jeff Langton, coach — Tommy Morrison (uncredited). Thanks: Jane Oliver, dedicatee. Filming Locations: Pasadena, California, USA; Philadelphia, Pennsylvania, USA. Production Companies: Chartoff-Winkler Productions; Star Partners III Ltd.; United Artists. Distributors: MGM/UA Distribution Company (1990) (USA) (theatrical); 20th Century–Fox Home Entertainment (2006) (USA) (DVD); 20th Century–Fox Home Entertainment (2009) (USA) (DVD) (Blu-ray) (The Undisputed Collection); MGM Home Entertainment (2009) (USA) (DVD) (Blu-ray) (The Undisputed Collection).

Cast — in credits order: Sylvester Stallone, Rocky Balboa; Talia Shire, Adrian; Burt Young, Paulie; Sage Stallone, Rocky Balboa, Jr.; Burgess Meredith, Mickey Goldmill; Tommy Morrison, Tommy "Machine" Gunn; Richard Gant, George Washington Duke; Tony Burton, Duke; James Gambina, Jimmy; Delia Sheppard, Karen; Michael Sheehan, Merlin Sheets; Michael Williams, Union Cane; Kevin Connolly, Chickie; Elisebeth Peters, Jewel; Hayes Swope, Chickie's Pal; Nicky Blair, Fight Promoter; Jodi Letizia, Marie (scenes deleted); Chris Avildsen, Druggy; Jonathan Avildsen, Druggy; Don Sherman, Andy; Stu Nahan, Fight Commentator; Al Bernstein, Fight Commentator; James Binns, James Binns (Rocky's Lawyer); Meade Martin, Las Vegas Announcer; Michael Buffer, Fight Announcer (3rd Fight); Albert J. Myles, Benson; Jane Marla Robbins, Gloria; Ben Geraci, Cab Driver; Clifford C. Coleman, Motorcycle Mechanic; Lou Filippo and Frank Cappuccino, Referees; Lauren K. Woods, Robert Seltzer, Albert S. Meltzer, John P. Clark, Stanley R. Hochman, Elmer Smith, Conference Reporters; Henry D. Tillman, Contender #1; Stan Ward, Contender #2; Brian Phelps, Mark Thompson, Paul Cain, Kent H. Johnson, Cindy Roberts, Reporters; Patrick Cronin, Dr. Rimlan; Helena Carroll, Woman Drinker; Tony Munafo, Bob Vasquez, Richard "Dub" Wright, Susan Persily, Gary Compton, John J. Cahill, Drinkers; LeRoy Neiman, Fight Announcer; Michael Pataki, Nicoli Koloff (archive footage); Jennifer Flavin, Tricia Flavin, Julie Flavin, Delivery Girls; Bob Giovane, Timmy; Carol A. Ready, Russian Woman; Katharine Margiotta, Woman in Dressing Room; Jeff Langton, Joe Sabatino, Daniel Epper, Del Weston, Mel Scott-Thomas, Billy D. Lucas, Alex Garcia, Curtis Jackson, Dale Jacoby, Clay Hodges, Richard C. Oprison, Kevin Bucceroni, John D'Martin, Rodney Frazier, Eric Hedgeman, Charles Hines, Kerry Judge, Billy D. Saunders, Boxers. Other credited cast listed alphabetically: G. Larry Butler, Boxing Match Attendee (uncredited); Jon Kuyper, Diana Lewis and Troy Martin, Reporters (uncredited); Kurt Leitner, Neighbor #1 (uncredited); Dolph Lundgren, Ivan Drago (archive footage) (uncredited); Paul Dion Monte, Boxer (uncredited); Ben Piazza, Doctor (uncredited); Kevin Rooney, Tommy's Title Fight Cornerman (uncredited); John Timmons, Cop #1 (uncredited); Gina Marie Turcketta, Kissing Girl (uncredited).

CHAPTER 21

The Power of One

Some time in the early 1990s, a young girl read a semi-autobiographical novel by Bryce Courtenay called *The Power of One*. The story of a young boxer in South Africa who used his athletic venue to make a statement against apartheid. Inspired by the tome, the young lady approached her father with the work and said, "Dad, why don't you do a good movie."

"Dad" was film producer Arnon Milchan, an Israeli-born stage producer who started producing films in the early 1970s. His early works included some stinkers and low-budget numbers, including *The Medusa Touch* (1976) and *Stripper* (1985). By 1991, though, he also had some quality films to his credit, including *Pretty Woman* (1990), *The War of the Roses* (1989), and *Guilty by Suspicion* (1991). His later works also included some memorable cinematic entries: *Falling Down* (1993), *Free Willy* (1993), *Under Siege* (1992), *Sommersby* (1993), *The Client* (1994), and *Natural Born Killers* (1994).

When *The Power of One* came to his attention, he saw a film that might be both prestigious and profitable — a producer's idea of perfection. He approached Warner Brothers with the idea, pitching Sean Connery for the pivotal role of "Doc." With Connery cast in a key role, Warner Brothers agreed to finance the project.

A film about apartheid in South Africa was suddenly on track. But it all started with a comment from a young reader. "That's the only reason the movie ever got made," Avildsen said.

After all, apartheid is not a typical movie topic. "Right," Avildsen said, sarcastically. "Just what we need. Another apartheid movie. People will flock to see that. People will sit around on Saturday night and say, 'Let's go see the apartheid movie.' Yeah, let's do that for sure."

"A movie like that, it's really incredible that it got made," Avildsen added.

Then the fabric started unraveling. First, Connery backed out, choosing instead to work in *Medicine Man*. Without Connery, Warner Brothers lost interest. By then, though, Milchan was determined to do the movie. He abandoned Hollywood and sought financing in France. He pulled off the deal, money was found, and Avildsen started working on the film in 1991.

One of his first duties was to scout locations. Although the story takes place in South Africa in 1935, economic sanctions prohibited the filmmakers from working there. Still, Avildsen's first trips to the African continent for the film were to South Africa. "I went to South Africa twice looking for actors, crew and locations that were mentioned in the book so that I would know better what to look for in Zimbabwe," Avildsen said.

On one of those flights, a fellow passenger in the first class section was South African icon Nelson Mandela and his wife. Avildsen and Mandela spent much of the flight talking about *Rocky,* boxing, and *The Power of One.* "He was a boxer once, and he was very interested in hearing about *Rocky.* He was also familiar with the book [*The Power of One*]. He couldn't have been more engaging."

Once in Johannesburg, Avildsen unpacked his High 8 camera, went to Alexandria township on the outskirts of town, and starting shooting on his tour. He also visited some schools that would have been like the ones his hero, P. K., would have attended. "That was fascinating," he said, as he got an up-close view of South African life that started his research for the film. He reinforced that research by watching *Goodbye Africa* and some other films made in South Africa during the 1930s, and some newsreel footage from the time. Some were memorable:

> One I'll never forget, sort of a Sunday afternoon custom in Johannesburg and lots of other towns I'm sure. There was a big park in town, and the whites would bring young black men there for public fighting, like gladiators. The white folks came out and had a picnic with their children and watched the blacks inside battling one another. It was an incredible experience. It felt like a visit to Nazi Germany.

Avildsen also tried to capture the visual impact of the area on film:

> The architecture was beige and heavy. And the whole place is built on gold mines. When you fly over it, everything is yellow dirt, like it's built on a honeycomb. That's where all the gold came from. That's also why they didn't have slavery. It was a lot cheaper not to have slaves and just keep the labor force the way they did.

Before he left, Avildsen met with Bryce Courtenay, the writer whose novel had inspired the film. Robert Mark Kamen, who worked with Avildsen on three *Karate Kid* films, adapted the story into a script. Avildsen knew in advance that such adaptations are not always successful. "If you've got a popular novel, chances are you've got a good story," Avildsen said. "But how do you translate that? Sometimes it's done well, sometimes it isn't. It's real tough to do because a book is so much longer and you can use your imagination, which has no budget limitations."

With the script started, Avildsen needed a star. His first choice for Giel Piet, the prisoner who prepares and trains the hero to be a boxer and is the ultimate victim of a race-based murder, was the actor who made *Lean on Me* so memorable: Morgan Freeman. Avildsen used Courtenay's novel to get the actor interested.

"I was in London working on *Robin Hood* when John was on his stopover to Johannesburg ...or Zimbabwe," Freeman recalled. "He told me he was working on a project, and he had the book *The Power of One* and told me to read it. So I did, and it was incredible."

"When I come back, I'll have a script for you," Avildsen told Freeman before leaving. Three weeks later, he returned with the script.

The cast was rounded out with one legend and a couple of unknowns. The legend was John Gielgud, who played the headmaster. Avildsen had worked with him once before in *The Formula*. Roger Ebert lauded Gielgud's performance as conveying the image of a man "happy in his academic ivory tower in the midst of upheaval."[1] The other actors also received accolades, with *Cinebooks* noting, "The cast is as good as it looks on paper, with shining lead performances." *Blockbuster* added, "Freeman steals the film as the hero's trainer."

Stephen Dorff landed the part of hero "P.K." Veteran European actor Armin Mueller-Stahl took the role of Doc, the part originally planned for Sean Connery. Other cast members were added, many of them coming from Africa. Several were found in Zimbabwe. Avildsen flew there after leaving Johannesburg, looking for locations and cast members.

The plot, set in the 1930s, involves a seven-year-old South African-born boy who is sent to a boarding school after his mother dies. A neo–Nazi group bullies the newcomer. He fights backs and triggers a year of personal battles.

Prior to entering school, his best friend as a child had been a young black boy. After graduating from school, he gets to know some Africans who are part of a growing civil rights political movement opposed to the apartheid system of government that controls South Africa. He becomes a symbol of that movement, with many believing him to be the mythical "Rain Maker" who will unite the tribes. His symbolic role boils down to winning a fight against the Nazi bully from his school days, a guy who became a corrupt cop in Johannesburg.

The role of the corrupt cop was played by Daniel Craig in his first screen appearance. Craig had originally been hired as a reader, i.e., someone to read the "other" part for people who auditioned for various roles during auditions in London. After observing him work, Avildsen approached Craig and said, "You're terrific. Why don't you be the bad guy?"

Despite the cast of largely unknown actors, and shooting in a strange location, filming went rather smoothly. As cinematographer Dean Semler said, "It was an enjoyable picture. We set the pace at the top, and I think John set a good atmosphere because he was very positive. He knew what he wanted. It was a very easy shoot, considering we had children, elephants, and foreign locations. It could have been very difficult."

The critics gave it mixed reviews. Leonard Maltin described it as "rah-rah mawkishness," an "offensive trivialization of a great subject," and "an ordeal to watch" that was "precisely what you'd expect when the director of *Rocky* and *The Karate Kid* tackles a movie about apartheid." Akins called it "a violent cartoon which trivializes apartheid."[2]

Roger Ebert complained that the film "continues the tendency of so many recent films about South Africa, like *Cry Freedom*, to embody the anti-apartheid struggle in a heroic white man, presumably so white Western audiences will have an easier time identifying."[3] He continued,

> *The Power of One* begins with a canvas that involves all of the modern South African dilemma, and ends as a boxing movie. Somewhere in between, it loses its way.... You can almost feel the film slipping out of the hands of its director, John G. Avildsen, as the South African reality is upstaged by the standard clichés of a fight picture ...
>
> It begins with a clear sense of the land and the attachment of all South Africans to it. It shows the symbiotic, if paternalistic, relationship of blacks and whites in rural areas. It gives some sense of the beginnings of apartheid. But then it turns into another movie about a bad bully.... [I]t diminishes evil by embodying it in one man who must be vanquished. By implying that his defeat is the defeat of the system, it avoids the real issue.... There are some nice touches... But how can you forgive a movie that begins by asking you to care who will win freedom, and ends by asking you to care who will win a fight?[4]

Others agreed. Mark Goodman referred to a statement often attributed to Samuel Goldwyn: "If you want to send a message, go to Western Union." "The intentions are honorable, and *Power* is topical," he added. "It is also, however, obvious for adults and too sophisticated for youngsters."[5]

Another critic wrote, "Avildsen draws good performances from the three actors who play P.K., as well as from the ever-reliable Freeman and Muller-Stahl, but subtlety is abandoned when he focuses on the ring and teen romance. The climax is a slugging match between PK and a former school bully which would make Rocky proud."[6]

Rita Kempley of the *Washington Post* had a similar opinion, calling the movie "an absorbing but awkward union of the two-fisted boxing movie with the moist-eyed British memoir."[7] Desson Howe was more blunt: "[It's] resounding bunk, candied over with the lush music of Johnny Clegg and hyped

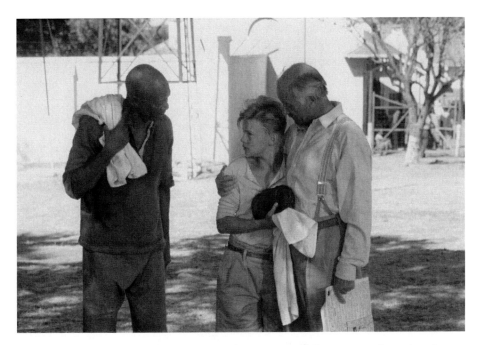

Morgan Freeman, Simm Fenton and Armin Mueller-Stahl in *Power of One* **(1992).**

to death by director John Avildsen." Clegg's music and Avildsen's direction, Howe said, made the film "a South African version of *The Sound of Music*."[8]

But a number of reviewers were favorably impressed. According to *Blockbuster*, it was a "slick but entertaining story." *CineBooks* praised it as "a rousing historical epic" and "compelling historical fiction [that] provides a rare look at South African culture, history, and politics." The film, the review noted, "uses the story of its protagonist to make its complex historical framework come grippingly alive."

Avildsen recalled attending screenings and being approached later by young people who said the film inspired them to join the Peace Corps. The film is still shown in schools, teaching youngsters about apartheid and racism.

Those positive elements didn't help the box office at the time, though. The real problem, as *Cinebooks* noted, was that the film was "largely unheralded and unseen." "I have no idea why *The Power of One* did no better than it did," Morgan Freeman said later. "But, on another hand, we don't have a lot of tolerance or desire to watch other people's misfortune. It is hard to think about paying seven dollars to watch a story about apartheid in South Africa."

Freeman's assessment seems accurate. The problem was topic. Audiences simply were not interested in a film about apartheid in South Africa. Still, the hindsight of history has generally viewed the film positively. As *CineBooks* concluded, "By necessity, the story is almost unremittingly downbeat, but *The Power of One* is nonetheless a powerful, engrossing, and enlightening tale that should not be missed."

Production Notes

Directed by: John G. Avildsen. Writers (WGA): Novel, Bryce Courtenay; Screenplay, Robert Mark Kamen. Producers: Graham Burke, executive producer; Roy Button, line producer; Greg Coote, executive producer; Arnon Milchan, producer; Steven Reuther, executive producer; Doug Seelig, associate producer. Original Music: Hans Zimmer. Cinematographer: Dean Semler. Editors: John G. Avildsen, Trevor Jolly. Casting Director: Caro Jones. Production Designer: Roger Hall. Art Directors: Martin Hitchcock, Kevin Phipps, Les Tomkins (supervising art director). Set Decorator: Karen Brookes. Costume Designer: Tom Rand. Make Up Department: Peter Frampton, key makeup artist; Colin Jamison, chief hair stylist; Amanda Knight, makeup artist; Lisa Tomblin, hair stylist. Production Managers: Kevin De La Noy, production supervisor; Doreen A. Dixon, post-production supervisor; Richard Gelfand, executive in charge of production; Rory Kilalea, production supervisor. Second Unit Directors or Assistant Directors: Chris Brock, additional second assistant director; Clifford Coleman, first assistant director; Peter Heslop, additional second assistant director; Tim Lewis, second assistant director; Alan Mullen, third assistant director; Adam Somner, second assistant director. Art Department: Barry Arnold, stand-by props; Dennis Bovington, construction coordinator — Zimbabwe; Keith Crossley, storyboard artist; Steve Fitzwater, construction coordinator — UK; David Guwaza, props — Zimbabwe; David Lusby, production buyer; Philip McDonald, set property master; Charles Torbett, property master; Abram Waterhouse, assistant to designer; Robin Heinson, painter; Peter Russell, draughtsman; Bradley Torbett, dressing propman. Sound Department: Jack Armstrong, boom operator; James A. Borgardt, adr editor; Gary Bourgeois, sound re-recordist; Fred Cipriano, sound effects editor; Doreen A. Dixon, supervising adr editor; Dean Drabin, foley mixer; Jerelyn J. Harding, adr editor; Robin Harlan, foley artist; Adam Jenkins, sound re-recordist; Jonathan Klein, foley editor; Dean Manly, assistant sound editor; Pat McCormick, dialogue editor; Scott Millan, sound re-recordist; Sarah Monat, foley artist; Ralph Osborn, dialogue editor; John Osborne, nature sounds — South Africa; Lauren Palmer, adr editor; Jeffrey Rosen, supervising sound editor; Trevor Rutherford, sound maintenance; Carolann Sanchez-Shapiro, assistant sound editor; Renee Tondelli, adr editor; Christine Tucker, adr mixer; Joel Valentine, sound effects editor; Clive Winter, production sound mixer. Special Effects Department: Paul Corbould, special effects; Garth Inns, special effects supervisor; Dominic Tuohy, special effects; Simon Cockren, special effects technician. Visual Effects Department: Glenn Campbell, matte cameraman; Paul Curley, matte artist; John Rauh, electronic compositor. Stunts: Eddie Stacey, stunt coordinator. Camera and Electrical Department: Adam Biddle, second assistant camera; Martin Evans, gaffer; John Flemming, second grip; Graham Hall, second assistant camera; Keith Hamshere, still photographer; Paul Kenward, first assistant camera; Martin Kenzie, camera operator; Clive Mackey, second assistant camera; Colin Manning, key grip; Mark O'Kane, Steadicam operator; Gary Pocock, dolly grip; Mike Roberts, additional camera operator; Paul Wells, assistant chief lighting technician; David Worley, additional camera operator; Jason Wren, first assistant camera. Casting Department: Pat Cordes, casting — South Africa; Barbara Harris, voice casting; Jack Jones, casting assistant; Karen Lindsay-Stewart, casting — U.K.; Paul Tingay, casting — Zimbabwe. Costume and Wardrobe Department: Ron Beck, costume supervisor; Janet Tebrooke, wardrobe —

women; Colin Wilson, wardrobe — men; Philip Maldonado, costumer (uncredited). Editorial Department: Donah Bassett, negative cutter; Douglas Brumer, associate editor; Richard Alan Elias, post-production assistant; Joanna Jimenez, assistant editor; Vladimir Goncharov, post-production assistant; William Marrinson, apprentice film editor; Barbara Miletich, post-production assistant; Hope Moskowitz, first assistant editor; Ben Palmer, apprentice film editor — UK; Bob Putynkowski, color timer; Stefanie Wiseman, assistant film editor; Russ Woolnough, assistant film editor — UK; Robert Yano, assistant film editor; Sarah Nean Bruce, post-production consultant (uncredited). Music Department: Bruce Fowler, orchestrator; Teresa García, assistant music editor; David Khabo, choir master; Laura Perlman, music editor; Jay Rifkin, music recordist; Hilton Rosenthal, music supervisor; Harrison White, playback singer (South African Choral singing). Transportation Department: Brian Hathaway, transportation coordinator; Coaster Nziramasanga, transportation captain. Miscellaneous Crew: Julie Adams, dialect coach; Peggy Ali, production secretary; John Alvin, maps — Africa; Gordon Arnell, unit publicist; Shauna Beal, assistant — Arnon Milchan; Lawrence Bibi, boxing scene editor; Linda Bowen, assistant production accountant; Bryce Courtenay, project consultant; Lucy Cressall, assistant production coordinator; Nick Daubeny, location manager; Clarie Davidson, drama coach; Gary Davis, systems analyst; Geraldine Ditano, assistant production accountant; Joyce Wilson Fetherolf, assistant — John G. Avildsen; Paul Fisher, location manager; Julie Gabriel, production secretary; Wm. A. Johnson, production associate — USA; Sally Jones, script supervisor; Tom Muzilla, boxing trainer; Sandra Nixon, production accountant; Carol Regan, production coordinator; Deborah Scott, assistant — Steve Reuther; Sue Sheldon, assistant production coordinator; Hilton Bales Smith, location manager; Mike Smith, supervising production accountant; Bill Wallace, boxing advisor; Linda J. Wilson, assistant — John G. Avildsen; Joel Freeman, production executive; Jim McCarthy, post-production accountant. Filming Locations: Surrey, England, UK; Burbank, California, USA; Zimbabwe. Production Companies: Alcor Films; Canal+; Regency Enterprises; Village Roadshow Pictures. Distributor: Warner Bros. Pictures.

Cast — in credits order: Nomadlozi Kubheka, Nanny; Agatha Hurle, Midwife; Nigel Ivy, P.K. Newborn; Tracy Brooks Swope, Mother; Brendan Deary, P.K. Infant; Winston Mangwarara, Tonderai Infant; Guy Witcher, P.K. Age 7; Tonderai Masenda, Tonderai; Cecil Zilla Mamanzi, Ranch Foreman; John Turner, Afrikaner Minister; Robbie Bulloch, Jaapie Botha; Gordon Arnell, Minister at Mother's Funeral; Jeremiah Mnisi, Dabula Manzi; Armin Mueller-Stahl, Doc; Paul Tingay, Grandfather; Hywell Williams, Captain; Michael Brunner, Cmdt. Van Zy; Clive Russell, Sgt. Bormann; Gert Van Niekirk, Lt. Smit; Morgan Freeman, Geel Piet; Simon Fenton, P.K. Age 12; Winston Ntshona, Mlungisi; Ed Beeten, Prison Commissioner; John Gielgud, St. John; Stephen Dorff, P.K. Age 18; Dominic Walker, Morrie Gilbert; Robert Thomas Reed, School Fight Opponent; Fay Masterson, Maria; Roy Francis, Referee; Clare Cobbold, Maria's Friend #1; Natalie Morse, Maria's Friend #2; Alois Moyo, Gideon Duma; John Osborne, Guard, School Gate; Simon Shumba, Man Without Pass; Stan Leih, Van Cop #1; Rod Campbell, Van Cop #2; Adam Fogerty, Andress Malan; Ian Roberts, Hoppie Gruenewald; Tony Denham, Boxing Partner; Marius Weyers, Prof. Daniel Marais; Eric Nobbs, City Cop #1; Edward Jordan, City Cop #2; Brian O'Shaughnessy, Col. Bretyn; Daniel Craig, Sgt. Botha; Faith Edwards, Miriam Sisulu; Raymond Barreto, Indian Referee; Liz Ngwenya, Nganga Ancient Woman; Andrew Whaley, Ticket Taker; Dominic Makuwachuma, Joshua; Lungani Sibanda, Student; Akim Mwale, Student; Pesedena Dinah, Student; Rosemary Chikobwe Sibanda, Student; Martha Gibson Mtika, Student; Joel Phiri, Student; Peggy Moyo, Student; David Khabo, Student; David Guzawa, Student; Robin Annison, Anita; Christien Anholt, Date at Dinner; Nigel Pegram, Man Guest #1; Jon Cartwright, Jacob; Rev. Peter Van Vuuren, Minister at Maria's Funeral; Marcia Coleman, Woman Guest; Banele Dala Moyo, Boy Who Reads. Other credited cast listed alphabetically: Garth Inns, Headmaster; Tyrone Jeffers, Student.

CHAPTER 22

8 Seconds

Lane Frost was a young athlete on a superstar path in an overlooked sport. In 1987, at the age of 23, he was one of the youngest national cowboy champions in the history of rodeo, the sport that has turned old-time cowboy skills into a competitive venture.

Sure, there were a few broken bones along the way, but Frost had literally held on through the rough rides on through the eight seconds of bucking bulls to rise to the top of the rodeo circuit. But then he died at the top of his game — gored and killed in July 1989 by one of the bulls that made him famous.

The tragedy of that story attracted the attention of country music performers and movie producers. Country superstar Garth Brooks, a rodeo aficionado, turned the story into a top hit with "The Dance." Meanwhile, Avildsen, producer Michael Shamberg, and scriptwriter Monte Merrick worked on a movie version of the story. Shooting on *8 Seconds* started in San Antonio, Texas, and other nearby small towns in the spring of 1993. The film made it to movie theaters in 1994.

The title — which did little to help sales — came from the time length a bull rider was required to stay on his bucking Brahma in order to qualify as having "ridden" the bull. "Ridden" is in quotation marks because all bull riders know that nobody ever really rides an angry bull. It's just a matter of how long you stay on. It's so difficult that eight seconds is considered an inordinately lengthy ride. That's why some commentators refer to the ride as "an eternity — all eight seconds of it."

Avildsen's preferred title was *Cowboy Up*, a phrase that meant manliness in rodeo slang. Another idea he liked was *No Guts, No Glory*. Either title would have been better than *8 Seconds*. Few people knew what that meant, he said, adding that "it sounded like somebody's sex life." The other two titles came closer to identifying the danger inherent to the sport. The problem was conveying that danger and drama on film. Too many people have seen too many cowboy movies to appreciate how truly difficult it is to ride a bull.

Avildsen tried. He had a good cast. Luke Perry had the lead role in his film debut. Although the real rodeo riders who worked on the film were unsure that Perry could pull it off, Frost's friend Tuff Hedeman ended up being impressed with the actor. "If that movie turns out any good," he later told a reporter, "it's Luke Perry's fault."[1]

Perry also impressed Avildsen: "I would love to see him take dance lessons. I think he could be a terrific dancer. He should learn to tap. You know, I've always wanted to do the Gene Kelly story. I could certainly see Luke going in that direction."[2]

Perry's contribution was a major one. He landed the role at a time when he wanted and needed a career boost. Perry became a TV star after *Beverly Hills 90210* premiered in 1990. The youth-based series had quickly become a success, particularly among the nation's youth. At the height of his popularity, he had to be rescued by police when he was mobbed by a crowd of 10,000 fans at an appearance at a shopping mall.

But, by 1993, critics were complaining that the show was losing its creative momentum.[3] Perry recognized the problem himself. "It's in trouble," he told *Entertainment Weekly*. "I know that the show is not great now. I believe it was a great show at one time. Then it went to being a good show. And now it's just another show. And for me to sit here and say that I'm unaware of that would be a big line of bulls—, and I don't do that."[4]

He also knew his days as a teen idol were numbered, saying "Come on, the hairline just won't have it. The best-case scenario for me is to get back to ground zero as an actor."[5]

8 Seconds offered him the opportunity to expand his acting into another medium while simultaneously shedding that teen-idol image. He was so dedicated to the project that, when the original studio (Fox) decided against producing it, Perry shopped it around to other companies. "The second it was brought to my attention, it was like Excalibur," he told *Entertainment Weekly*. "It was the sword that was stuck in the stone. I couldn't believe they were just letting it sit there." He knew the story was a good one, he added, because "I felt it in my nuts."[6]

Cynthia Geary from TV's *Northern Exposure* played his love interest Kellie. Stephen Baldwin took the supporting role of fellow cowboy Tuff Hedeman, who in real life had won three championship titles himself. Other cast members included James Rebhorn, Carrie Snodgress, Red Mitchell, Ronnie Claire Edwards, and Linden Ashby.

On the surface, it was a rodeo movie, but like many of Avildsen's movies, it was no ordinary success story. Avildsen explored the inner turmoil that motivated Frost. What he found wasn't pretty.

Frost was driven, the movie argued, by a futile attempt to satisfy his demanding father, a man who was himself a former champion bronco rider. Unable to be good enough for dad, Lane turns to his adoring fans and almost destroys his marriage. That conflict is the heart of the story, causing Roger Ebert to note, "The movie is really more the story of the marriage than a story of rodeo."[7]

In the film, Lane meets Kellie, a champion barrel racer, at one of his rodeo appearances. She takes the lead, gets to know him, and introduces him to her mother. They soon get married, even though both of them are too young to understand what they're getting into.

Neither anticipates how Lane's career will explode. As he becomes more successful in the arena, he spends more time on the rodeo circuit and with friend Tuff Hedeman, signing autographs and posing for pictures. Eventually he gets too close to some of the "buckle bunnies" who frequent the circuit. One "buckle bunny" who ends up in bed with Lane was a little-known actress named Renee Zellweger in her film debut. Country music duo Kix Brooks and Ronnie Dunn also appear as themselves.

Kellie is often left alone, living in a used trailer instead of the house Lane's father wanted to build for the couple. Eventually, the strain on the marriage becomes too much. Ebert liked this aspect of the film, writing, "The story of the marriage is actually the best and most original thing in *8 Seconds*.

Luke Perry as Lane Frost in *8 Seconds* (1994).

Most movies idealize young love and dismiss the practical problems of living happily ever after.... But Perry and Geary do a good job of making the young couple believable."[8]

But the rodeo scenes were critical to the believability of the film, and much of that rested on the shoulders of Luke Perry. Well, on his rear end, actually. He had to be believable when riding those bulls. Perry wanted to do the film and started riding bulls to prepare for the role even before the film deal had been signed. "Luke Perry ... learned how to ride bulls on his own," Avildsen remembered. "He was hoping that it would turn into a movie."

Avildsen, though, was reluctant to let his star do his own stunt riding for the film. "I thought it was a crazy idea, and we shouldn't have our actor doing it," he told *Entertainment Weekly*. "But Luke was very insistent." Perry finally won the debate. "Luke and I got together, and he convinced me that it was safe," Avildsen said, "because I thought it was nuts to have our star doing it because it was about a guy who got killed doing it."[9]

When film editor Doug Seiling requested more footage of Perry and Baldwin riding the bulls, Avildsen agreed to shoot some more scenes of the duo in action. "We got footage of Luke riding three more bulls," Avildsen said. "He jumps off at the end, and the bull kicks his shoulder and dislocates his shoulder. 'Okay,' I said. 'That's enough of that.'" The kick came dangerously close to the back of his head. Perry had a slightly different memory of the event. "Aww, I got thrown on my shoulder. But it was the very last shot, so the timing couldn't have been better."[10]

That timing was not accidental: Avildsen had agreed to film him on the bulls only if it would be the last footage shot. "That way, if he got hurt, it wouldn't interfere with the film," Avildsen said.[11]

They likely would have done better if Tuff Hedeman had been the rider for most of those scenes, but he didn't look like Perry or Baldwin. Hedeman, Frost's best friend, had an impressive rodeo career. From 1986 to 1993, he was among the world's top four professional bull riders, an amazing streak of eight consecutive years. Among rodeo fans, he developed a reputation comparable to Larry Mahan, the "Babe Ruth" of rodeo cowboys. He was also a paid consultant for the film.[12]

Hedeman reportedly objected to some of the scenes, particularly the dialogue. Another consultant, Lane's widow Kellie Frost, was also on the payroll. She apparently played a major role in the positive portrayal of Lane's image. On the rodeo circuit, Lane's "showboating ways" were considered "plain bad luck."[13]

Still, once the film was completed, it had one major fan: Luke Perry. The actor hoped that the movie had demonstrated that he could perform roles that went beyond the teen-idol image he had cultivated in *Beverly Hills 90210*.

"I feel like I got a monkey off my back, and I can make my decisions appropriately," he told *Entertainment Weekly.* He raved about the movie's theme, saying, "It's man and beast. And it wasn't about his superhero-like character — it was about a human being." Perry even applied the lessons from the film to his own life: "You've gotta know how good you are at something, and you have to be realistic with yourself," he said. "I know I've got a lot to learn. But I'm better than I thought I was."[14]

Another Avildsen fan was Stephen Baldwin. Baldwin, perhaps better known for his role as Bill Cody on TV's *The Young Riders* and as Barney Rubble in the *Flintstones* movie, played the athletic Hedeman. By the time filming had ended, Baldwin was a fan of Avildsen and his directing style: "John is a great director. He's tough. That's what I like about him. He knows what he wants, and he won't back down."[15]

Ebert complained that "oddly enough it's the rodeo footage that needs improvement."[16] *Variety* film critic Todd McCarthy agreed, saying the film was "a smooth, sappy ride through the life of a great bucking bull rider." It was, he added, "sweet, sentimental and rose-colored to a fault [but] has none of the grit, dust and bruises that virtually define the sport. "Avildsen and lenser Victor Hammer don't come up with any new visual angles on the rodeo."[17]

Avildsen strongly disagrees with those who question the camerawork in the film. He employed cameras that had never been used to shoot rodeo footage before. He provided hand-held, wide-angle cameras to the rodeo clowns in the arena, instructing them to hold the cameras at knee level. The result was a view of the action that had never been presented on film before.

McCarthy also complained about scenes that were omitted: "The elaborate preparation for a rider's quick trip in the arena are largely glossed over, and the vivid immediacy of the man-vs-beast contests is softened by the gross extension of the rides; even the title is false, in that the rides are made to last upwards of 25 seconds before the buzzer sounds."[18]

Weinberg was even more critical: "While the world awaits a true classic in the genre of 'rodeo' movies, this stands alone to prove just how silly and dull the sport is."[19] Similarly, Brown noted that the Garth Brooks tune about Frost, "The Dance," was missing from the soundtrack and, he added, "there's more action in that song than in this lame biopic."[20]

The vantage point is that of a fan in the stands, with little explanation of the intricacies of the sport. The hero seems like a natural who has little trouble riding the bulls; it's the fame that he has to learn to handle. The riding is just too easy, and the audience never appreciates how difficult the task is. As Ebert noted, "Even a duel with a dreaded bull that has thrown more than 300 riders is set up for an inevitable outcome."[21]

Others complained about the overly reverential treatment of the main character. Richard Harrington of the *Washington Post* wrote, "This movie feels as though it were filmed in a home on the range, so seldom is heard a discouraging (or disparaging) word. Frost's brief life is observed through rose-colored lenses that deny him all but the most obvious bruises."[22] Brown called it "a sappy, soapy Western for the Sassy set."[23]

Playboy magazine gave the film a positive review. And it also appears to be popular in prisons.

What makes the film somewhat different is the death of the hero, an ending that evoked memories of *Brian's Song*. Harrington observed that the death comes "as something of a shock, if only because the film has so accentuated the positive."[24] Stovall liked the scene: "The film redeems itself somewhat by its downbeat ending."[25] Ebert agreed, writing that the ending "tempts us to like the movie simply because we feel sympathy for the characters."[26]

The climax is the death of Lane Frost. To rodeo fans, that part of the plot was no surprise. Nor was it that unusual for a John Avildsen film; Rocky, after all, lost his first fight. However, to the rest of the audiences — those more accustomed to happy Hollywood endings — Frost's death came as a shock — accentuated, no doubt, by the fact that New Line Cinema never mentioned the death in their promotions. *Billboard* reviewer Eric Boehlert reported after watching the movie in Manhattan, "Moments after Frost was gored by a bull, his casket appeared on screen and the audience gasped."[27]

The movie has an additional ten minutes of footage after Frost's funeral, as it builds to its climax. Tuff Hedeman keeps riding, eventually winning the world championship. And, in his final championship ride, he stays on the bull for a full 16 seconds — eight extra seconds in memory of Lane Frost.

Billboard's Eric Boehlert lauded its "heartland theme" that "doubles as a valentine to the Plains states, celebrating their traditions, heroes and music."[28] He added, "That a studio would opt to immortalize that sort of cowboy legend may mean Hollywood is finally reaching out to people who have been buying country records for generations." But the publication described it as "essentially a *Brian's Song* for the rodeo circuit" and complained that it was "occasionally soft in the middle."[29]

Similarly, Harrington wrote, "Thrown by overly reverential performances and a lightweight script, *8 Seconds* never gets far out of the gate."[30] Ebert agreed: "There's a certain slackness in *8 Seconds*, a feeling that a lot of the material has been included simply because it happened in real life — not because it adds much to the story. The whole character of the best friend, Tuff, seems like a distraction."[31]

Blockbuster called it "a routine sports tale, but Perry has some good moments, and kids will undoubtedly enjoy." Stovall was unimpressed, saying "the plot is perfunctory."[32] Bloom simply wrote that it "doesn't really cut the mustard."[33] McCarthy said it "plays more like a reassuring, inspirational TV movie than a big-screen attraction."[34] Peter Rainer found the entire plot lackluster:

> Frost never sinks low enough to make his rise exciting; his ordeals ... are standard. The screenwriter, Monte Merrick, must have recognized this. At one point he has one of the characters remark on how much their lives resemble a country-western song. Actually, their lives resemble a bad country song. The good ones don't indulge in all this processed heartbreak.[35]

The strongest criticism came from Scott Weinberg, who called it "one of the laziest and most superficial sports movies ever made."[36] He complained about the director, the cast, the script, and — well — everything. "The only real entertainment value to be found in *8 Seconds* is this: Watch the movie, and continually scratch your head while asking yourself this question, 'Why was this movie ever made?'"[37]

Los Angeles Times critic Peter Rainer complained that Avildsen "knows something about inspirational movies and he appears to have forgotten most of it here."[38] Pulver complained that the film got "standard Avildsen *Rocky* rah-rah treatment."[39] Weinberg added, "It's evident that director John Avildsen ... is on complete 'sports montage auto-pilot,' since every scene will instantly remind you of an earlier, better movie — most likely one of Avildsen's own."[40]

McCarthy didn't like "the caution and reverence with which the film approaches virtually every scene."[41] Brown had a similar complaint: "[Avildsen] keeps the reins slack in what amounts to a cowboys 'n' codependency weeper."[42] Stovall complained, "Avildsen remains a proponent of the point-and-shoot school of direction."[43]

Avildsen's reputation also suffered on the set. Observers described his directing style as "dictatorial" and recounted shouting matches between him and film consultant Cody Lambert.[44] Tuff Hedeman summed up his experience by saying, "I'm just glad that's over. I'd a whole lot rather been at a rodeo somewhere."[45]

The public seemed to agree. The rodeo-based plot simply didn't appeal to most moviegoers, and *8 Seconds* did not do well at the box office. Part of the problem was that moviegoers and critics didn't know exactly what type of film it was.[46]

Despite the lukewarm critical and public response, the movie still had a cultural impact — particularly with the country music nightclub industry. Country nightspots had seen their heydays following the release of *Urban Cowboy* in 1979, but things had died down since then. Nightclub owners were looking for new ways to get young country music fans bellying up to their bars.

Some saw an answer in *8 Seconds*— real bulls instead of mechanical ones. Further, the tie-in to "The Dance," the Garth Brooks tune about the young rider, seem to offer a built-in appeal to country fans even if the song was never used in the movie.

An Orlando bar installed a bullpen where adventurous young cowboys could try their hand at riding a real bull. The nightspot was coyly renamed ":08," using the official stopwatch time as its logo.

The novelty of the attraction worked for a while, as crowds flocked to the bar, its bullpen, and the music it featured. Eventually, though, most people figured out why riding a bull was so difficult. And dangerous. And that bullpen took up a lot of valuable real estate without bringing in much money.

Production Notes

Directed by: John G. Avildsen. Writers (WGA): Written by Monte Merrick. Producers: Danny DeVito, co-producer; Cyd LeVin, executive producer; Tony Mark, co-producer; Michael Shamberg, producer; Jeffrey Swab, executive producer. Original Music: Bill Conti. Cinematographer: Victor Hammer. Editor: J. Douglas Seelig. Casting Director: Caro Jones. Production Designer: William J. Cassidy. Art Director: John Frick. Set Decorator: Jenny C. Patrick. Costume Designer: Deena Appel. Make Up Department: Desne J. Holland, key makeup artist; Tracey Lea Roden, assistant hair stylist; Tracey Lea Roden, assistant makeup artist; Doreen Vantyne, hair stylist. Production Managers: Sara King, post-production supervisor; Tony Mark, unit production manager; Eric McLeod, production supervisor; Second Unit Directors or Assistant Directors: Clifford C. Coleman, first assistant director; Scott Metcalfe, second assistant director; Jon C. Scheide, second second assistant director. Art Department: Amanda Anderson, art department coordinator; Tiger Baker, bull replica designer & artist; Joe Barrow, carpenter; Adam Braid, set dresser; Jennifer Bristol, painter; Rodney Brown, carpenter; John V. Burson, construction coordinator; Chuy Carrera, additional swing gang; Melissa Farnham, art department intern; Charlotte Garnell, assistant set decorator; Charlotte Garnell-Scheide, assistant set decorator; John R. Helton, scenic artist; Julian Hernandez, additional swing gang; Robert Janecka, property master; Michael Kocurek, set dresser; Mike Kocurek, set dresser; Jason Krohmer, carpenter; Michael Leonard, co-lead person/set dresser; Cole Lewis, lead scenic; Lisa Lopez, assistant set decorator; Jay F. McCuin, assistant propmaster; Elizabeth Jane Mcnamara, set dresser/shopper; Ron Perkins, carpenter; E. Colleen Saro, lead person; Kristin Schaffner, art department intern; David Solis, art department intern; Elizabeth Yeager, property assistant. Sound Department: Wayne Bell, sound mixer — second unit; Jim Brookshire, dialogue editor; Craig Clark, dialogue editor; Harry Cohen, sound designer; Gilbert R. Cuellar, Jr., cable person; David Farmer, sound effects editor; William Freesh, sound re-recording mixer; Michael Scott Goldbaum, sound mixer; Tom Gonta, foley mixer; Michael Goodman, adr editor; Robert Guastini, adr recordist; James Hare, sound re-recording assistant; Jeff Levison, stereo sound engineer — DTS; Joseph A. Mayer, supervising adr editor; Brian Risner, sound effects editor; Gary Rizzo, sound re-recording assistant; Paul Rodriguez, manager of sound services; Joanie Rowe, foley artist; Joseph T. Sabella, foley artist; Allan Schultz, dialogue editor; Ann Scibelli, sound effects editor; Tony Sereno, sound re-recording mixer; Cathie Speakman, adr editor; Cathie Speakman, dialogue editor; Ken Teaney, sound re-recording mixer; Jeff Vaughn, adr mixer; Jerome R.

Vitucci, boom operator; Sondra West, livestock sound consultant; Steven D. Williams, supervising adr editor; Steven D. Williams, supervising sound editor; Harry Woolway, assistant sound editor. Special Effects Department: Bart Dion, special effects coordinator; Dennis Dion, special effects; Bill Wynn, special effects second man. Visual Effects Department: Edwin Armstrong, electronic optical effects; Steve Borden, electronic optical effects; John Galt, electronic optical effects; Joseph Grimm, electronic optical effects; Bruce Manning, electronic optical effects; Douglas Nickel, electronic optical effects; James Pearman, electronic optical effects; Edward Quirk, electronic optical effects; John Rauh, electronic compositing; Michael Schlitt, electronic optical effects; Karin Skouras, film recording; Wayne Weiss, electronic optical effects; J. Richard West, electronic optical effects. Stunts: Billy Bob Black, Eric D. Bogany, Mark Cain, Troy Crow, Cody Custer, David Fournier, Kellie Frost, Casey Gates, Tuff Hedeman, Guy Hohman, Cody Lambert, Brett Leffew, Tyler Magnus, Ty Murray, Jason N. Pearce, Jim Sharp, Kelly Slover, Ben Stevenson III, Jim Bob Stoebner and Art Watson, stunts; David Alvarado, stunts — rodeo rider; Michael Litteral, rodeo stunts; Mike H. McGaughy and Brian Joseph Moore, stunt coordinators. Camera and Electrical Department: Benjamin T. Allen, video assist production assistant; Ron Allen, additional grip; Steven G. Ambrose, lighting technician; Colin Anderson, first assistant camera; Layton Blaylock, additional camera operator; Mark Braun, first assistant camera — second unit; Scott Carley, additional grip; Robert Chambers, dolly grip; Ian Ellis, additional assistant camera; William E. Fetherolf, video assist production assistant; Jim Givens, additional assistant camera; Dwayne Hargo, arena cameramen; Bill Hayes, additional assistant camera; Kirk Heard, camera production assistant; Tony Hoffman, additional assistant camera; Dawn Laurel, second assistant camera; Ken Lamkin, camera operator; Carl W. Lenhart, best boy grip; Jimmy Lindsey, additional assistant camera; Greg Lomas, grip; Michelle Madison, second assistant camera; Ross A. Maehl, additional photographer; Mark Mims, grip; Jonathan Moore, video assist operator; Glenn E. Moran, best boys electric; Mike Munic, additional grip; Randy Nolen, Steadicam operator; Mike O'Brien, grip; Van Redin, unit photographer; Robert B. Reynolds, best boys electric; Peter D. Roome, camera operator; Kelly Scroggins, additional assistant camera; Alex Skvorzov, gaffer; Eric T. Smith, camera operator — arena; Mark Stanley, key grip; Zane Streater, additional grip; Rick Tatum, lighting technician; Joseph D. Urbanczyk, main camera operator — re-shoots; Maliz van Ooyen, second assistant camera — location; Peter J. Verrando, video playback operator; Ralph Watson, camera operator. Casting Department: Jo Edna Boldin, location casting; Barbara Harris, adr voice casting; Kim Horridge, extras casting; Kelly Kernan, casting assistant; D. Reina, casting assistant; Barbara Williamson, casting assistant. Costume and Wardrobe Department: Christine Cantella, wardrobe assistant; Tangi Crawford, costume supervisor; Melanie Armstrong Fletcher, costumer; Deborah Fox, seamstress; Janice Janacek, set costumer; Amy Maner, costumer; William May, wardrobe production assistant; Francine Pons, seamstress; David Swope, set costumer; Yvonne Wilburn, wardrobe assistant. Editorial Department: Edward R. Abroms, first assistant editor; Jerry Behrens, editor — end montage; James Carter, color consultant; Syd Cole, negative cutter; Marie Hélène Desbiens, negative cutter; Joe Fineman, executive in charge of post-production; Pamela Hilse, post-production coordinator; Mato, color timer; Mel Riser, apprentice editor; Pam Winn, post-production consultant; William Yeh, second assistant editor. Music Department: Tony Brown, executive music supervisor; Eric Cowden, music editor; Lee De Carlo, score mixer; Toby Emmerich, music supervisor; Jack Eskew, orchestrator; Patrick Giraudi, additional music editor; Daniel J. Johnson, co-music editor; Ken Johnson, music editor; Nathan Kaproff, music contractor; Steve Livingston, music editor; Chris McGeary, assistant music editor; Kathy Nelson, executive music supervisor; Dawn Soler, music supervisor. Transportation Department: Julian T. Arredondo, driver; Don Breneman, driver; Henry Castillo, transportation captain; Vince De Amicis, driver; Rolando De Hoyos, driver; Emilio M. Gonzales, driver; Kevin Holland, picture car coordinator; Kevin Hudis, driver; David Lifton, driver; Joseph Lockwood, driver; Esteban Rodrìguez, driver; Angie Saenz, driver; Peter Sebring, transportation coordinator; Jesus F. Tellez, driver. Miscellaneous Crew: Diana Johnson, production accountant; Doug Adams, Randy Baczewski, Jarrod Benke, Travis Beuhl, Vernon Blocker, Eric D. Bogany, Daniel Brock, George Crenshaw, Shane Ferguson, Clyde Kimbro, Mel Kimbro, Robert Kunz, Jerome Mcclure, David Mills, Lanny Oliphant, Don Price, Zane Price, Bobby Reynolds, David Smith and Fred J. Yancy, chute cowboys; Joel Adams, Amy Lindsay, Brian Wasiak and Sarah Wiggins, stand-ins; Julie Adams, dialect coach; Mac Altizer, Sammy Andrews, Benny Beutler, Sammy Catalina, George Haynes, Clarence John, Bubb Riggs and Lance Young, stock contractors; Liz Amsden, contract administrator; Jimmy Anderson, Leon Coffee, Miles Hare, Gary Hedeman, Brian Henry, Eric T. Smith and Mark Swingler, bullfighters; Diana Atkinson, Liz Landers, Tra'chell Mcdougal and Gary Shurig, craft services; Justin Garrick Bell, assistant location manager; Billy Bob Black, Eric D. Bogany, Mark Cain, Troy Crow, Cody Custer, David Fournier, Kellie Frost, Casey Gates, Tuff Hedeman, Guy Hohman, Cody Lambert, Brett Leffew, Tyler Magnus, Ty Murray, Jason N. Pearce, Jim Sharp, Kelly Slover, Ben Stevenson III, Jim Bob Stoebner and Art Watson, bullriders; Margaret Blatner, production attorney; Amy Cadenhead Calcote, Jeff Mayse, Daniel J. Shaw, Martha Waters and Courtney Wulfe, production assistants; Helen Caldwell, script supervisor; Michael R. Casey, location manager; Stephanie Bloch, assistant — Stephen Baldwin; Syd Cole and Marie Hélène Desbiens, positive assemblers; Tony Dinizo, promotion manager; Leon Dudevoir, production executive; James Fain, Clyde Frost, Bob Peterson and Sue Rosoff, end montage contributors; Jill A. Felice, assistant — Tony Mark; Joyce Wilson Fetherolf, assistant — John G. Avildsen; Cynthia Garcia Walker, assistant production accountant; Holly Hagy, assistant production coordinator; Tony Hoffman, product placement; Linda Kelly-Sunday, location assistant; Gary Leffew, bullriding instructor; Stella Lohmann, assistant location manager; Pearl A. Lucero, production coordinator; Douglas E. Madison, effects assistant; Julie Mankowski, accounting assistant; Mike Mayberry and Samantha Torres, production interns; David Mills and Joey Wallace, chaps; Deborah Moore, executive charge of production; Paul Prokop, production controller; Daniel Ramos, assistant — John G. Avildsen; Sherry Rosen, administrative assistant — Luke Perry; Diane L. Sabatini, assistant — Michael Shamberg; Mark Sellers, choreographer; Carla Santos Shamberg, assistant — Michael Shamberg; Brad Stephens, publicist; David Stewart, personal assistant — Luke Perry; Marcia Tangen, nurse; Bill Watson, animal wrangler; Linda Wilson, assistant — John G. Avildsen. Filming Locations: Boerne, Texas, USA; Del Rio, Texas, USA; Helotes, Texas, USA; Pendleton, Oregon, USA; San Antonio, Texas, USA; Seguin, Texas, USA; San Diego, California, USA. Production Companies: Jersey Films; New Line Cinema. Distributors: New Line Cinema (1994) (USA) (theatrical); Fox Network (1999) (USA) (TV) (broadcast premiere).

Cast — in credits order: James Rebhorn, Clyde Frost; Cameron Finley, Young Lane; Carrie Snodgress, Elsie Frost; Dustin Mayfield, Teenage Lane; Clyde Frost, Couple #1; Elsie Frost, Couple #2; Luke Perry, Lane Frost; Stephen Baldwin, Tuff Hedeman; Red Mitchell, Cody Lambert; Gabriel Folse, Amarillo Cowboy; Joe Stevens, Amarillo Cowboy; Clint Burkey, Travis; Cynthia Geary, Kellie Frost; Ronnie Claire Edwards, Carolyn Kyle; John Swasey, Drunk Cowboy; Jim Gough, Official Nacogdoches; Mike Hammes, Police Officer; Jonathan Joss, Medic Del Rio; Danny Spear, Kellie's Father; Paul Alexander, TV Reporter; Daniel Ramos, Bartender; George Michael, Himself; Linden Ashby, Martin Hudson; Tonie Perensky, Buckle Bunny; Coquina Dunn, Buckle Bunny; Renée Zellweger, Buckle Bunny; John Growney, Himself; Ed Kutts, Rodeo Announcer; Boyd Polhamus, Rodeo Announcer; Hadley Barrett, Rodeo Announcer; Kix Brooks, Brooks & Dunn; Ronnie Dunn, Brooks & Dunn; Troy Lee Klontz, Brooks & Dunn; Daniel James Milliner, Brooks & Dunn; James Henry Gunn, Brooks & Dunn; Tommy Greywolf, Brooks & Dunn; Barry Francis Lederer, Brooks & Dunn; Daniel Lee McBride, Brooks & Dunn;

Terry McBride, McBride & The Ride; Ray Herndon, McBride & The Ride; Billy Thomas, McBride & The Ride; Gary Morse, McBride & The Ride; Jeff Roach, McBride & The Ride; Vince Gill, The Vince Gill & Karla Bonoff Band; Karla Bonoff, The Vince Gill & Karla Bonoff Band; Kenny Edwards, The Vince Gill & Karla Bonoff Band; Michael G. Botts, The Vince Gill & Karla Bonoff Band; J.D. Martin, The Vince Gill & Karla Bonoff Band. Other credited cast listed alphabetically: Lori Heuring, Bridesmaid

CHAPTER 23

Inferno (Desert Heat)

As of this writing, *8 Seconds* was the last film to bear John Avildsen's name as director. It was not, however, the last film he made.

In 1999 he directed a Jean Claude Van Damme vehicle with the working title of *Coyote Moon.* His version had a different plot than the movie as released. In Avildsen's version, a key character (Van Damme's Indian friend) was a ghost who inspired the lead character. Avildsen's original cut offered the plot with that mystical touch. But Van Damme didn't like that approach and had it recut, Avildsen removed his name as director, replacing it with the pseudonym "Danny Mulroom." The Van Damme version never made it to the theaters; but was released directly to video in the United States as *Inferno.* International audiences saw it under the title *Desert Heat,* and that's the one that seems to be most popular when appearing on American cable channels.

Van Damme—nicknamed "The Muscles from Brussels"—used his impressive physique to establish a solid if unspectacular career as an action hero in more than a dozen films. His most popular performance was in *Timecop,* a science-fiction adventure in which he goes back in time to arrest a criminal and thus change a horrible future that awaits mankind. Other films included *Lionheart, Knock Off, Legionnaire,* and *The Quest* (which he wrote and directed).

Van Damme had high hopes for the film when production started. He considered it similar to *Pulp Fiction,* the John Travolta-Samuel Jackson vehicle that was bloody but popular with audiences. He thought *Inferno* had more action than *Legionnaire* with the added touch of some good love scenes. "It's crazy, it's sexy, it's funny, it's cyncial," he told newspaper reporters before post-production had been completed.[1]

The title *Coyote Moon* came from a reference in the script to an Indian legend about the coyote and its erratic behavior during the full moon. Such a full moon highlights the opening scene, and the Indian friend refers to Van Damme as "coyote."

The film caught both the director and the star during a downward spin. Avildsen's stock was still down after the box-office disappointment of *8 Seconds* and he had not worked on a film in four years. Van Damme's previous effort *Legionnaire* had been released directly to video. At the time, the direct-to-video marketing ploy was considered a unique approach. By the time *Inferno* hit the shelves, the ploy was viewed as a way of salvaging money on a weak product.

The actor was hoping for better luck with this one. Although Van Damme served as producer, he sought outside help from Evzen Kolar (producer of *Double Impact*), and veteran Lawrence Levy. Kolar-Levy Productions, in turn, joined with Van Damme's Long Road Entertainment to handle the project. *Legionnaire* also carried the "Long Road Entertainment" label.

The cast had a number of lesser known actors and actresses, but included one of Avildsen's favorites, Pat Morita, who worked with Avildsen in *The Karate Kid*. Morita played a local who spent his days in the cafe waiting for his true love to return. Others in the cast included Danny Trejo, who played Van Damme's best friend (and was supposed to be a ghost), and Gabrielle Fitzpatrick, better known for her role opposite Jackie Chan in *Mr. Nice Guy*. Filming was done on location in the Mojave Desert over an eight-week period in 1998.[2]

The film's plot is not original at all, but was a remake of the Japanese film *Yojimbo*. (Avildsen plays with that piece of trivia in the film. At one point, a bus driver tries to get a date with a waitress by inviting her to watch *Yojimbo* with him.) Van Damme plays Eddie Lomax, a military vet with a dark past who travels to an unnamed town in the southwest to give his motorcycle to a long-time Indian friend and to get the friend's approval to commit suicide. Before he has a chance to kill himself, he is beaten by a group of local ruffians who steal his gun and the motorcycle. One ruffian lingers to finish him off with a shot to the head.

The young hoodlum (portrayed by Avildsen's son Jonathan) can't pull the trigger and shoots into the ground beside Van Damme instead. With the help of his Indian friend, Van Damme recuperates and then heads into town to retrieve his friend's motorcycle. Before leaving, the Indian friend has some advice: get the two gangs working against each other.

Van Damme finds his way to a local diner where he meets Rhonda, a waitress, and discovers that the town is controlled by two rival gangs. Members from one of those gangs were behind the robbery.

A jet plane flies over the town twice, supposedly from a nearby airbase. The first time is when Van Damme walks into town alone. Because of its speed, he does not hear it approaching from behind and is startled when it sails past him. The incident sets up the later climax with the villain.

Before he begins his quest, our hero first seeks to arm himself. He spots his stolen gun for sale at a local shop run by two gang members. He kills both men, retrieves his gun, and rescues the owner of the shop, who had been imprisoned in a back room.

He then takes his friend's advice. He goes to a nearby town and attacks members of the rival gang, killing several, rescuing two girls, and leaving the survivors believing that the rival gang was behind the attack. The grateful girls later reward Van Damme with a two-on-one sexual tryst, a gratuitous scene which only makes the profanity-laced film more confusing. In Avildsen's original cut this scene drew a standing ovation from the test audience. "The only other time I saw that happen was when we tested *Rocky*," Avildsen said.

The attack sparks a gang war. Van Damme and his Indian friend watch the initial fighting, waiting for a time to attack both groups. They eventually do, with some success, but the Indian is captured and killed. He dies, asking Van Damme to name his first child after him.

After the fight, Van Damme relates the story to Rhonda, telling her about the Indian's final words. Rhonda finds the story somewhat unbelievable, because — as she tells him — his Indian friend had died ten years ago. The inclusion of that scene in the early cut of *Desert Heat* was a mistake. That scene was shot by Avildsen as part of his ghost treatment. No other reference to his friend's death is subsequently made in the film.

Still, Rhonda adds to the excitement, because she has somehow learned that the survivors of both gangs are planning to ambush Van Damme when he returns to town. Before the climactic fight scene, Van Damme sets up a booby trap in his room. The resulting explosion kills a number of gang members, and Van Damme picks the others off until only two are left.

One is the young kid who couldn't kill him. Van Damme sends him away. The other is the leader of the gang, who gets the drop on him. A passing jet plane provides all the distraction Van Damme needs to get the advantage back and to defeat the villain.

Rhonda runs to him and they embrace. Behind his back, the villain is re-arming himself and about to shoot Van Damme. Rhonda sees the move and twists her body to protect her lover. Before the villain can shoot, the local townspeople kill him.

The entire incident turns out to be an economic boon for the small town. Its livelihood had long been dependent upon the tourist industry, particularly UFO enthusiasts who came there in search of some mysterious aircraft spotted in the areas years before. When the UFOs failed to reappear, the tourists also stayed away.

But Van Damme and Morita provide the answer. Morita disposes of all of the 28 bodies killed in the various melees. Tabloid newspapers subsequently report that 28 people mysteriously disappeared in this UFO haven. That's enough to spark a revival of the tourist trade, and to bring Bertie — Morita's true love — back to town.

Dreams play a significant role in the plot. Early in the film, Van Damme has a dream in which the Devil tells him to kill himself. Morita has two dreams, one about a glorious day in which Van Damme triumphs and one in which he loses the second fight. In the end, Van Damme and Rhonda ride off into the sunset on his red motorcycle, joined on the journey by the Indian friend on an identical bike.

The *Coyote Moon* version is the only version that was presented to test audiences. It tested well. But Van Damme didn't like it, so the movie went back to the cutting room. The recut version was never tested. Avildsen offered to pay for the test, betting that his version would test better. But that never happened. Instead, *Coyote Moon* was put on the shelf and the world saw *Desert Heat*.

Reviews were scarce and the few that did get published were cruel. Keith Phipps called the film "a direct-to-video movie from top to toe, and not a very good one at that."[3] Mark Reddy complained that *Desert Heat*, was "just lousy acting and worse action."[4]

Part of the criticism was targeted toward Van Damme as an over-the-hill action hero. "Its attempts at broad humor clash with its Native American subplot, while making the film's violence seem in poorer taste," Phipps wrote. "What's worse, even the violence is unsatisfying by Van Damme standards. Looking a bit spent, the pugilistic Belgian barely moves, instead falling back on gunplay, the aging martial-arts star's best friend. For anyone looking to see how the mighty have fallen, *Desert Heat* should be required viewing."[5]

Despite his attempts at removing his name from the film, Avildsen also came under criticism. "Instead of one man's personal triumph through hard work and determination, Avildsen has created the view of one man's triumph through killing a lot of people, and done it badly," Phipps wrote.[6] Reddy was more direct, writing, "The direction is hideously sloppy."[7]

Avildsen not only directed the film, but simultaneously taped the entire production process with his digital camera.. After he left the set, he edited his home movies into a mini-documentary called *What I Did Last Summer: The Making of* Coyote Moon.[8] According to the documentary, the film encountered at least two production problems. The first was a simple cost-efficiency problem. To be truly menacing, the gang members had be adorned with the requisite tough-guy tattoos associated with their careers. However, applying those tattoos took an hour each day for each gang member. Avildsen and the producer had to discuss the feasibility of doing this, since it involved paying overtime to all cast members. There was a debate over whether the budget could handle the overtime.

The second problem appeared to indicate that the cast didn't have a great deal of respect for Van Damme. The actor had a cocaine addiction that he was feeding during production. Avildsen's documentary depicts Van Damme frequently blowing and picking his nose. In fact, Avildsen ends his documentary with a section called "Nose to the Grindstone," which quickly replays all of those incidents that were captured on camera. It was a way for the director to document his star's cocaine addiction. The point was perhaps summarized by one incident in which Van Damme picked his nose, causing one observer to say, "A holy moment. We have many of those."

In the end, the documentary seems to be a comment on the film itself. It's not a film intended to be appreciated, but merely one to poke fun at.

As for *Coyote Moon*, it remains on a bookshelf in Avildsen's home. "My feeling is that my version would have been successful," he said.

Production Notes

Directed by: John Avildsen as Danny Mulroon (director's cut). Writer: Tom O'Rourke Screenplay. Producers: Evzen Kolar, Lawrence Levy and Jean-Claude Van Damme, producers; Joseph Merhi and Bennett R. Specter, executive producers; Richard G. Murphy and Ken Solarz, co-producers; Jay Sedrish, line producer; Samuel Hadida, producer (uncredited). Original Music: Bill Conti. Cinematographers: Ross A. Maehl. Editor: J. Douglas Seelig. Casting Directors: Cathy Henderson and Dori Zuckerman. Production Designer: Michael Novotny. Art Director: Roger L. King. Costume Designer: Mayes C. Rubeo. Make Up Department: Katalin Elek, makeup artist. Production Manager: Jay Sedrish, unit production manager. Second Unit Directors or Assistant Directors: Clifford C. Coleman, assistant director; David Hallinan, second assistant director; Michelle Jaeger, dga trainee; Steve Stafford, second unit director. Art Department: Gert Broekema, Tiffany Cowsill, Stephen McCumby, Tim Scheu and Lee Thomson, set dressers; Darrin Fletcher, storyboard artist; Wayne Lindholm, lead carpenter; Steven Schalk, property master; Samuel J. Tell, leadman. Sound Department: Vanessa Theme Ament, foley artist; Rusty Amodeo, sound effects editor; Ken Beauchene, boom operator; Nicholas James, supervising adr editor; Itzhak Magal, sound; Derek Marcil, sound re-recording mixer; Charles Maynes, sound effects editor and sound effects recordist; Andre Perreault, sound re-recording mixer; Christopher Sposa, sound utility. Special Effects Department: William Curtin, special effects; Boyd Lacosse, special effects pyro; Rudy Perez, special effects coordinator; Edward Romero, special effects technician. Visual Effects Department: Nadine Casamayou, assistant editor — BFTRE; Brent O. Coert, production coordinator — BFTRE; Hitoshi Inoue, digital artist — BFTRE; Fred Lacayanga, I/O coordinator — BFTRE; Travis Langley, technical supervisor — BFTRE; Michael Latschislaw, digital artist — BFTRE; Josh Saeta, digital artist — BFTRE; Perry Santos, visual effects producer; Gunther Schatz, digital artist — BFTRE; Kerry Shea, production manager — BFTRE; Martha Soehendra, digital artist — BFTRE; Derick Tortorella, technical supervisor — BFTRE; Todd Vaziri, lead digital artist — BFTRE; Christopher Dusendschon, in-show optical process and effects compositor — THDX (uncredited); Christopher Dusendschon, optical element Hazeltine colorist — THDX (uncredited). Stunts: William H. Burton, Clarke Coleman, Gilbert B. Combs, Craig Davis, Thomas Dewier, Richard Epper, Jon H. Epstein, Tim Gilbert, Evzen Kolar, Tim Trella and Christopher J. Tuck, stunts; Bobby J. Foxworth, stunt coordinator;

Randy Hall, stunt double — Mr. Van Damme; Steve Stafford, aerial director; Steve Stafford, aerial stunts. Camera and Electrical Department: Neil Jacobs, still photographer; Calvin Maehl, gaffer; Doug Schwartz, first assistant camera; Joseph M. Setele, first assistant camera — "b" camera; Miguel Sánchez, electrician; David J. Frederick, director of photography — second unit (uncredited). Casting Department: Chadwick Cohn, casting assistant. Editorial Department: Cecilia Hyoun, first assistant editor; Mato, color timer; Cherylin Primero, editorial intern; Damon Reeves, assistant editor; Issam Tahan, post-production logistics. Music Department: Marc Bonilla, composer — song "White Dog"; Jack Eskew, orchestrator; Ron Finn, music arranger — "Amazing Grace" and "Battle Hymn of the Republic"; Ron Finn, music editor; Ron Finn, musician — "Amazing Grace" and "Battle Hymn of the Republic"; Ashley Irwin, orchestrator; Laura Karpman, music arranger — "Amazing Grace"; Laura Karpman, musician — "Amazing Grace"; Stacy McAdams, music arranger — hymns; Chris McGeary, music editor; Ted Perlman, music producer — "All Roads Lead to You"; Brian Tarquin, composer — song "Firestorm." Transportation Department: Tony Barattini, driver — set dressing department; Paul Burlin, driver; Glenn Midcap, transportation; Brian Joseph Moore, driver; Derek Raser, transportation coordinator; George A. Sack, driver. Miscellaneous Crew: William Curtin, weapons armorer; Marlene Hart, production coordinator; Gary Kurashige, set medic; Peter Malota, fight choreographer; Tom Paczkowski, key office production assistant; Perry Santos, assistant — John Avildsen; Anthea Strangis, assistant production coordinator; Charles Thornton, Jr., jet pilot. Filming Locations: Lancaster, California, USA; Mojave Desert, California, USA; Mountain, California, USA. Production Company: Long Road Productions. KPI Productions: Davis-Films; Lomax Productions; PM Entertainment Group. Distributors: Columbia Tri-Star Home Video; Viacom.

Cast — in credits order: Jean-Claude Van Damme, Eddie Lomax; Pat Morita, Jubal Early; Danny Trejo, Johnny Six Toes; Gabrielle Fitzpatrick, Rhonda Reynolds; Larry Drake, Ramsey Hogan; Vincent Schiavelli, Mr. Singh; David "Shark" Fralick, Matt Hogan; Silas Weir Mitchell, Jesse Hogan; Jonathan Avildsen, Petey Hogan; Jaime Pressly, Dottie Matthews; Bill Erwin, Eli Hamilton; Ford Rainey, Pop Reynolds; Kevin West, Vern; Priscilla Pointer, Mrs. Henry Howard; Robert Symonds, Henry Howard; Paul Koslo, Ives; Brett Harrelson, Buck; Jeff Kober, Beserko; Gregory Scott Cummins, Leon; Neil Delama, Lester; Nikki Bokal, Carol Delvecchio; Kelly Ewing, Rose Delvecchio; Lee Tergesen, Luke; Other credited cast listed alphabetically; Steve Adell, Joe Bob; Erik Aude, Soldier; Natalie Barish, Old Woman Buyer; Philip Bruns, Old Man Buyer; Ray Chang, Mr. Chang; Evelyn Guerrero, Bertie Early; Jim Hanks, Tour Bus Driver; Lisa McCullough, Irma; Cynthia Palmer, Woman on the Bus; Michael Papajohn, Creep; Ed Trotta, Jack; Don Wood, Guard.

Epilogue

John Avildsen might best be described as semi-retired. He is on board for a future film project called *Stano*. The proposed plot involves an underdog in baseball — a theme Avildsen had handled well in *Rocky* and *The Karate Kid* films. As of this writing, that project is yet to be made.

Avildsen is also listed as the director of record for the unreleased dark comedy *Me*. The plot involves a family dealing with a child injured in a baseball accident. The film is based on a play by the late Gardner McKay, who became famous as the star of the popular television show *Adventures in Paradise* (1959–1962).

A third future project is *Angel One*. Details on it remain sketchy.

Avildsen also gets calls for work in cable, particularly for re-editing of his own films. With the constant demands of television for filling specific time slots (with cuts at the proper time for commercials), he still works on his own projects.

He also spends some time working with film students. That included a two-week stint as a guest lecturer at universities and workshops at a number of schools. In 2006, he led a film workshop at Indian Mountain School in Lakeville, Connecticut. "It's the only school I ever graduated

John G. Avildsen, 2013 (courtesy Anthony Avildsen).

from, so I have really happy memories of this place," he said at the time. "I got kicked out of practically every place I went, except this place!"[1]

His time at the forefront of Hollywood films may be past, but he still has an influence on the industry. The *Rocky* franchise, for example, seems to be endless — although that may be due to Sylvester Stallone's ties to the character. That would explain the release of the sixth film in the series, *Rocky Balboa*.

The Karate Kid remains a popular franchise, one that was revived in 2010 with Harald Zwart as director and Jaden Smith — son of superstar Will Smith — in the title role. Smith showed Avildsen the film in advance, seeking the director's blessing before it reached mass audiences. Avildsen was impressed with the performance of Jaden in the title role, but didn't think that Jackie Chan's back story as the mentor (losing his family in an automobile accident) was as effective as that of Pat Morita's Miyagi (his family dying in an internment center while he was winning the Medal of Honor in World War II). The plot differed a bit from the original, with young Smith playing a 12-year-old Dre who moves to Beijing with his mother (yep, you're not in California any more). Dre finds himself at odds with the culture and the class bully until a local handyman (Jackie Chan) teaches him karate. This version uses the plot as the basis of an examination of Chinese culture, but there's enough similarity in plot and acknowledgment of Avildsen's vision to warrant the use of the same title. As director Zwart noted, "You have to see the movie to understand why we kept it [the title]"[2]

John Avildsen has left an indelible mark on films, with *Rocky*, *The Karate Kid*, and more. And maybe more to come.

Filmography

Director

2012   *Me.* (pre-production)
2011   *Stano* (pre-production)
1999   *Inferno* (as Danny Mulroon)
1998   *A Fine and Private Place*
1994   *8 Seconds*
1992   *The Power of One*
1990   *Rocky V*
1989   *The Karate Kid Part III*
1989   *Lean on Me*
1988   *For Keeps*
1987   *Happy New Year*
1986   *The Karate Kid Part II*
1984   *The Karate Kid*
1983   *A Night in Heaven*
1982   *Traveling Hopefully* (documentary short)
1981   *Neighbors*
1980   *The Formula*
1980   *Murder Ink* (TV pilot)
1978   *Slow Dancing in the Big City*
1976   *Rocky*
1975   *W.W. and the Dixie Dancekings*
1975   *Fore Play*
1973   *Save the Tiger*
1972   *The Stoolie*
1971   *Cry Uncle*
1971   *Okay Bill*
1970   *Guess What We Learned in School Today?*
1970   *Joe*
1969   *Turn on to Love*
1965   *Light Sound Diffused* (documentary short)
1964   *Smiles* (short)

Assistant Director

1967   *Hurry Sundown*
1963   *Greenwich Village Story*

Cinematographer

1972   *The Stoolie*
1971   *Cry Uncle*
1971   *Okay Bill*
1970   *Guess What We Learned in School Today?*
1970   *Joe* (photographed by)1969; *Out of It* (director of photography)
1969   *Turn on to Love*
1965   *Light Sound Diffused* (documentary short)

As Editor

1992   *The Power of One*
1990   *Rocky V*
1989   *The Karate Kid Part III*
1989   *Lean on Me*
1988   *For Keeps*
1986   *The Karate Kid Part II*
1984   *The Karate Kid*
1983   *A Night in Heaven*
1982   *Traveling Hopefully*
1981   *Neighbors* (supervising editor)
1978   *Slow Dancing in the Big City*
1971   *Cry Uncle*
1971   *Okay Bill*

1970   *Guess What We Learned in School Today?*
1965   *Light Sound Diffused* (documentary short)

Writer

1971   *Cry Uncle* (additional dialogue)
1971   *Okay Bill*

Producer

2007   *Dancing into the Future* (video documentary) (producer)
1989   *Lean on Me* (executive producer)
1978   *Slow Dancing in the Big City* (producer)
1969   *Out of It* (associate producer)
1965   *Mickey One* (assistant producer)
1965   *Light Sound Diffused* (documentary short) (producer)

Camera Operator

1978   *Slow Dancing in the Big City*
1972   *The Stoolie*

Appearances as Himself

2008   *Mr. Firth Goes to Washington* (documentary) Himself— Interviewee
2006   *In the Ring* (video documentary) Himself
2006   *The Rise of Two Legends* (video short) Himself

2006   *Tribute to James Crabe* (video documentary short) Himself
2005   *Make Your Own Damn Movie!* (video documentary) Himself— Director
2005   *Biography* (TV series documentary) Himself
_____*Sylvester Stallone* (2005) Himself
2004   *Super Secret Movie Rules* (TV series documentary) Himself
_____*Sports Underdogs* (2004) (Himself
2004   *The Way of the Karate Kid* (video documentary short) Himself
2003   *A Decade Under the Influence* (documentary) Himself
2002   *Magic Time: A Tribute to Jack Lemmon* (video documentary short) Himself
1997   *Sports on the Silver Screen* (TV documentary) Himself— Academy Award Ceremony (uncredited
1993   *The Troma System* (short) Himself
1977   *The 49th Annual Academy Awards* (TV special)   Himself— Winner: Best Director

Other

2004   *The Way of the Karate Kid* (video documentary short) (special thanks)
1964   *Black Like Me* (assistant to director)
1963   *Greenwich Village Story* (assistant director)
1963   *Greenwich Village Story* Alvie

Chapter Notes

Chapter 1

1. Alvarez, M. J. (1971). Cry Uncle. *Variety*, 18.
2. Lloyd, A., Fuller, G., & Dresser, A. (1983). *The illustrated who's who of the cinema*. New York: Macmillan, p. 20.
3. Carlton, B. (2000, Feb. 13). Avildsen cast as UAB film lecturer. *Birmingham News*, 1F, 4F.

Chapter 2

1. Bodnar, John (2003). *Blue-collar Hollywood: Liberalism, democracy, and working people in American film*. Baltimore: John Hopkins University Press, p. xv. See also Arnold, Gary (1970, Aug. 20). Parable of "Joe," *The Washington Post*; Goodman, Mark (1970, July 27). Jonah in a hard hat. *Time Magazine*.
2. The kids at Cannon (1970, Aug. 31). *Time Magazine*.
3. McKinley, Jesse (1999, Aug. 25). Norman Wexler, 73, writer of "Saturday Night Fever" (obit). *The New York Times*, B7.
4. Emery, Robert J. (2002). *The directors: Take two* (pp. 115–143). New York: Allworth Press.
5. Gallagher, John Andrew (1989). *Film directors on directing*. Westport, CT: Praeger.
6. Emery, 2002.
7. *Ibid.*
8. *Ibid.*, p. 121.
9. Berkvist, Robert (2006, Dec. 14). Peter Boyle, 71, is dead; Roles evoked laughter and anger. *New York Times*, A33; Peter Boyle (1970, Oct. 16). *Life Magazine*. Perlstein, Rick (2007, Feb. 8). Who's afraid of Peter Boyle. Inthese-

times.com, http://www.inthesetimes.com/article/3013/.
10. Berkvist, 2006.
11. Emery, 2002, p. 122.
12. Hoberman, J. (2000, July 30). Off the hippies: "Joe" and the chaotic summer of '70. *New York Times*, D8.
13. Muller, Eddie (1999). The big leak: An uneasy evening with the Noir legend. http://www.eddiemuller.com/tierney.html.
14. Emery, 2002.
15. Berkvist, 2006.
16. Nystrom, Derek (2004, Spring). Hard hats and movie brats: Auteurism and the class politics of the New Hollywood. *Cinema Journal*, 43, 18–41.
17. Gallagher, 1989, pp. 5–6.
18. *Ibid*, p. 6.
19. Karney, Robyn (1993). *The Hollywood who's who: The actors and directors in today's Hollywood*. New York: Continuum, p. 19.
20. Hoberman, J. (2000, July 30). Did you see this? 37 years ago. *New York Times*.

Chapter 3

1. Avildsen, John G., with David Odell, Allen Garfield & Lloyd Kaufman (1999). Audio commentary track: *Cry Uncle* DVD supplement. Troma Team Video.
2. Baker, Robert A. & Nietzel, Michael T. (1985). *Private eyes 101 knights: A survey of American detective fiction*. Bowling Green, KY: Bowling Green State University Popular Press, p. 145.
3. Disick, David (1999). *Producer David Disick recalls* (*Cry Uncle* DVD supplement),

Troma Team Video; Hessel, Lee (1999). *Producer Lee Hessel takes aim at Lloyd* (*Cry Uncle* DVD supplement). Troma Team Video.

4. Gallagher, John Andrew (1989). *Film directors on directing*. Westport, CT: Praeger, p 6.

5. Avildsen, et al., 1999.

6. Disick, 1999.

7. Avildsen, et al., 1999.

8. *Ibid.*

9. Kaufman, Lloyd (1998). *All I needed to know about filmmaking I learned from* The Toxic Avenger. New York: Berkley Boulevard Books, p. 88.

10. Avildsen, et al., 1999.

11. Thompson, Howard (1971, Aug. 18). The screen: "Cry Uncle" combines sex and whodunit. *New York Times.*

12 Avildsen, et al., 1999.

13. *Ibid.*

14. Kanfer, Stefan (1971, Sept. 20). "Wild blue yonder," *Time Magazine.*

15. Emery, Robert J. (2002). *The directors: Take two.* New York: Allworth Press, p. 123.

16. Avildsen, et al., 1999.

17. *Ibid.*

Chapter 4

1. Mason, Jackie, & Gross, Ken (1988). *Jackie, oy! Jackie Mason from birth to rebirth.* New York: Little, Brown.

2. Emery, Robert J. (2002). *The directors: Take two* (pp. 115–143). New York: Allworth Press, p. 124.

3. Miller, Frederic P., Vandome, Alice F., & McBrewster, John (2010). *Kojak.* Beau-Bassin, Mauritius: Alphascript.

4. Macomber, Shawn (2008, Apr.). The ultimate Jackie Mason. *American Spectator, 41(3),* 16–20.

5. Reynolds, Tom (2004, Mar. 29). Interesting but slow pathos masquerading as comedy. www.imbd.com.

6. Quoted by Emery, 2000, p. 124.

7. Emery, 2000.

8. *Ibid.*, p. 124.

Chapter 5

1. Freedland, Michael (1985). *Jack Lemmon.* New York: St. Martin's Press, p. 122.

2. *Ibid.*

3. *Ibid.*, pp. 123–124.

4. *Ibid.*, p. 124.

5. *Ibid.*, p. 122.

6. *Ibid.*, p. 123.

7. *Ibid.*, p. 124.

8. *Ibid.*, pp. 124–125.

9. *Ibid.*, p. 121.

10. *Ibid.*, p. 122.

11. *Ibid.*, p. 124.

12. *Ibid.*, p. 123.

13. *Ibid.*

14. *Ibid.*

15. *Ibid.*, p. 122.

16. *Ibid.*, p. 126.

17. *Ibid.*

18. Null, Christopher (2002). Save the Tiger. www.filmcritic.com.

19. Frith, Walter (1996). Save the Tiger (1973). us.imbd.com/Reviews/96/9640.

20. Quoted by Freedman, 1985, p. 126.

21. Quoted by Freedman, 1985, p. 126.

22. Karney, Robyn (1993). *The Hollywood who's who: The actors and directors in today's Hollywood.* New York: Continuum, p. 18.

23. *Ibid.*, p. 273.

24. Frith, 1996.

25. Freedman, 1985, p. 127.

26. Kael, Pauline (1976). *Reeling.* Boston: Little Brown.

27. Karney, 1993, p. 19.

28. Null, 2002.

29. Freedland, 1985, p. 129.

30. *Ibid.*, pp. 129–130.

31. Blockbuster (1991). *The greatest movies of all time.* Blockbuster Entertainment, p. 173.

Chapter 6

1. Gallagher, John Andrew (1989). *Film directors on directing.* Westport, CT: Praeger, p. 8.

2. *Ibid.*

3. Emery, Robert J. (2000). *The directors: Take two.* New York: Allworth Press, p. 126.

4. Winters, Richard (2003, Nov. 29). Makes sex seem as exciting as cement. *Internet Movie Database,* imdb.com.

5. Gallagher, 1989.

6. Quoted by Gallagher, 1989, p. 9.

7. Winters, 2003.

8. Malin, Wayne (2005, Dec. 23). Poor sex farce. *Internet Movie Database,* imdb.com.

9. Quoted by Emery, 2000, p. 127.

Chapter 7

1. Alvarez, M. J. (1975). W.W. and the Dixie Dancekings. *Variety*, 20.
2. Reynolds, Burt (1994). *My life*. New York: Hyperion, p. 191.
3. *Ibid*.
4. Alvarez, 1975.
5. Reynolds, 1994, p. 191.
6. Karney, Robyn (1993). *The Hollywood who's who: The actors and directors in today's Hollywood*. New York: Continuum, p. 394.
7. Reynolds, 1994, p. 193.
8. Friskics-Warren, Bill (2008, Sept. 3). Jerry Reed, 71, country singer and actor. *New York Times*, A21.
9. Quoted by Gallagher, John Andrew (1989). *Film directors on directing*. Westport, CT: Praeger, p. 9.
10. Reynolds, 1984, pp. 192–193.
11. Karney, 1993, p. 383.
12. Alvarez, 1975.
13. Reynolds, 1984, pp. 191–192.
14. *Ibid.*, p. 192.
15. *Ibid*.
16. *Ibid*.
17. *Ibid*.
18. *Ibid*.
19. *Ibid.*, p. 190.
20. *Ibid.*, pp. 194–195.
21. *Ibid.*, p. 196.
22. Alvarez, 1975.
23. Canby, V. (1975, July 24). "W.W." is a pleasant summer surprise. *New York Times*, 18:1.
24. Reynolds, 1985, p. 195.
25. Canby, 1975.
26. Karney, 1993, p. 384.
27. *Ibid*.
28. Quoted by Gallagher, 1989, p. 9.

Chapter 8

1. Speier, Michael (2001, Apr. 9). DVD: Rocky. *Variety*, 18.
2. Wood, Robin (1986). *Hollywood from Vietnam to Reagan*. New York: Columbia University Press, p. 166.
3. *Ibid.*, p. 170.
4. Blockbuster (1991), p. 183. See also Review (1977, Jan. 29). *America, 136*, 87–88; Review (1977, Aug. 13). *America, 137*, 78–80; Review (1977, Jan. 13). *Senior Scholastic, 109*, 27;

Review (1977, Apr. 11). *Newsweek, 89*, 70–72; Review (1977, Feb.). *Seventeen, 36*, pp. 118–119.
5. Stallone, Sylvester (1999, June 28). Knockout punch: Making *Rocky* in 1976. *Newsweek, 133(26)*, 64.
6. Medavoy, Mike, & Young, Josh (2002). *You're only as good as your next one*. New York: Pocket Books.
7. *Ibid.*, p. 45.
8. *Ibid*.
9. Nashawaty, Chris (2002, Feb. 22). The right hook. *Entertainment Weekly*, 80–85.
10. Speier, 2001.
11. Nashawaty, 2002.
12. Medavoy & Young, 2002, p. 45
13. Speier, 2001.
14. Medavoy & Young, 2002, pp. 45–46.
15. *Ibid*, p. 48.
16. *Ibid*.
17. Nashawaty, 2002.
18. *Ibid.*, p. 82.
19. *Ibid*.
20. *Ibid*.
21. *Ibid*.
22. *Ibid*.
23. Grove, Christopher (2002, Mar. 19). Genre pix finally get their moment in the sun. *Variety*, 6.
24. Quoted by Nashawaty, 2002.
25. Karney, Robin (1993). *The Hollywood who's who: The actors and directors in today's Hollywood*. New York: Continuum, p. 444.
26. *Ibid*.
27. Brumley, Al (2001, Apr. 24). *Rocky* DVD reveals why "You can't beat a starving actor." *Dallas Morning News*, online.
28. Nashawaty, 2002, p. 83.
29. Karney, 1993, p. 444.
30. Brumley, 2001.
31. Speier, 2001.
32. Nashawaty, 2002.
33. Bettencourt, Scott (2002, July 9). Composer/director partnerships. *Film Score Monthly*, 1–8.
34. Medavoy & Young, 2002, p. 48.
35. Nashawaty, 2002.
36. Medavoy & Young, 2002.
37. *Ibid*.
38. *Ibid*.
39. Carlton, B. (2000, Feb. 13). Avildsen cast as UAB film Lecturer. *Birmingham News*, 1F, 4F.
40. Quoted by O'Neil, Tom (2001). *Movie awards*. New York: Praeger, p.12.
41. Medavoy & Young, 2002, p. 49.

42. *Ibid.*

43. *Ibid.*, pp. 49–50.

44. *Ibid.* p. 50.

45. *Ibid.*

46. *Ibid.*

47. *Ibid.*, pp. 50–51.

48. Nye, Doug (2001, Apr. 27). "Rocky" celebrates 25 years with DVD. *Birmingham News Punch*, 27–28.

49. Medavoy & Young, 2002, p. 51.

50. Karney, 1993, p. 444.

51. Griffin, Daniel (2007, November 21). The Karate Kid. *Film as art: Daniel Griffin's guide to cinema.* www.uashome.alaska.edu/~dfgriffin/website/index.htm.

52. Hakari, A. J. (2000). The Karate Kid. *Classic Movie Guide.* www.classicmovieguide.com.

53. Nashawaty, 2002.

54. O'Neil, 2001, p. 387.

55. *Ibid.*

56. Kael, Pauline (1980). *When the lights go down.* New York: Henry Holt.

57. Siskel, Gene (1977, Mar. 30). *Tempo: Before the decision, a champ makes the rounds,* 2–1, 2–3.

58. *Ibid.*, pp. 2–1.

59. *Ibid.*

60. O'Neil, 2001.

61. Medavoy & Young, 2002, p. 52.

62. Nashawaty, 2002.

63. Quoted by Ciabattari, Jane (2001, Apr. 22). "Now I'm a giver instead of a taker." *Parade Magazine*, p. 5.

64. Nashawaty, 2002.

65. Karney, 1993, p. 444.

66. Quoted by Ciabattari, 2001, p. 4.

67. Brumley, 2001; Speier, 2001.

68. Speier, 2001, p. 18.

69. Breznican, Anthony (2003, Sept. 28). "Rundown" star gives two thumbs up. *Birmingham News* (AP story), 1F, 7F.

70. Speier, 2001, p. 18.

71. Quoted by Culhane, John (1977, Mar. 27). The man who coached "Rocky" to victory. *New York Times,* AR1.

Chapter 9

1. Felsen, Milt (2000). Interview with the authors, Birmingham, AL. Other unattributed quotes from Felsen in this chapter are from the same interview.

2. Cieply, Michael (1988, Oct. 5). A tale of two studio chiefs: Fox's Goldberg makes it *Big* with "white-bread" tastes. *Los Angeles Times*, C7.

3. Morek, Christian (1993, Sept. 1). Culkin cut from "Rich" deal at WB. *Variety,* 13.

4. Sickels, Robert C. (2002). 1970s disco daze: Paul Thomas Anderson's *Boogie Nights* and the last golden age of irresponsibility. *Journal of Popular Culture, 35,* 4.

5. Freedland, Michael (1985). *Jack Lemmon.* New York: St. Martin's Press, p. 124.

6. Franklin, D. P. (2006). *Politics and film: The political culture of film in the United States.* Lanham, MD: Rowman & Littlefield

7. Avildsen, John. (2002). An interview with the authors, Los Angeles.

8. Sefcovic, Enid M. I. (2002). Cultural memory and the cultural legacy of individualism and community in two classic films about labor unions. *Critical Studies in Media Communication, 19,* 329–351.

Chapter 10

1. Gallagher, John Andrew (1989). *Film directors on directing.* Westport, CT: Praeger, p. 14.

2. *Ibid.*

3. Quoted by Pollock, Dale (1980, Aug. 14). Anxious production companies eye 3-week-old actors' strike, L.A. Times–Washington Post News Service, as published in the *Sarasota Herald-Tribune*, 8-D.

4. Quoted by Thomas, Bob (1978, Dec. 3). Slow dancing in the big city. Associated Press wire story, as published in *Daily News* (Bowling Green, Kentucky), 7-C.

5. *Ibid.*

6. Arnold, Gary (1978, Dec. 26). "Slow Dancing in Big City" remake of "Lady and the Tramp," L.A. Times–Washington Post Service, as published in *Tri City Herald*, 5.

7. Smith, Steven (1979, Jan. 25). "Rocky" ripoffs: One works, the other doesn't. *Eugene Register-Guard*, 13D.

8. Dinicola, Dan (1978, Dec. 29). "Slow Dancing" is mushy, hackneyed. *Schenectady Gazette,* 10.

9. Roberts, Sam (1989, Apr. 2). Jimmy Breslin goes Hollywood, family and all. *New York Times* (as reprinted online, pp. 1–3).

10. Associated Press (1977, Oct. 23). State

has bring 'em back alive project. *The Modesto Bee*, B-9.

11. Avildsen, John G., with David Odell, Allen Garfield and Lloyd Kaufman (1999). Audio commentary track (*Cry Uncle* DVD supplement), Troma Team Video.

12. Yager, Fred (1980, June 11). These movies you see ... critics may see differently. Associated Press, as published in *Eugene Register-Guard*, D-1.

13. Quoted by Thomas, 1978, p. 7-C.

14. von Maurer, Bill (1979, Feb. 20). Slow Dancing goes nowhere fast. *The Miami News*, 5C.

15. Anderson, George (1979, Jan. 4). Too slow. *Pittsburgh Post-Gazette*, 11.

Chapter 11

1. Manso, Peter (1994). *Brando: The biography*. New York: Hyperion, p. 858.

2. Schickel, Richard (1991). *Brando: A life in our times*. New York: Atheneum, p. 195.

3. Manso, 1994, p. 847.

4. *Ibid.*, pp. 849–850.

5. Quoted in Manso, 1994, p. 849.

6. *Ibid.*, p. 858.

7. *Ibid.*

8. *Ibid.*

9. *Ibid.*, p. 859.

10. *Ibid.*, p. 858.

11. *Ibid.*, p. 859.

12. *Ibid.*, p. 858.

13. *Ibid.*

14. *Ibid.*, p. 859.

15. *Ibid.*

16. Schickel, 1991, p. 195.

17. Brando, Marlon, & Lindsey, Robert (1994). *Brando: Songs my mother taught me.* New York: Random House, p. 415.

18. *Ibid.*

19. *Ibid.*, pp. 415–416.

20. Manso, 1994, p. 859.

21. *Ibid.*

22. *Ibid.*

23. *Ibid.*, p. 860.

24. *Ibid.*

25. *Ibid.*

26. Karney, Robin (1993). *The Hollywood who's who: The actors and directors in today's Hollywood.* New York: Continuum.

27. Manso, 1994, p. 860.

Chapter 12

1. Ebert, Roger (1981, Jan. 1). Neighbors. *Chicago-Sun Times.*

2. Woodward, Bob (1984). *Wired: The short life and fast times of John Belushi.* New York: Simon & Schuster.

3. *Ibid.*, pp. 201–202.

4. Emery, Robert J. (2000). *The Directors: Take two.* New York: Allworth Press, p. 134.

5. Gallagher, John Andrew (1989). *Film directors on directing.* Westport, CT: Praeger.

6. Woodward, 1984.

7. *Ibid.*

8. *Ibid.*

9. *Ibid.*

10. *Ibid.*, p. 261.

11. Bettencourt, Scott (2002, April 25). The missing: A partial chronology of rejected film scores. *Film Score Monthly*, www.filmscoremonthly.com/articles/2002/25.

12. Brillstein, Bernie, & Rensin, David (1999). *Where did I go right? You're no one in Hollywood unless someone wants you dead.* Boston: Little, Brown, pp. 200–203.

13. Woodward, 1984, p. 232.

14. Gallagher, 1989, p. 15.

15. Brillstein & Resnin, 1999.

16. Gallagher, 1989, p. 15.

Chapter 13

1. Quoted by Blank, Ed (1989, Mar. 24). Director of "Lean on Me" hoped for color-blind audience. *Pittsburgh Press*, C4.

2. Quoted by Emery, Robert J. (2000). *The directors: Take two.* New York: Allworth Press, p. 135.

3. The diary of an actress and her pain (1986, Apr. 27). *Philadelphia Inquirer*, K1.

4. Ebert, Roger (1983, Nov 24). A Night in Heaven. *Chicago Sun-Times.*

5. Emery, 2000, p. 135.

6. *Ibid.*, pp. 135–136.

7. Quoted by Blank, 1989, p. C4.

8. Henderson, Mark (1983, Nov.19). Hollywood uses body talk to sell "Night in Heaven." *Ottawa Citizen*, 44.

9. Canby, Vincent (1983, Nov. 19). Review: Night in Heaven. *New York Times.*

10. Sheffield, Skip (1983, Nov. 22). "Night in Heaven": Woman finds love, self-worth. *Boca Raton News*, p. 4C.

11. Henderson, 1983, p. 44.
12. Walentis, Al (1983, Nov. 19). "Night in Heaven" turns beefcake into turkey. *Reading Eagle*, p. 17.
13. McClane, Mike (1983, Nov. 25). "A Night in Heaven" is a stripped down bore. *Gainesville Sun*, p. 20.
14. Sheehan, Henry (1983, Nov. 29). A Night in Heaven. *The Boston Phoenix*, p. 10.
15. *Ibid.*
16. Canby, 1983.
17. Henderson, 1983, p. 44.
18. *Ibid.*
19. Emery, 2002, pp. 135–136.
20. Walentis, 1983, p. 17.
21. Dangaard, Colin (1983, Nov. 4). Atkins' Night In Heaven: Love scenes almost real. *Ottawa Citizen*, p. 90.

Chapter 14

1. Rifkin, Glenn (1992, Febr. 16). All about/martial arts: The black belts of the screen are filling the dojos. *New York Times*, 10.
2. Locke, Sondra (1998). *The good, the bad & the very ugly: A Hollywood journey.* New York: William Morrow.
3. McGilligan, Patrick (1999). *Clint: The life and legend.* New York: St. Martin's Press.
4. Greydanus, Steven D. (2005, Aug. 7). The Karate Kid. *National Catholic Register.*
5. Molloy, Tim (2005a, November 26). Pat Morita, 73, actor known for "Karate Kid" and "Happy Days." *New York Times*, A12.
6. Hakari, A. J. (2000). The Karate Kid. *Classic Movie Guide.* www.classicmovieguide.com.
7. Variety staff (1984). The Karate Kid. *Variety.*
8. Griffin, Daniel (2007, November 21). The Karate Kid. *Film as art: Danel Griffin's guide to cinema.* uashome.alaska.edu/~df griffin/website/index.htm.
9. Eggers, Dave (2007, June 11). Commando. *New Yorker, 83(16),* 72.
10. Greydanus, 2005.
11. Ebert, Roger (1984, Jan. 1). The Karate Kid. *Chicago Sun-Times.*
12. Clee, Andrea (1999). The Karate Kid. *Movie Gazette Review.* www.movie-gazette.com/cinereviews/199.
13. Hakari, 2000.

14. *Ibid.*
15. Clee, 1999.
16. Canby, Vincent (1986, June 20). Karate Kid Part II. *New York Times*, 17.
17. Rayns, Tony (2007). "The Karate Kid." In John Pym, ed. (1999). *Time Out film guide* (p. 559). London: Time Out Guides.
18. Griffin, 2007.
19. *Ibid.*
20. Greydanus, 2005.
21. Ebert, 1984.
22. Griffin, 2007.
23. Ebert, 1984.
24. Ebert, Roger (1989, June 30). The Karate Kid Part III. RogerEbert.com.
25. Hakari, 2000.
26. Greydanus, 2005.
27. Quoted by Lipton, Mike, & Brener, Howard (2005, Dec. 12). Pat Morita. *People, 64(24),* p. 79.
28. Quoted by Molloy, Tim (2005b, Nov. 26). Pat Morita, Mr. Miyagi from 'Karate Kid,' dies at 73. *Birmingham News,* 6A.
29. Weintraub, Jerry (2011). *When I stop talking, you'll know I'm dead.* New York: Hatchette, p. 210.
30. Dowd, Maureen (2009, June 21). Obama's fly move. *New York Times*, WK9.
31. Greydanus, 2005.
32. Ebert, 1984.
33. Clee, 1999.
34. Ebert, 1984.
35. Griffin, 2007.
36. *Ibid.*
37. Molloy, 2005, A12.
38. Ebert, 1984.
39. *Ibid.*
40. *Ibid.*
41. Genzlinger, Neil (2004). It's Karate, Kid! The Musical. *New York Times*, D2.
42. Spare times (2004, June 4). *New York Times*, 34,
43. Richardson, Christopher (1998). The Miyagi Method: a new vision for religious educators. *Journal of Beliefs & Values: Studies in Religion & Education, 19,* 219–230.
44. Swansburg, John (2012, Aug. 3). Amazing lost footage from *The Karate Kid. Slate,* www.slate.com/blogs/browbeat/2012/08/03.
45. Labrecque, Jeff (2012, Aug. 3). "Karate Kid": John Avildsen's rehearsal tapes "...are the best! ... around!!" PopWatch, EW.com.

Chapter 15

1. Peretta, Don (2009). The Karate Kid: Part II. In John Pym, ed. (1999). *Time Out film guide* (p. 559). London: Time Out Guides, p. 559.

2. Armstrong, Derek (2009). The Karate Kid Part II. allmovie.com, www.allmovie.com/work/the-karate-kid-part-ii-26949/review.

3. Peretta, 2009, p. 559.

4. Armstrong, 2009.

5. *Ibid.*

Chapter 16

1. Quoted by Gallagher, John Andrew (1989). *Film directors on directing*. Westport, CT: Praeger, p. 17.

2. *Ibid.*, p. 16.

3. *Ibid.*

4. *Ibid.*, p. 17.

5. Siskel, Gene (1987, Aug. 22). Falk not happy about 'New Year.' *Philadelphia Daily News*, articles.philly.com/1987-08-22/entertainment/26167188_1_adult-film-love-story-happy-new-year/4.

6. Falk, Peter (2006). *Just one more thing.* New York: Carroll & Graf, p. 286.

7. *Ibid.*, p. 271.

8. Weintraub, Jerry (2011). *When I stop talking, you'll know I'm dead.* New York: Hatchette.

9. Canby, Vincent (1987, Aug. 7). Film: "Happy New Year." *New York Times.*

10. *Ibid.*

11. Siskel, 1987.

12. Quoted by Gallagher, 1989, p. 16.

13. Quoted by Gallagher, 1989, p. 16.

14. Siskel, 1987.

15. Falk, 2006, p. 269.

Chapter 17

1. Gallagher, John Andrew (1989). *Film directors on directing* (pp. 17–18). Westport, CT: Praeger, p. 17.

2. Quoted by Willistein, Paul (1988, Jan. 28). Ringwald nears adulthood with "For Keeps." *The Morning Call* as syndicated in *Boca Raton News*, p. 8W.

3. Hollywood film carries strong pro-life message (2008, April). *The Forerunner*, http://www.forerunner.com/forerunner/X0443_Hollywood_film.html.

4. Armstrong, Doug (1988, Jan. 15). Pregnant-teen film loaded with clichés. *Milwaukee Journal*, p. 6D.

5. *Ibid.*

6. Healy, Michael (1988, Jan. 28). But movie makes light of serious teen subject. *Los Angeles Daily News* as syndicated in *Boca Raton News*, p. 8W.

7. Kehr, Dave (1988, Jan. 15). The issues bog down juvenile 'For Keeps.' *Chicago Tribune.*

8. Willistein, Paul (1988, Jan. 16). Teens deserve better than "For Keeps." *The Morning Call.*

9. "Hollywood film carries...," 2008.

10. Quoted by Gallagher, 1989, p. 18.

11. Willistein, 1988, Jan. 16.

12. Willistein, 1988, Jan. 26, p. 8W.

13. Molly Ringwald films public service ad (1988, Mar. 3). *Ocala Star-Banner*, p. 2A.

14. Weinburg, Marc (1988, Mar.). For Keeps (review). *Orange Coast Magazine, 14 (3),* 238–239.

15. Healy, 1988, p. 8W.

Chapter 18

1. Finke, Nikki (1989, Mar. 3). Lean on Me: A modern myth? *Los Angeles Times.*

2. *Ibid.*

3. *Ibid.*

4. *Ibid.*

5. *Ibid.*

6. *Ibid.*

7. *Ibid.*

8. *Ibid.*

9. *Ibid.*

10. Ebert, Roger. (1989). Review: Lean on Me. *Chicago Sun Times.*

11. *Ibid.*

12. *Ibid.*

13. *Ibid.*

14. *Ibid.*

15. Schickel, Richard (1989, Mar. 13). Tough love. *Time Magazine*, p. 82.

16. *Ibid.*

17. Ebert, 1989.

18. *Ibid.*

19. Karney, Robyn (1993). *The Hollywood who's who: The actors and directors in today's Hollywood.* New York: Continuum.

20. mrpsycholeojoey87 (2011). Lean on Me. YouTube.com.

21. Finke, 1989.

22. Young, Jon (1989, Nov.). Lean on me. *Video, 13,* 78.

23. Hyman, Irwin A. (1989, Nov.). Lean on me. *The Education Digest, 55,* 20–22.

Chapter 19

1. Ebert, Roger (1989, June 30). The Karate Kid Part III. RogerEbert.com.

2. *Ibid.*

3. Black, Ben (2007, Mar. 31). Review: The Karate Kid Part III. BadMovies.org http://www.badmovies.org/othermovies/karatekidiii/.

4. Ebert, 1989.

5. *Ibid.*

6. Brenner, Paul (n.d.). The Karate Kid Part III. *All Movie Guide.*

7. Miller, Adrienne (2009, May 18). The Karate Kid Part III. *Bonsai Galore.*

8. Eyre, Jane (2008, Apr. 29). Use this DVD as a coaster. Amazon.com.

9. Heckman, Melissa K. (2008, Feb. 8). Can't look away. Amazon.com.

10. Bagula, Roger L. (2009, June 16). One sequel too far. Amazon.com.

11. Eyre, 2008.

12. Weinberg, Scott (1998). Review: The Karate Kid Collection. Joblo.com http://www.joblo.com/dvdclinic/dvd_review.php?id=749.

13. Black, 2007.

14. Ebert, 1989.

15. Knight, Sean R. (2008, May 5). A serious review, without sarcasm. Amazon.com.

16. Miller, 2009.

17. Bagula, 2009.

18. Van Vorst, Ethan D. (2008, Nov. 21). Not "that" bad, but not as good as some say. Amazon.com.

19. Ebert, 1989.

20. Scott, Walter (2009, Nov. 29). Personality parade. *Parade,* 2.

21. Miller, 2009.

22. Weinberg, 1998.

23. Ebert, 1989.

24. Haflidason, Almar (2001, Sept. 18). Review: The Karate Kid Part III. *BBC Film Reviews,* http://www.bbc.co.uk/films/2001/09/18/karate_kid_3_1989_dvd_review.shtml.

25. Bechtel, Mark, & Pappu, Sridhar (2004, June 12). Sports beat. *Sports Illustrated, 100(15),* 30.

26. Griffin, Daniel (2007, Nov. 21). The Karate Kid. *Film as art: Daniel Griffin's guide to cinema.* www.uashome.alaska.edu/~dfgriffin/website/index.htm.

27. Greydanus, Steven D. (2005, Aug. 7). The Karate Kid. *National Catholic Register.*

Chapter 20

1. Medavoy, Mike, & Young, Josh (2002). *You're only as good as your next one.* New York: Pocket Books, pp. 126–127.

2. *Ibid.,* p. 46.

3. Nye, Doug (2001, Apr. 27). "Rocky" celebrates 25 years with DVD. *Birmingham News Punch,* 27–28.

4. McTiernan, John (1995). An interview with Jean Bodon.

5. Quoted by Nashawaty, Chris (2002, Feb. 22). The right hook. *Entertainment Weekly,* p.84.

6. Nye, 2001, p. 28.

7. *Ibid.,* p. 27.

8. Mathews, Jack (1991, Jan. 31). Declining expectations. *Los Angeles Times,* E3.

9. Grant, Edmond (1991, Mar.-Apr.). Film reviews: Rocky V. *Films in Review, 42(3–4),* 118–119.

10. Kermode, Mark (1991, Sept.). Rocky V. *Sight & Sound, 1(5),* 58.

11. Karney, Robin (1993). *The Hollywood who's who: The actors and directors in today's Hollywood.* New York: Continuum, p. 445.

12. Brumley, Al (2001, Apr. 24). *Rocky* DVD reveals why 'You can't beat a starving actor. *Dallas Morning News,* online; Speier, Michael (2001, Apr. 9). DVD: Rocky. *Variety,* 18.

Chapter 21

1. Ebert, Roger (1992, Mar. 27). The Power of One. *Chicago Sun-Times.*

2. Akins, P.T. (1992, Apr. 16). Movies: The Power of One. *Rolling Stone,* p. 628.

3. Ebert, 1992.

4. *Ibid.*

5. Goodman, Mark (1992, Apr. 6). The Power of One. *People, 37,* 16.

6. Brown, Geoff (1992, Sept.). Reviews: *The Power of One. Sight & Sound, 2(5),* p. 57.

7. Kempley, Rita (1992, Mar. 27). The Power of One. *Washington Post.*

8. Howe, Desson (1992, Mar. 27). The Power of One. *Washington Post.*

Chapter 22

1. Quoted by Reid, Jan (1993, Nov.). Tuff-stuff. *Texas Monthly, 21(11),* 138–145.

2. Quoted by Schwarzbaum, Lisa (1994, Mar. 11). Luke before he leaps. *Entertainment Weekly, 213,* 16–21.

3. *Ibid.*

4. *Ibid.*

5. *Ibid.*

6. *Ibid.,* p. 17.

7. Ebert, Roger (1994, Feb. 25). Review: 8 Seconds. *Chicago Sun-Times.*

8. *Ibid.*

9. Quoted by Schwarzbaum, 1994.

10. *Ibid.*

11. Reid, 1993.

12. *Ibid.*

13. *Ibid.,* p. 141.

14. Schwarzbaum, 1994.

15. Baldwin, Stephen (2004, May 16). Interview with the author. Birmingham, AL.

16. Ebert, 1994.

17. McCarthy, Todd (1995). Eight Seconds. *Variety Film Reviews, 1993–1994,* 2–14–94.

18. *Ibid.*

19. Weinberg, Scott (1998). 8 Seconds. *Apollo Movie Guide,* 2284.

20. Brown, Joe (1994, Feb. 25). 8 Seconds. *Washington Post,* 13.

21. Ebert, 1994.

22. Harrington, Richard (1994, Feb. 25). 8 Seconds. *Washington Post,* 13.

23. Brown, 1994.

24. Harrington, 1994.

25. Stovall, Natahsa (1994, Mar. 1). 8 Seconds. *Village Voice, 39(9),* 58

26. Ebert, 1994.

27. Boehlert, Eric (1994, Feb. 26). 8 Seconds. *Billboard, 106(9),* 38.

28. *Ibid.*

29. *Ibid.*

30. Harrington, 1994.

31. Ebert, 1994.

32. Stovall, 1994.

33. Bloom, Phillipa (1994). 8 Seconds, *Empire, 65,* 12.

34. McCarthy, 1995.

35. Rainer, Peter (1994, Feb. 25). 8 Seconds: This true rodeo story lacks true grit. *Los Angeles Times,* 8.

36. Weinberg, 1998.

37. *Ibid.*

38. Rainer, 1994.

39. Pulver, Andrew (1994, Nov.). Reviews: 8 Seconds. *Sight & Sound, 4(11),* 43–46.

40. Weinberg, 1998.

41. McCarthy, 1995.

42. Brown, 1994.

43. Stovall, 1994.

44. Reid, 1993, p. 141.

45. *Ibid.*

46. Kermode, Mart, & Dean, Peter (1995, Apr.). Video: 8 Seconds. *Sight & Sound, 5(4),* 60–63.

Chapter 23

1. Carey, Lynn (1998, Sept. 4). Jean-Claude Van Damme is "Off" and running. *Contra Costa* (CA) *Times.*

2. Pesselnick, Jill (1998, June 22). Van Damme pic ignites. *Variety,* 13.

3. Phipps, K.(2001). *Desert Heat.* www// theonionavclub.com/reviews/.

4. Reddy, Mark (2001). *Desert Heat.* www. amazing-colossal.com.

5. Phipps, 2001.

6. *Ibid.*

7. Reddy, 2001.

8. Avildsen, John (2000). *What I did last summer: The making of* Coyote Moon. Los Angeles: Avildsen Home Production.

Epilogue

1. Tuohy, Laurel (2006, Nov. 2). Youthful filmmakers thrive at Indian Mountain School. *Lakeville Journal,* B4.

2. The Karate Kid (2010, Jan. 22). *USA Today,* 2D.

Bibliography

Alvarez, M. J. (1971). Cry Uncle. *Variety,* 18.
_____. (1975). W.W. and the Dixie Dancek-ings. *Variety,* 20.

Akins, P.T. (1992, Apr. 16). Movies: The Power of One. *Rolling Stone,* 628.

Anderson, George (1979, Jan. 4). Too slow. *Pittsburgh Post-Gazette,* 11.

Armstrong, Derek (2009). The Karate Kid Part II. allmovie.com www.allmovie.com/ work/the-karate-kid-part-ii-26949/review.

Armstrong, Doug (1988, Jan. 15). Pregnant-teen film loaded with clichés. *Milwaukee Journal,* 6D.

Arnold, Gary (1970, Aug. 20). Parable of "Joe," *The Washington Post.*
_____. (1978, Dec. 26). "Slow Dancing in Big City" remake of "Lady and the Tramp," L.A. Times–Washington Post Service, as published in *Tri City Herald,* 5.

Associated Press (1977, Oct. 23). State has bring 'em back alive project. *The Modesto Bee,* B-9.

Avildsen, John (2000). *What I did last sum-mer: The making of* Coyote Moon. Los Angeles: Avildsen Home Production.

Avildsen, John G., with David Odell, Allen Garfield & Lloyd Kaufman (1999). Audio commentary track: *Cry Uncle* DVD sup-plement. Troma Team Video.

Baker, Robert A., and Michael T. Nietzel (1985). *Private eyes 101 knights: A survey of American detective fiction.* Bowling Green, KY: Bowling Green State University Pop-ular Press.

Bechtel, Mark, and Sridhar Pappu (2004, June 12). Sports beat. *Sports Illustrated, 100(15),* 30.

Berkvist, Robert (2006, Dec. 14). Peter Boyle, 71, is dead; Roles evoked laughter and anger. *New York Times,* A33.

Bettencourt, Scott (2002, July 9). Com-poser/director partnerships. *Film Score Monthly,* 1–8.
_____. (2002, Apr. 25). The missing: A partial chronology of rejected film scores. *Film Score Monthly,* www.filmscore monthly.com/articles/2002/25.

Black, Ben (2007, Mar. 31). Review: The Karate Kid Part III. *BadMovies.org* http:// www.badmovies.org/othermovies/karate kidiii/

Blank, Ed (1989, Mar. 24). Director of "Lean on Me" hoped for color-blind au-dience. *Pittsburgh Press,* C4.

Blockbuster (1991). *The greatest movies of all time.* Blockbuster Entertainment.

Bloom, Phillipa (1994). 8 Seconds, *Empire, 65,* 12.

Bodnar, John (2003). *Blue-collar Hollywood: Liberalism, democracy, and working people in American film.* Baltimore: Johns Hop-kins University Press.

Boehlert, Eric (1994, Feb. 26). 8 Seconds. *Billboard, 106(9),* 38.

Brando, Marlon, and Robert Lindsey (1994). *Brando: Songs my mother taught me.* New York: Random House.

Breznican, Anthony (2003, Sept. 28).

"Rundown" star gives two thumbs up. *Birmingham News* (AP story), 1F, 7F.

Brillstein, Bernie, and David Rensin (1999). *Where did I go right? You're no one in Hollywood unless someone wants you dead.* Boston: Little, Brown.

Brown, Geoff (1992, Sept.). Reviews: The Power of One. *Sight & Sound, 2(5),* p. 57.

Brown, Joe (1994, Feb. 25). 8 Seconds. *Washington Post,* 13.

Brumley, Al (2001, Apr. 24). *Rocky* DVD reveals why "You can't beat a starving actor." *Dallas Morning News,* online.

Canby, Vincent (1975, July 24). "W.W." is a pleasant summer surprise. *New York Times,* 18:1.

_____ (1983, Nov. 19). Review: Night in Heaven. *New York Times.*

_____ (1986, June 20). Karate Kid Part II. *New York Times,* 17.

_____ (1987, Aug. 7). Film: "Happy New Year." *New York Times.*

Carey, Lynn (1998, Sept. 4). Jean-Claude Van Damme is "Off" and running. *Contra Costa* (CA) *Times.*

Carlton, Bob. (2000, Feb. 13). Avildsen cast as UAB film lecturer. *Birmingham News,* 1F, 4F.

Ciabattari, Jane (2001, Apr. 22). "Now I'm a giver instead of a taker." *Parade Magazine,* 5.

Cieply, Michael (1988, Oct. 5). A tale of two studio chiefs: Fox's Goldberg makes it *Big* with "white-bread" tastes. *Los Angeles Times,* C7.

Clee, Andrea (1999). The Karate Kid. *Movie Gazette Review.* www.movie-gazette.com/cinereviews/199.

Culhane, John (1977, Mar. 27). The man who coached "Rocky" to victory. *New York Times,* AR1.

Dangaard, Colin (1983, Nov. 4). Atkins' Night In Heaven: Love scenes almost real. *Ottawa Citizen,* 90.

The diary of an actress and her pain (1986, April 27). *Philadelphia Inquirer,* K1.

Dinicola, Dan (1978, Dec. 29). "Slow Dancing" is mushy, hackneyed. *Schenectady Gazette,* 10.

Disick, David (1999). *Producer David Disick recalls* (*Cry Uncle* DVD supplement), Troma Team Video.

Ebert, Roger (1981, Jan. 1). Neighbors. *Chicago Sun-Times.*

_____ (1983, Nov. 24). A Night in Heaven. *Chicago Sun-Times.*

_____ (1984, Jan. 1). The Karate Kid. *Chicago Sun-Times.*

_____ (1989). Review: Lean on Me. *Chicago Sun-Times.* http://www.joblo.com/dvdclinic/dvd_review.php?id=749.

_____ (1989, June 30). The Karate Kid Part III. *RogerEbert.com.* 27.

_____ (1992, March 27). The Power of One. *Chicago Sun-Times.*

_____ (1994, Feb. 25). Review: 8 Seconds. *Chicago Sun-Times.*

Eggers, Dave (2007, June 11). Commando. *New Yorker, 83(16),* 72.

Emery, Robert J. (2002). *The directors: Take two.* New York: Allworth Press.

Falk, Peter (2006). *Just one more thing.* New York: Carroll & Graf.

Finke, Nikki (1989, Mar. 3). Lean on Me: A modern myth? *Los Angeles Times.*

Franklin, D. P. (2006). *Politics and film: The political culture of film in the United States.* Lanham, MD: Rowman & Littlefield

Freedland, Michael (1985). *Jack Lemmon.* New York: St. Martin's Press.

Friskics-Warren, Bill (2008, Sept. 3). Jerry Reed, 71, country singer and actor. *New York Times,* A21.

Frith, Walter (1996). Save the Tiger (1973). us.imbd.com/Reviews/96/9640.

Gallagher, John Andrew (1989). *Film directors on directing.* Westport, CT: Praeger.

Genzlinger, Neil (2004). It's Karate, Kid! The Musical. *New York Times,* D2.

Goodman, Mark (1970, July 27). Jonah in a hard hat. *Time Magazine.*

_____ (1992, Apr. 6). The Power of One. *People, 37,* 16.

Grant, Edmond (1991, Mar.-Apr.). Film reviews: Rocky V. *Films in Review, 42(3–4),* 118–119.

Griffin, Daniel (2007, Nov. 21). The Karate Kid. *Film as art: Daniel Griffin's guide to cinema.* www.uashome.alaska.edu/~dfgriffin/website/index.htm.

Greydanus, Steven D. (2005, Aug. 7). The Karate Kid. *National Catholic Register.*

Grove, Christopher (2002, Mar. 19). Genre pix finally get their moment in the sun. *Variety,* 6.

Haflidason, Almar (2001, Sept. 18). Review: The Karate Kid Part III. *BBC Film Reviews,* http://www.bbc.co.uk/films/2001/09/18/karate_kid_3_1989_dvd_review.shtml.

Hakari, A. J. (2000). The Karate Kid. *Classic Movie Guide.* www.classicmovieguide.com.

Harrington, Richard (1994, Feb. 25). 8 Seconds. *Washington Post,* 13.

Healy, Michael (1988, Jan. 28). But movie makes light of serious teen subject. *Los Angeles Daily News* as syndicated in *Boca Raton News,* 8W.

Henderson, Mark (1983, Nov.19). Hollywood uses body talk to sell "Night in Heaven." *Ottawa Citizen,* 44.

Hessel, Lee (1999). *Producer Lee Hessel takes aim at Lloyd* (*Cry Uncle* DVD supplement). Troma Team Video.

Hoberman, J. (2000, July 30). Off the hippies: "Joe" and the chaotic summer of '70. *New York Times,* D8.

_____ (2000, July 30). Did you see this? 37 years ago. *New York Times.*

Hollywood film carries strong pro-life message (2008, April). *The Forerunner,* http://www.forerunner.com/forerunner/X0443_Hollywood_film.html.

Howe, Desson (1992, Mar. 27). The Power of One. *Washington Post.*

Hyman, Irwin A. (1989, Nov.). Lean on me. *The Education Digest, 55,* 20–22.

Kael, Pauline (1976). *Reeling.* Boston: Little, Brown.

_____ (1980). *When the lights go down.* New York: Henry Holt.

Kanfer, Stefan (1971, Sept. 20). "Wild blue yonder." *Time Magazine.*

The Karate Kid (2010, Jan. 22). *USA Today,* 2D.

Karney, Robin (1993). *The Hollywood who's who: The actors and directors in today's Hollywood.* New York: Continuum.

Kaufman, Lloyd (1998). *All I needed to know about filmmaking I learned from* The Toxic Avenger. New York: Berkley Boulevard Books.

Kehr, Dave (1988, Jan. 15). The issues bog down juvenile "For Keeps." *Chicago Tribune.*

Kempley, Rita (1992, Mar. 27). The Power of One. *Washington Post.*

Kermode, Mark (1991, Sept.). Rocky V. *Sight & Sound, 1(5),* 58.

_____, and Peter Dean (1995, Apr.). Video: 8 Seconds. *Sight & Sound, 5(4),* 60–63.

The kids at Cannon (1970, Aug. 31). *Time Magazine.*

Lipton, Mike, & Brener, Howard (2005, Dec. 12). Pat Morita. *People, 64(24),* 79.

Lloyd, A., Fuller, G., & Dresser, A. (1983). *The illustrated who's who of the cinema.* New York: Macmillan, p. 20.

Locke, Sondra (1998). *The good, the bad & the very ugly: A Hollywood journey.* New York: William Morrow.

Manso, Peter (1994). *Brando: The biography.* New York: Hyperion.

Mason, Jackie, and Ken Gross (1988). *Jackie, oy! Jackie Mason from birth to rebirth.* New York: Little, Brown.

Mathews, Jack (1991, Jan. 31). Declining expectations. *Los Angeles Times,* E3.

McCarthy, Todd (1995). Eight Seconds. *Variety Film Reviews, 1993–1994,* 2–14–94.

McClane, Mike (1983, Nov. 25). "A Night in Heaven" is a stripped down bore. *Gainesville Sun,* 20.

McGilligan, Patrick (1999). *Clint: The life and legend.* New York: St. Martin's Press.

McKinley, Jesse (1999, Aug. 25). Norman Wexler, 73, writer of "Saturday Night Fever" (obit). *The New York Times,* B7.

Medavoy, Mike, and Josh Young (2002). *You're only as good as your next one.* New York: Pocket Books.

Miller, Adrienne (2009, May 18). The Karate Kid Part III. *Bonsai Galore.*

Miller, Frederic P., Vandome, Alice F., & McBrewster, John (2010). *Kojak.* Beav-Bassin, Mauritius: Alphascript.

Molloy, Tim (2005a, Nov. 26). Pat Morita, 73, actor known for "Karate Kid" and "Happy Days." *New York Times,* A12.

_____ (2005b, Nov. 26). Pat Morita, Mr. Miyagi from "Karate Kid," dies at 73. *Birmingham News,* 6A.

Molly Ringwald films public service ad (1988, Mar. 3). *Ocala Star-Banner,* p. 2A.

Morek, Christian (1993, Sept. 1). Culkin cut from "Rich" deal at WB. *Variety,* 13.

Muller, Eddie (1999). The big leak: An uneasy evening with the Noir legend. http://www.eddiemuller.com/tierney.html.

Nashawaty, Chris (2002, Feb. 22). The right hook. *Entertainment Weekly,* 80–85.

Null, Christopher (2002). Save the Tiger. www.filmcritic.com.

Nye, Doug (2001, Apr. 27). "Rocky" celebrates 25 years with DVD. *Birmingham News Punch,* 27–28.

O'Neil, Tom (2001). *Movie awards.* New York: Praeger.

Pesselnick, Jill (1998, June 22). Van Damme pic ignites. *Variety,* 13.

Peter Boyle (1970, Oct. 16). *Life Magazine.*

Phipps, K.(2001). *Desert Heat.* www//theonionavclub.com/reviews/

Pollock, Dale (1980, Aug. 14). Anxious production companies eye 3-week-old actors' strike," L.A. Times–Washington Post News Service, as published in the *Sarasota Herald-Tribune,* 8-D.

Pulver, Andrew (1994, Nov.). Reviews: 8 Seconds. *Sight & Sound, 4(11),* 43–46.

Pym, John, ed. (1999). *Time Out film guide.* London: Time Out Guides.

Rainer, Peter (1994, Feb. 25). 8 Seconds: This true rodeo story lacks true grit. *Los Angeles Times,* 8.

Reddy, Mark (2001). *Desert Heat.* www.amazing-colossal.com.

Reid, Jan (1993, Nov.). Tuffstuff. *Texas Monthly, 21(11),* 138–145.

Reynolds, Burt (1994). *My life.* New York: Hyperion.

Richardson, Christopher (1998). The Miyagi Method: a new vision for religious educators. *Journal of Beliefs & Values: Studies in Religion & Education, 19,* 219–230.

Rifkin, Glenn (1992, Feb. 16). All about/martial arts: The black belts of the screen are filling the dojos. *New York Times,* 10.

Roberts, Sam (1989, Apr. 2). Jimmy Breslin goes Hollywood, family and all. *New York Times* (as reprinted online, pp. 1–3).

Schickel, Richard (1989, March 13). Tough love. *Time Magazine,* p. 82.

_____ (1991). *Brando: A life in our times.* New York: Atheneum.

Schwarzbaum, Lisa (1994, Mar. 11). Luke before he leaps. *Entertainment Weekly, 213,* 16–21.

Scott, Walter (2009, Nov. 29). Personality parade. *Parade,* 2.

Sefcovic, Enid M. I. (2002). Cultural memory and the cultural legacy of individualism and community in two classic films about labor unions. *Critical Studies in Media Communication, 19,* 329–351.

Sheehan, Henry (1983, Nov. 29). A Night in Heaven. *The Boston Phoenix,* 10.

Sheffield, Skip (1983, Nov. 22). "Night in Heaven": Woman finds love, self-worth. *Boca Raton News,* 4C.

Sickels, Robert C. (2002). 1970s disco daze: Paul Thomas Anderson's *Boogie Nights* and the last golden age of irresponsibility. *Journal of Popular Culture, 35,* 4

Siskel, Gene (1977, March 30). Tempo: Before the decision, a champ makes the rounds, *Chicago Tribune,* 2–1, 2–3.

_____ (1987, Aug. 22). Falk not happy about "New Year." *Philadelphia Daily News,* articles.philly.com/1987-08-22/entertainment/26167188_1_adult-film-love-story-happy-new-year/4.

Smith, Steven (1979, Jan. 25). "Rocky" ripoffs: One works, the other doesn't. *Eugene Register-Guard,* 13D.

Spare times (2004, June 4). *New York Times,* 34,

Speier, Michael (2001, Apr. 9). DVD: Rocky. *Variety*, 18.

Stallone, Sylvester (1999, June 28). Knockout punch: Making *Rocky* in 1976. *Newsweek, 133(26),* 64.

Stovall, Natahsa (1994, Mar. 1). 8 Seconds. *Village Voice, 39(9),* 58

Thomas, Bob (1978, Dec. 3). Slow dancing in the big city. Associated Press wire story, as published in *Daily News* (Bowling Green, Kentucky), 7-C.

Tuohy, Laurel (2006, November 2). Youthful filmmakers thrive at Indian Mountain School. *Lakeville Journal*, B4.

Variety staff (1984).The Karate Kid. *Variety*.

von Maurer, Bill (1979, Feb. 20). Slow Dancing goes nowhere fast. *The Miami News*, 5C.

Walentis, Al (1983, Nov. 19). "Night in Heaven" turns beefcake into turkey. *Reading Eagle*, 17.

Weinburg, Marc (1988, Mar.). For Keeps (review). *Orange Coast Magazine, 14 (3),* 238–239.

Weinberg, Scott (1998). 8 Seconds. *Apollo Movie Guide,* 2284.

_____. (1998). Review: The Karate Kid Collection. Joblo.com

Weintraub, Jerry (2011). *When I stop talking, you'll know I'm dead.* New York: Hatchette.

Willistein, Paul (1988, Jan. 16). Teens deserve better than "For Keeps." *The Morning Call*.

_____. (1988, Jan. 28). Ringwald nears adulthood with "For Keeps," *The Morning Call* as syndicated in *Boca Raton News*, 8W.

Winters, Richard (2003, Nov. 29). Makes sex seem as exciting as cement. *Internet Movie Database*. imdb.com.

Wood, Robin (1986). *Hollywood from Vietnam to Reagan.* New York: Columbia University Press.

Woodward, Bob (1984). *Wired: The short life and fast times of John Belushi.* New York: Simon & Schuster.

Young, Jon (1989, Nov.). Lean on me. *Video, 13,* 78.

Index

239